BETWEEN NANOWORLDS AND GLOBAL CULTURE

science +
Fiction

jovis

This volume was published in the context of the exhibition

science + fiction
Between Nanoworlds and Global Culture

Artists and scientists on
Cultural identities
Brain research
Nanotechnology
Science and the public

Edited by Stefan Iglhaut and Thomas Spring
Commissioned by VolkswagenStiftung Hanover

Sprengel Museum Hanover
Center of Art and Media Technology (ZKM) Karlsruhe
caesar, center for advanced european studies and research, Bonn
Deutsches Hygiene-Museum Foundation
The Nobel Museum, Stockholm
The Deutsches Museum, Munich

Assistant editor: Anna Echterhölter
Photography: Michael Herling / Aline Gwose
Translations: Robin Benson / Adam Blauhut / Joseph O'Donnell /
Felicity Gloth / Catherine Kerkhoff-Saxon / Lucinda Rennison
Design: Gewerk, Berlin
Type-setting: Satzinform, Berlin
Production: Bookwise, Munich

jovis Verlag GmbH
Kurfürstenstraße 15/16
10785 Berlin

www.jovis.de

ISBN 3-936314-22-5

BETWEEN NANOWORLDS AND GLOBAL CULTURE

science + fiction

ARTISTS AND SCIENTISTS ON
CULTURAL IDENTITIES
BRAIN RESEARCH
NANOTECHNOLOGY
SCIENCE AND THE PUBLIC

EDITED BY
STEFAN IGLHAUT AND THOMAS SPRING

IN COOPERATION WITH
SPRENGEL MUSEUM HANOVER
CENTER OF ART AND MEDIA TECHNOLOGY KARLSRUHE
CAESAR, CENTER OF ADVANCED EUROPEAN STUDIES
AND RESEARCH, BONN
DEUTSCHES HYGIENE-MUSEUM FOUNDATION
THE NOBEL MUSEUM, STOCKHOLM
THE DEUTSCHES MUSEUM, MUNICH

JOVIS

LIST OF ILLUSTRATIONS

CONTENTS

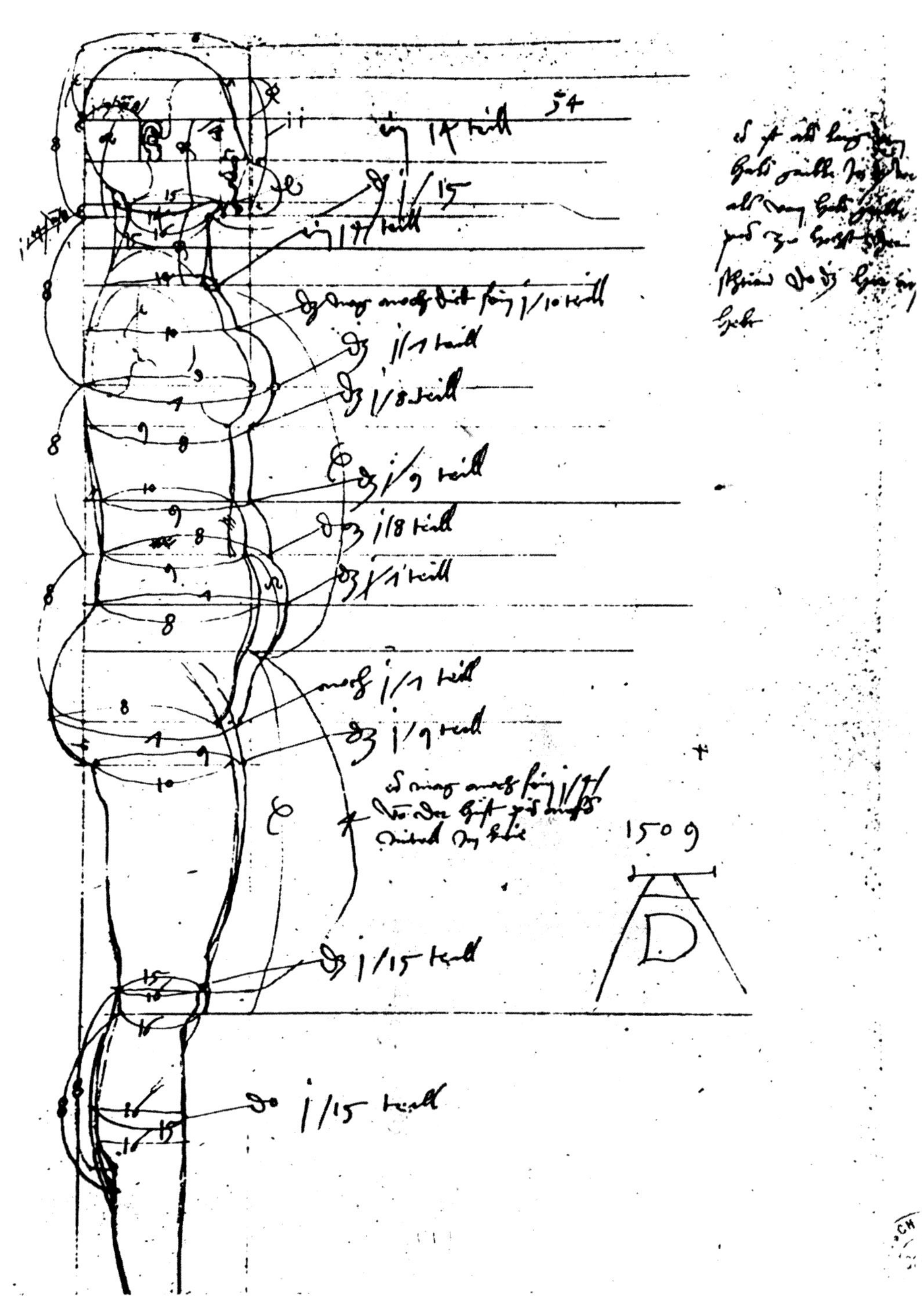

Albrecht Dürer *Study of Proportions from the Dresden Sketch Book,* 1509; WALL INSTALLATION SKETCHES SCIENCE/ART

It is time to rethink the links between art and science, to redraw the traditional boundaries within which, from a scientific viewpoint, aesthetic problems are at best a decorative accessory to the production of scientific knowledge, which is essentially an autonomous process. Here art is degraded to a "purely compensatory entity responsible for the transformation of scientific output into the beautiful, the subjective or the mad" (Peter Geimer).

If we recognize the necessity of linking art and science in a way that is convincing for both sides, our attention will first be drawn to the past, primarily to the Renaissance, in search of the causes of the division. During this period, art and science began to drift apart, leaving behind correlations and intimacies as they charted out their cold course of specialization. They not only moved into separate buildings, they did not allow their former partners to enter, either. And yet one must look to the present too, for today science still appears to lack the necessary, not to say passionate, interest in a relationship of this kind. The arts are put in charge of feeling, sensuousness, form and expression – those things that lie on the outer perimeter of the natural sciences, which many believe spur on the world today.

The VolkswagenStiftung has endeavored to thaw out a relationship that for centuries now has been in a deep freeze. It has invited artists and scientists to grapple with key issues of contemporary scientific research. The result is the exhibition "science + fiction". Spanning nanoworlds and globalized culture, it represents a new format designed to transcend the conventional means of representing science. It shifts the focus to the cultural and societal preconditions of knowledge as well as the scientific basis of our everyday worlds. It is a modern *Wunderkammer* (cabinet of curiosities) in the age of globalization. "Science + fiction" is a tightrope act, communicating science, presenting art and reflecting upon different forms of knowledge production.

Given the complexity of the research issues portrayed, it appeared most sensible to develop the works of art in direct cooperation with relevant scientific institutions. The exhibition emerged from a close collaboration between artists and scientists of different disciplines. The Munich-based artists M + M, Ars Viva winner Christoph Keller, the Dutch studio Atelier van Lieshout, the artistic duo Christa Sommerer & Laurent Mignonneau, and the Berlin artists Dellbrügge & de Moll were invited to work with scientists who in many instances were recipients of funding from the VolkswagenStiftung. In their respective pavilions, the participants tackled a variety of topics: science and everyday life, brain research, nanotechnology, globalization, intercultural understanding as well as the future of the knowledge based society. In the process of drawing closer, interacting and accepting one another, it became evident that both scientific and artistic research had at least one thing in common: the attempt to understand different realities.

The works of art are flanked by an installation created by the Berlin exhibition agency gewerk. As a kind of framework structure, it juxtaposes artistic and scientific images, and it offers to the visitors additional information on the central themes of the exhibition. The artists' associative worlds are supplemented by recorded statements on research matters, laboratory findings and historical excursions, thus placing artistic output on a scientific or scholarly foundation. Works by Ingo Günther, Peter Kogler, Max Bill, Ken Lum and other artists are also shown.

As a research-funding organization, the VolkswagenStiftung is not only breaking new ground with the exhibition, but this latter is an integral component of the foundation's vision and strategy. The exhibition is, above all, an experiment – one that initiates a dialogue between artists and researchers and aims to put sensory experience on an equal footing with rational thought. In the end, viewers must judge for themselves whether

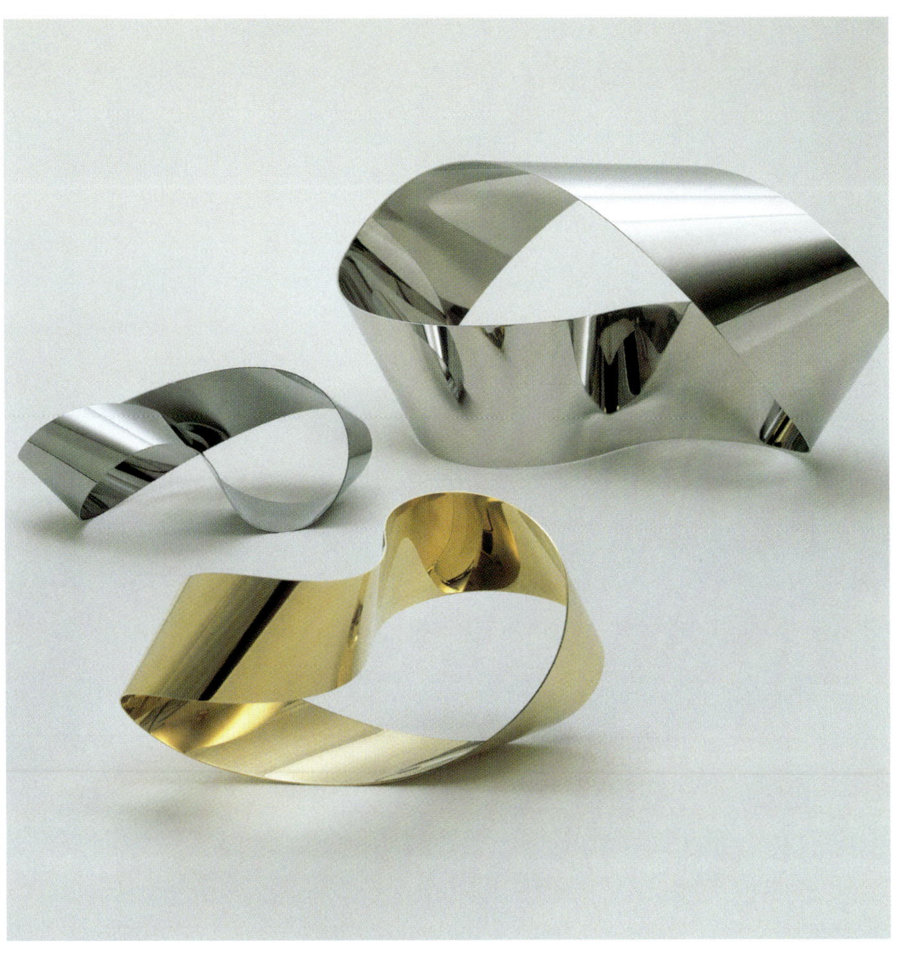

Max Bill *unendliche schleife für drei positionen* (infinite ribbon for three positions) 1974–75;
MODEL IDEAS SATELLITE

the concept has been realized successfully, whether art and science can be linked convincingly, whether art and science as different systems of knowledge production can give birth to a new mode of representation when combined, and whether the interventions of art and science offer new potential. And yet it seems certain that the subjective and creative aspects of art and the objective systematics of research can be mutually enhancing. The exhibition's irritating moments and breaks with convention mean that it opens up new vistas and provides intellectual stimulus.

The organizers are indebted to the artists and researchers involved in making the original idea into a reality. In addition, I would like to express my thanks to the board of trustees of the VolkswagenStiftung as well as the exhibition advisory board, made up of professors Christina von Braun, Horst Bredekamp, Andreas Engel, Jörg Kotthaus, Martin Roth, Wolf Singer and Peter Weingart. I also wish to thank the cooperating institutions and their directors and staff members, especially Prof. Ulrich Krempel and the Sprengel Museum in Hanover, Prof. Peter Weibel and the Center for Art and Media Technology Karlsruhe, Prof. Karl-Heinz Hoffmann and caesar, the center for advanced european studies and research, Bonn, Dr. Klaus Vogel and Dr. Gisela Staupe at the Deutsches Hygiene Museum Foundation, Prof. Svante Lindqvist and Dr. Ulf Larsson at the Nobel Museum, Stockholm, Prof. Wolf Peter Fehlhammer and Dr. Walter Hauser at the Deutsches Museum in Munich. Special thanks also go to the project directors, Stefan Iglhaut and Thomas Spring, and their associate Anna Echterhölter, and also to the exhibition designers, Jens Imig and Stefan Rothert, and their team at gewerk. Finally, I wish to express my gratitude to the staff members of the VolkswagenStiftung for their continued interest and commitment in support of the exhibition idea.

STEFAN IGLHAUT / THOMAS SPRING
BETWEEN SCIENCE+FICTION: IMAGES OF ART AND SCIENCE

> Art is all that remains to those
> who do not want to give science the last word.
>
> Marcel Duchamp

What is real? What is artificial? What is objective? "Science+fiction" is an exhibition that takes as its central theme our perception of reality in science and art. It questions artists and scientists alike and traces the hidden pathways that link current research with our fantasies, hopes and desires.

The exhibition was developed for the 40th anniversary of the VolkswagenStiftung. Artists and scientists were invited to discuss with one another and give visual form to topics that affect all of us: where is the border between the other and the self in a globalized world? What opportunities does the new transculture offer? How do our brains enable us to perceive the world? What is the significance of altering materials on a molecular level? What promises does scientific culture hold? What errors does it make?

Science and art enter into an experimental relationship. Scientific images and topics are transformed into art, and works of art are counterbalanced in their confrontation with scientific facts and narratives. Images, objects, preserved organs and a variety of media allow viewers to consider the focal points of scientific research from a number of perspectives and discover its cultural prerequisites in a modern *Wunderkammer* of knowledge and art.

"It has been repeatedly stressed that art and science, though separated by many trenches, share the same creative core. Well into the 18th century, the unity of art and science – in the sense of the Greek *Techne* – was the normal state of affairs, and not their separation. Mathematicians took art lessons, and artists studied math. No engineer worth his salt would have been able to say whether he was a utilitarian or a fine artist. Industrialization irrevocably ended this unity, but whenever great scientists tested their creative skills, they remembered the obsessive, order-giving rationality of the artist" (Horst Bredekamp).

In the 18th century, the famous Royal Society, though an academy of science, was still admitting members with purely literary qualifications. The situation was reversed in the 19th century. On a visit to an airplane exhibition in 1912, a young Marcel Duchamp was moved to remark to his fellow artists Brancusi and Leger: "La peinture est morte. Qui pourra faire mieux que cette hélice? Dis-moi tu en serais capable, toi?" Even so, grappling with a world increasingly shaped by science and technology, the 20th century produced a new type of painting, and Marcel Duchamp responded to the changed situation with the development of his "ready-mades". His ironic play with cultural contexts and their power of definition made possible entirely new ways of understanding art. Duchamp was able to get the better of science with this revolution: "Art is all that remains to those who do not want to give science the last word."

For this reason "science+fiction" has not been conceived as a science exhibition in the tradition of a "Public Understanding of Science". It does not intend to promote understanding or to celebrate a success story. Rather, it is an experiment based on an actual encounter and a real dialogue between art and science (that is to say, between artists and scientists) – an experiment that could well have ended in a monologue or the kitsch of scientific realism. The exhibition does not seek out, identify and show existing works of art with a scientific motif, but grapples with two fields that began drifting apart in the Renaissance and have come to oppose each other culturally.

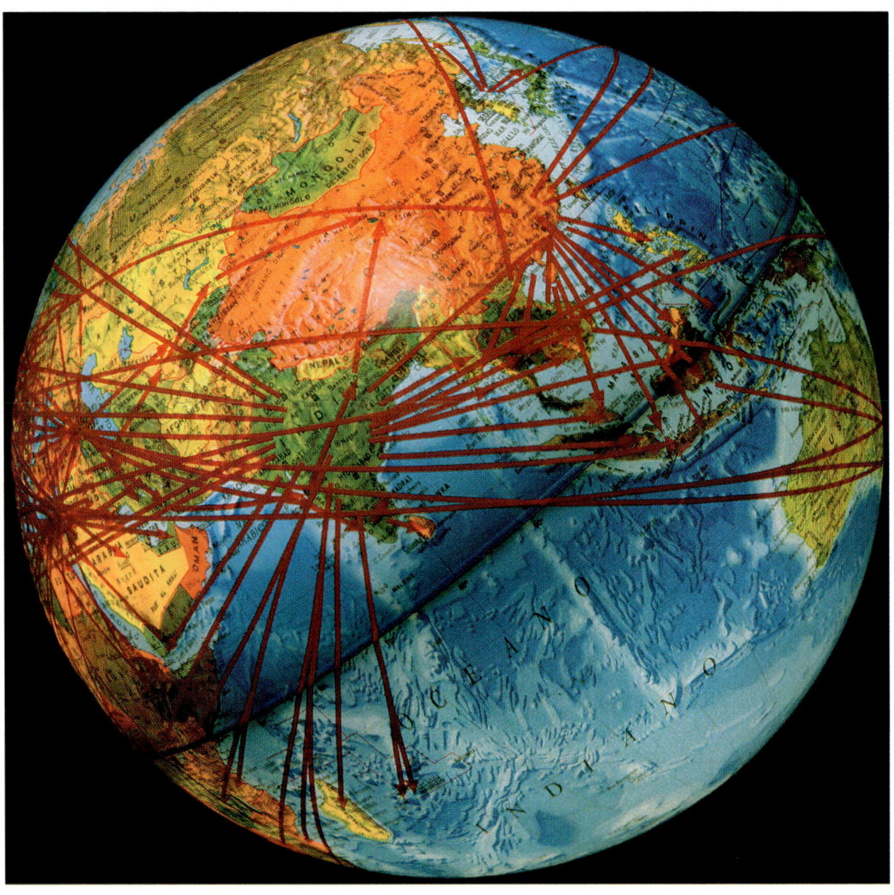

Ingo Günther, *Globus* from the project *Republic of Refugees*. The lines indicate migration waves, used by the artist to stress the migrants' incredible potential: "Grasped as a transglobal network and equipped with their own state, refugees could well become the socio-economic, politico-ideological avant-garde of the new millennium" (www.refugee.net); GLOBALIZATION SATELLITE

Thematic guidelines laid the foundation for the workshops with artists and scientists and were the starting point for the works of art. The objective was to initiate communication and discovery processes and to overcome inhibitions as the participants clarified their stand on the phenomenon of science. Not understanding, no longer understanding, no longer wanting to understand and misunderstanding were important stages along the way.

From the very start, fields were chosen in which the VolkswagenStiftung has been active as a research-funding organization, stimulating scientific discourse: constructs of "foreign" and "native" cultural identities in the process of globalization; the dynamics and adaptivity of neuronal systems; the physics, chemistry and biology with single molecules.

The selection was made with an eye toward scientific significance, visitor interest, general relevance, and suitability for artistic treatment. The parameters were science, everyday life, and the future of science. Artists were invited to study the objects, methodologies and findings of the fields in question. Thus scientists were confronted with an alien view and autonomous depiction of their disciplines. Both sides were compelled to leave their traditional realms. "Science+fiction" shows science and art as borderline phenomena and as illusory constructs. It presents art as a parallel formation to science, and science as art.

The project is based on the altered situation in science as expressed in the many discussions and analyses of our "knowledge society". This term describes a society whose functional systems are largely grounded in the production of scientific knowledge: politics, economy, media, law and culture are inconceivable without science these days. Conversely, science has been transformed too, and there has been a loss of the social distance between science and society that had thus far seemed necessary. The developments are paradoxical. As knowledge has saturated society more fully, living conditions have become more experimental, the future more open. The ascent of the concept of self-organization, which characterizes all areas of our lives and all fields of knowledge, has gone hand in glove with a globalization process spurred on by science and technology. The changed inner structure of science is being intensely debated these days, seen as the difference between Mode I and Mode II of knowledge production. In this discussion, the old scientific culture of modernism is portrayed as centralized and oriented toward fundamental principles. The new, postmodern production of knowledge in Mode II is decentralized, local, application-oriented and multifaceted. Its goal is socially robust knowledge: "In contrast to the past, now it is not only science that speaks to society, but society to science. This dialogue results in a new type of knowledge, and all of society participates in its production, not only scientists. Apparently, the more a society understands research with its uncertainties and risks, the more it intervenes in the realm of science. Public involvement in science may prove to be an essential factor in the future, since it lends knowledge reliability and legitimacy," states Dieter Simon of the Berlin-Brandenburg Akademie der Wissenschaften.

Against this backdrop, "science + fiction" sought to initiate a discussion among artists and scientists. The works of art shown at the exhibition resulted from the interaction between artists, designers, curators and scientists. Depending on the topic and the temperament of the participants, the interaction was characterized by varying degrees of intensity. The participants not only discussed the significance of images and the content of complex computer-animated representations ("Do atoms really look like that?"). They also debated their ability to generalize models or the varying degrees of simplification necessary to render a topic intelligible.

Artists and scientists construct their own worlds, and these are supported by the respective functional systems in a more subtly differentiated reality. In one instance, when the participants suggested to a natural scientist that he portray his discovery by means of art, he declined theatrically. Later, the very same scientist admitted being an "artist" himself.

Conversely, it was important for many artists that their methods be regarded as "scientific". Prejudices, distinctions, and unexpected cultural links have lent, and continue to lend, vitality to the field.

The communicability or non-communicability of modern research with its links to other disciplines also left its mark on the project. As Brecht once said, art does not need the sciences, but rather encounters them as extremely present societal phenomena.

The project "science + fiction" explores the permeability of these worlds, their transitional areas and mutual influences. Cultural knowledge of the exhibition topics is not defined as a neatly-sorted system, but rather as a cluster of scientific knowledge, art, science fiction, myths and public discourse. Popular culture is the place where collective fantasies and outstanding individual achievements meet and find a common echo. The demonstrable knowledge in the field of nanotechnology is supplemented by a wide range of scientific fantasies and literary exaggerations that have, in their turn, influenced research work. This is an example of a scientific subject in its aggregate cultural states: "Popular culture is a seismograph for change. It records upheavals and shifts, both material and ideological; shock waves passing through society; technological and social conditions; strategies, hopes and fears. Science fiction is one of the most interesting of all genres, since it is the freest and most innovative," according to Kai Kaschinski and Christoph Spehr. By juxtaposing science with science fiction and showing the conflict between scientific research and art, the exhibition mines a rich vein of material.

In addition to the art that emerged from exposure to scientific fields, an installation entitled "Framework" was developed to provide background information on the central topics and create links via scientific artifacts, preserved organs, images and texts.

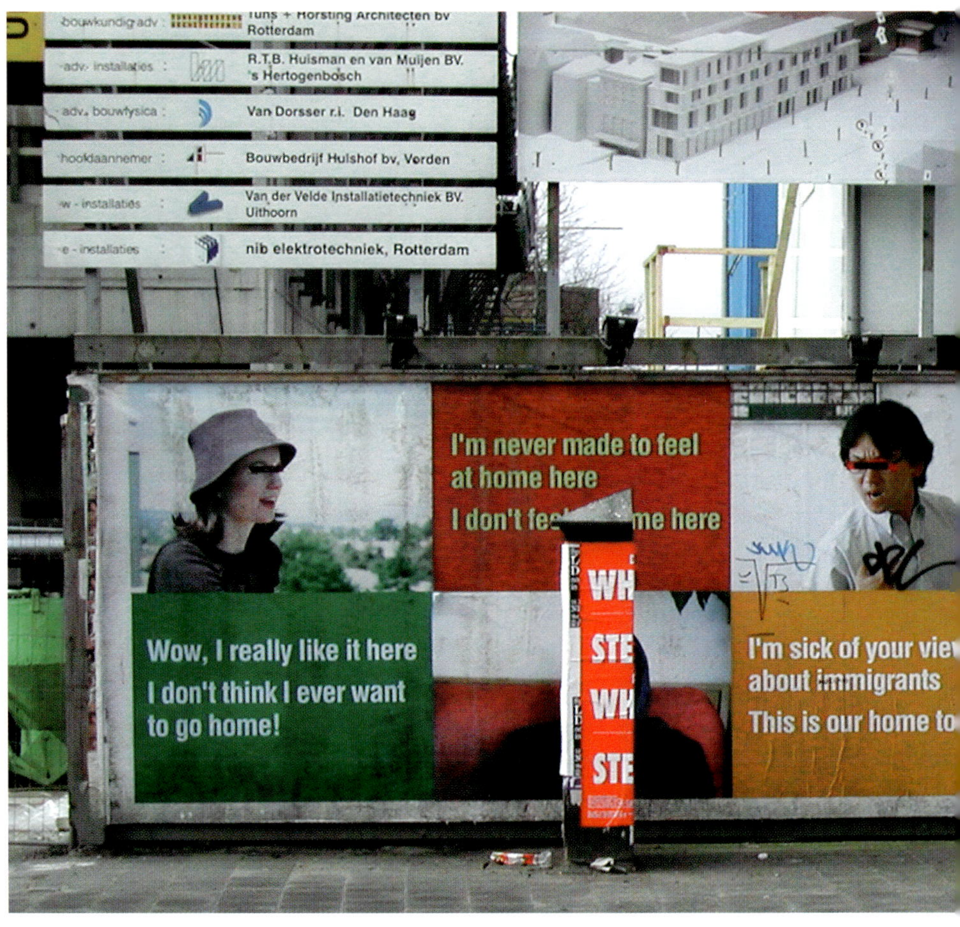

Ken Lum, *There is no place like home*. Billboard for the exhibition *Unpacking Europe: Towards a Critical Reading* by Salah Hassan and Iftikhar Dadi. It stands in front of the Museum Boijmans Van Beuningen in Rotterdam. The project appeared in different urban spaces all over the world.
HOME SATELLITE

"Framework" presents sciencefiction film stars such as Frankenstein and Master Yoda, rap videos, graffiti art, and even models from the *Wunderkammer*. With works of art by Max Bill, Ingo Günther, Peter Kogler and Ken Lum, it examines worlds of societal and scientific imagery. The installation confronts visitors not only with scientific discoveries, but also with diverse means of expressing cultural knowledge as well as numerous cross-references between science and our everyday lives. Visitors can trace intriguing developments, e.g. depictions of the atom since antiquity; Descartes' mechanistic concept of the body as a source of popular fantasies about human machines; illustrations from the field of nanotechnology that borrow material from science fiction films.

The Berlin-based exhibition company "gewerk" designed "Framework"; it was also responsible for the formal parameters of the artistic works. It developed the matrix of modular elements with which all participants were required to work. These elements are pieced together to form presentation islands, pavilions, displays etc., or dismantled into individual parts. The system has made "science+fiction" into a kind of experiment in which artists and scientists struggle, under the same conditions, to find the optimal way to portray their subject matter. The results remain controversial, complementing each other with their differing perspectives, making "science+fiction" an art exhibition and a science exhibition in one.

In addition to documenting the exhibition, this catalog contains survey texts on the central scientific themes as well as talks and interviews with artists concerning their understanding of their work. Essays on the relationship between science and art in the context of the museum treat the subject in greater depth. The catalog is supplemented by the volume *science+fiction Bilder und Texte*, which offers extensive material on the chosen topics.

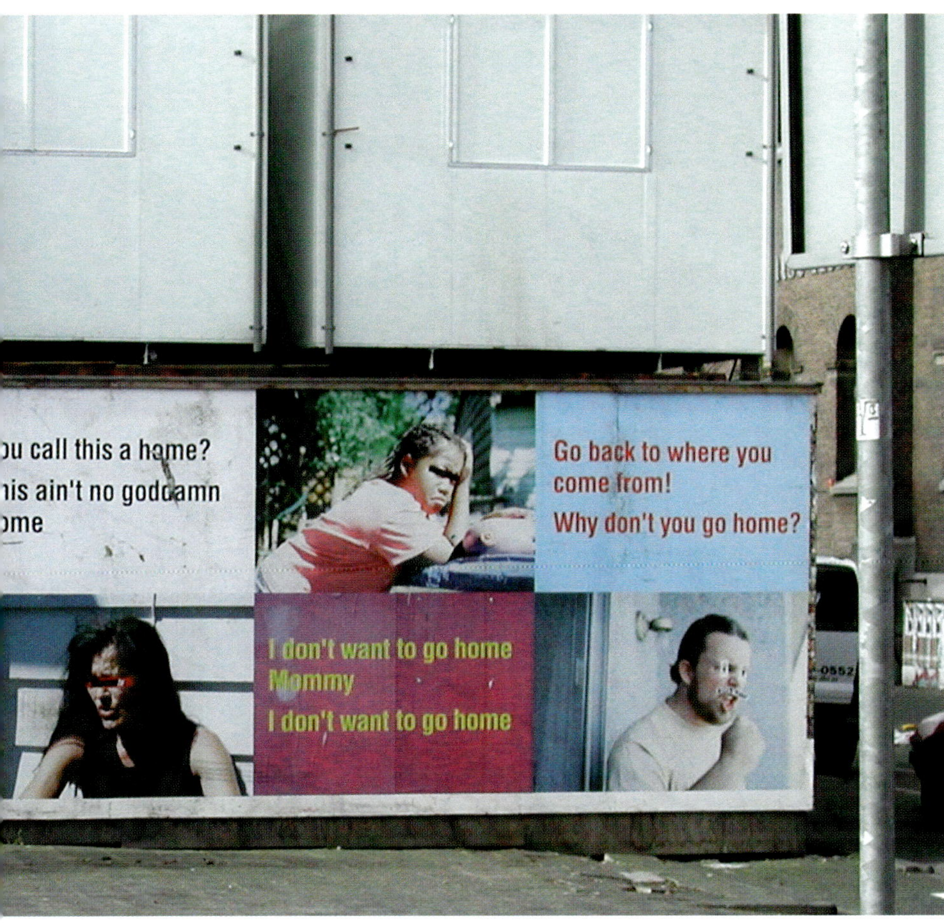

In the late 17th century, Gottfried Wilhelm Leibniz dreamt of popularizing science through a universal, theater-like museum that would bring together entertainment, information and an element of wonder. Leibniz's dream of unifying art and science remains the unattainable goal of this project. It brings into play a little of the combinatorics of science and fiction and the wonder and knowledge captured in the idea of the historical *Wunderkammer*.

ULRICH KREMPEL
NEW IMAGES OF THE WORLD: WHAT IS PERMITTED TO SCIENCE AND
WHAT CAN ART DO IN AN EXHIBITION?

The Academy of Exhibitions

Science and art, which have a programmatic encounter in this exhibition, have been coupled for longer than we are wont to believe. Their programmatic encounters go back to a time when they were engaged in a struggle to emancipate themselves, in German absolutist society, from the tutelage of the princes and the clergy. Both as a value and as an end in themselves, independent research and the free artistic formulation of new ways of seeing the world were initially a Renaissance project, one that was subsequently adopted by the Enlightenment and its utopias. Indeed, in Gottfried Wilhelm Leibniz' view they went hand in hand, as when he outlined his idea for an academy of exhibitions for the sciences and the arts, as a place in which to demonstrate social progress and provide entertainment and instruction. In 1675, Leibniz elaborated on his concept of the exhibition as a modern form of communication. "Let us assume that some persons of rank who have some understanding of marvellous curiosities and novelties, especially machines, wanted to show these to the public.
"In order to cover the costs incurred, they would need to have sufficient funds at their disposal... Apart from those taking care of the financial side of such an enterprise, people would be needed who could contribute to its success with new inventions. However, as a large circle might easily generate confusion, I think it would be advisable to limit its number to two or three dedicated people, *Maîtres du Privilège*; others would be engaged only for a certain time... The people thus committed would be painters, sculptors, joiners, watchmakers and similar groups of people. As the enterprise progressed, one could also gradually include mathematicians, engineers, architects, magicians, faith healers, musicians, poets, publishers, typesetters, engravers and others as the need arises. One could, for example, give a demonstration of a magic lantern – that would make a fine start – and show attempts to fly; one could also present model meteorites, the most diverse optical phenomena; an illustration of the celestial vault with its stars; comets; a globe such as the one designed by Gottorp in Jena; fireworks, fountains, vessels of unusual shape; mandrakes and other rare plants. Unusual and rare animals. The Cercle Royal. Models of animals. A regal apparatus for a horse race with artificial horses. Raffles. Illustrations of acts of war. One could construct fortifications of wood; on the stage: compassion, acts of cruelty, et cetera – all as reproductions of real events. The superintendent responsible for constructing the fortifications could explain the course of the battles illustrated... Exhibition rooms showing natural phenomena or art. Fights, illustrations of swimming. Extraordinary tightrope walkers; highly dangerous leaps... From England, one could invite the man who is able to swallow fire, et cetera (provided he is still alive). In the evening one could watch the moon and the other stars through a telescope."[1]
Showing kommercial wisdom, Leibniz combined his idea with the academy's prerogative to hold exhibitions, thereby ensuring that the exhibition would be regarded as an educational enterprise. "It would be a source of wonder, inspiring people to come up with inventions of their own and enjoy beautiful sights. It would instruct them in countless new fields that are both useful and intellectually stimulating... All those who wanted to publicly demonstrate a new invention or an ingenious plan could come along and make it known to others and, at the same time, benefit from this".[2]
In retrospect, the utopian quality of this exhibition institute has stood the test of time less well than some other aspects of his concept. Contemporary organizers of large-scale exhibitions on natural or cultural history themes tend to favor extraordinary or

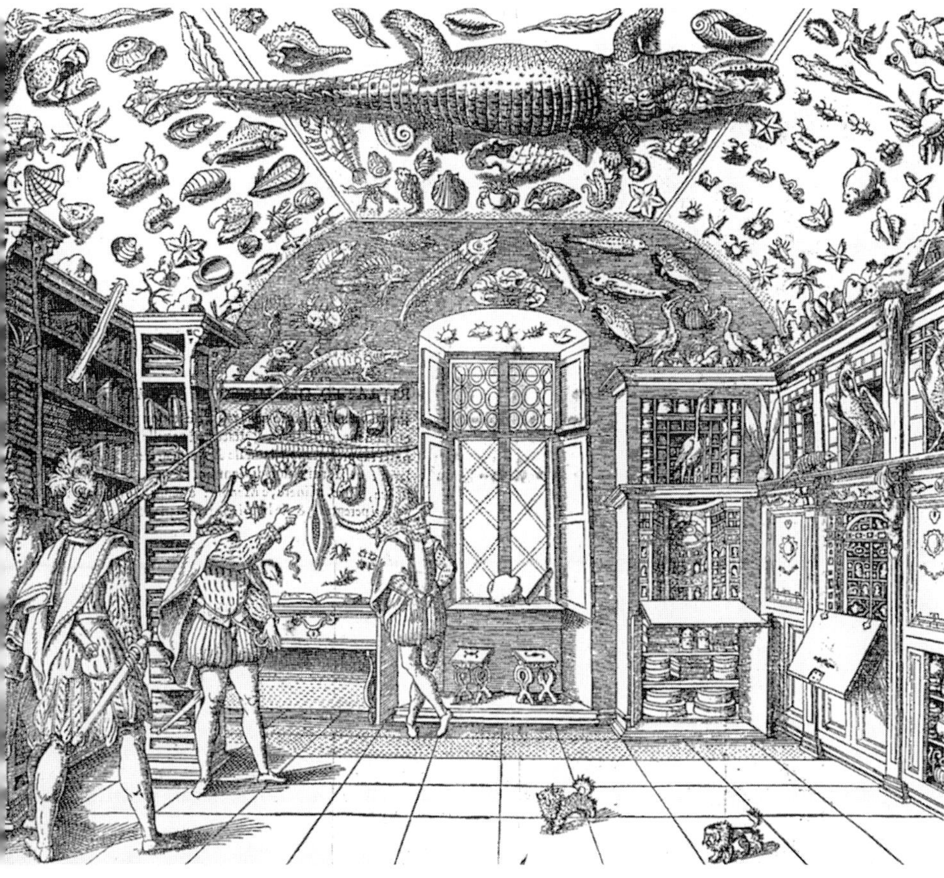

Ferrante Imperato *View of the Museum,* taken from: *Historia Naturale*, 1672, Frontispiece, copperplate engraving. The *Wunderkammer* recalls the old practice of presenting artistic and scientific objects and artifacts together under one roof; SATELLITE WUNDERKAMMER II

highly dangerous events, aiming for a popular appeal that promises maximum success. This practice appears to have its theoretical origins in Leibniz' proposals. Furthermore, the arbitrary manner in which some of the subject areas of entertainment and instruction are combined calls to mind such theoretical changelings as the "infotainment" of the late 20th century.

Leibniz' utopian vision combines entertainment, the acquisition of knowledge and his notion of education in an encyclopedic project that encompasses the entire spectrum of memorable and remarkable events within society. He believed in a chronological continuum of development and the progressive accumulation of objects and facts worth seeing and knowing. Education and information were considered valuable and directly useful both to the individual and society. A very important aspect of Leibniz' concept is the introduction of the mediator, a knowledgeable person who, by virtue of his own understanding of science or art, paves the way for others. Leibniz' idea not only seems to have been inspired by that of the sacred guardian, but also to anticipate that of the exhibition curator. Leibniz places the mediator alongside the inventor, magician, technician, scientist, craftsman and charlatan as well as the general public, the audience and society's elite. In addition to providing more education and information for all, his *Maîtres du Privilège* bring the social estates together in harmony; moreover, the general desire to learn about objects and the world in the spirit of rational discovery is already contained in the act of imparting knowledge.

Where do we stand today? What can we expect from an encounter between art and science at a time when we tend to feel overwhelmed by the systematics of the sciences in all their subtle complexity, and when the ethical questions directed at research are gaining in urgency? Didn't art and science also come together in the past (from the standpoint of art, at least) in scenarios that often seemed playful, in ironic satires and with the serious intention of borrowing work strategies and worlds of imagery from one another? And doesn't today's art, with its symbolic practical values, present an opportunity to illuminate the state of scientific knowledge by posing new questions?

Over the course of time, the arts have increasingly had to face the fact that they have forfeited some of their seemingly inalienable functions to newly-developed technologies and rapidly developing sciences. The zoological and botanical illustrations of reality, the topographical description of the world, the portrait, the artistic exploration of the micro and macro worlds made accessible to us by the sciences – these are all areas that the fine arts have largely had to abandon to the new technical media of photography and film, to cite but two examples.

This may be one reason why 20th century artists, in countless ironic adaptations of the poses and methods of the exact sciences, recalled that long-lost world in which there was common ground between the two. At the same time, the traditional role of the artist has clearly changed. No formulator of eternal truths has taken the stage, nobody who can assert the absolute truth of artistic knowledge. The diagnostic eye of the painters of Verism, *Neue Sachlichkeit* and Critical Realism implies knowledge of the norms of appearances and their deviations; it predates the attitude of the Pop Artists who evoke, collect and reproduce a world dominated by man-made objects, rendering them intelligible in alienated form. Gathering and examining found and collected objects, establishing similarities and deviations, and developing ideas from the world of objects are just as much pseudo-scientific strategies as is the use of the *objet trouvé* to describe contemporary worlds of images. And where the sciences and the arts actually have collaborated on shared themes (observing and recording the myths of everyday life, thematizing and assessing human conditions and concepts of perception in the acts of seeing and knowing etc.), the boundaries between their speculative activities have become blurred and difficult to distinguish.

Artists have repeatedly shown a predilection for applying playful irony to pre-existing roles. When Damien Hirst organized his longitudinal sections of real cows and lambs into ensembles of showcases for people to enter, the allusion to the presentational form of the anatomical cabinet was just as evident as an allusion to the attitude of the scientist who, overcoming the temporal nature of things and living beings, is able to conserve that which is destined for transience. At the same time, Hirst is serious about overturning the traditional role of the artist: in an operation that seems to transcend death, he manipulates and dissects a dead creature, preserving its anatomical features, and displaying the inner organs or the digestive system, for example, in an orderly arrangement as they appear naturally from his specimen's dissected side. Here, however, the artist-anatomist is also the director of a magic ritual which rescues the dead object from the hands of death and commits it to eternal life in an extraterrestrial state, in which it floats in the conserving fluids of a vessel that now encloses the dissected animal. The artist appears as the successor to that presumptuous scientist who – with God-like certainty – destroys and preserves life and even perverts the natural course of things.

Even the establishing of a – real or imitation – drugstore at an art exhibition evokes the systematics of medical diagnostics and their reflection in drugstore practice. Such a setting also appears as a well-arranged presentation of the embodiment of human knowledge. Although it will be unintelligible to those who enter by chance or without any background knowledge, it will remain comprehensible as an assembly of items of scientific knowledge. Just as the *cella* of the ancient temple was clearly a preliminary form of the modern museum with its collection of ennobled objects, what we find here is a collection of things presented as a sacred chamber of human knowledge. In its inaccessibility and untouchable quality as a presentation of exhibits, this collection is only accessible to the adoring eye of the uninitiated. Here, one begins to under-

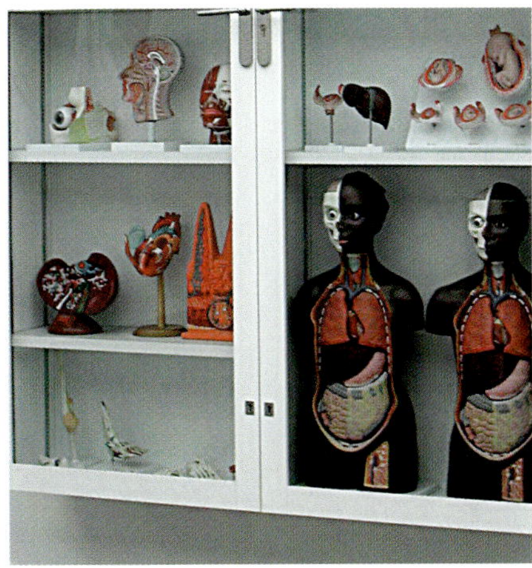

Damien Hirst *Trinity,* 2000, Hamburger Bahnhof, Staatliche Museen Preußischer Kulturbesitz Berlin

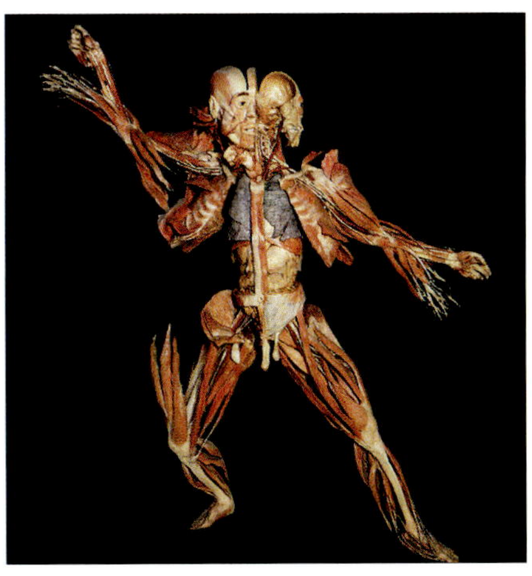

Gunther von Hagens *The Lasso Thrower*, plastinate

stand just how much the scenic staging of such rooms presupposes the artist playfully performing a role which he simultaneously limits to that of ironically producing a citation. For unlike the scientist, the artist works in the symbolic space of art. And only here does the presumptuous pose of the artist become truly understandable; here, amidst all the objects he himself has created, amongst objects that are only suitable for aesthetic use.

Gunther von Hagens' Beuys-Hat

Fama reports that the classical pharmaceuticals representative visiting doctors' surgeries always has to devote special attention to the "artistic doctor", namely the doctor who finds personal fulfillment in making music, writing or painting, or in the enlightened appreciation of the arts. Making music and art seems to be important here not only as a means of compensating for a tough job, but also as a vestige of the traditional ideal of enjoying a comprehensive humanistic education. Even today, this educational ideal is used by some natural scientists and students of medicine to justify their inclination for holistic and, at times, artistic concepts. The relationship between natural-scientific knowledge and an artist-like appearance almost assumes the form of a grotesque caricature in the case of corpse plastinator Gunther von Hagens, who appears in public dressed in Beuys-style clothing, hat included. Von Hagens' exhibition propagates his own scientific work, and is a new platform for presenting durable anatomical specimens of the human body. However, his procedure is a departure from the laconic presentation of the standard specimen (as is still evident in Damien Hirst's animal specimens), since he stages his conserved products as sculptures in three-dimensional space. Von Hagens celebrates his own dexterity and leads the spectator in a completely different direction from the one in which he purports to be going; his figures are exhibited to achieve maximum effect as allusions to classical sculptural poses. They do not aim to impart anatomical knowledge. Presented in flamboyant poses, they reach out into the space around them, dancing, flying and fluttering, but for all that, they mark time. This kind of display works only momentarily; the exhibits self-destruct, in fact, in the very act of presentation. (The master's laboratory had to supply new specimens during the course of the exhibition.) Hence, the display betrays a total lack of respect on the part of the scientist or the artist for the object or the work.

Von Hagens' neo-baroque dance of death makes use of revealing "naked" corpses that pose for spectators. Planned as a travelling exhibition, it is touring the civic halls and congress centers of Europe. This spectacle is a very individual and – from a scientific point of view – extremely dubious approach to the human being as an object of artistic or scientific interest.

And even if the inventor of the latest process for lending supra-subjective permanence to anatomical specimens justifies his enterprise by claiming that he is fulfilling an educational mission, his work nevertheless places his exposition closer to the show booth of a Doctor Caligari and the freak shows of the past than to the intellectual ambitions of the exhibition in its established form as a medium of reflection. This is in no way altered by the Beuys-style hat that the master of the dancing dead dons for his public appearances, presumably as a subliminal reference to the subjective iconography of the famous sculptor and, indeed, to the proximity of Beuys' art world to the fields of transience and the metaphysical superelevation of simple materials. Here, "science" has reached a crossroads which may and will see it depart radically from the emancipatory presentation of objects, objet trouvés, materials and specimens with a scientific connotation. Von Hagens wants to make people shudder and to create that combination of disgust and amazement that grips us when we see traffic accidents with burning cars in our towns and cities. Moreover, his mode of displaying exhibits cannot teach us anything genuinely new, and certainly nothing that we will not find in fact, or as a statement, in the form of the glass people at the Dresden Museum of Hygiene. His objects merely possess the magic of the original and the ostensibly playful stances in which he presents his patchwork corpses. Unlike the late Drs. Frankenstein and Hackethal, this particular scientist already seems to have transcended human death in his dancing poses. And yet the pose only eternalizes that single moment in which the mortal material is captured and displayed. But perhaps the death of organic matter has never been more manifest than in the remains of these anonymous dead humans.

The Objective Seen Subjectively?

This exhibition is based on a dialogue between art and science, mediated through active human beings who come together to discuss scientific strategies and possibilities of understanding one another correctly. They also debate the problems of adequately imparting ideas and knowledge or cunningly planned public appearances.

Sensory perception is the basis of all human activity, whether everyday, artistic or scientific. Artists fulfill their duty to subjective perception when they include themselves in these processes, more distinctly as individually and subjectively perceiving and acting persons than would ever be possible for a scientist.

It is hardly surprising, then, that the artists participating in this project have encountered reservations on the part of scientists. Ralf de Moll, who speaks of reservations about the "unprofessional context" of an art exhibition for presenting aspects of scientific research, is but one example. After all, it is precisely the objectivity of the sciences which is recognizable in its manifold determinations in the approach taken by the exhibiting artists. So when Christoph Keller (like the other artists involved in the exhibition) in his statement initially attests the sciences a "clear definition of objectivity" whilst referring to his own artistic work as involving more of a dialectically conceived "relationship between the person making the statement and the environment", he is going quite some way towards describing the strategy of artistic reflection on the fields of work, research strategies, results and responsibilities of the scientist. And this approach goes much further than the corresponding discourse in scientific institutes and research projects. From there, however, it is often but a short path to the serious reservations vis-à-vis the staff working in the scientific establishment when M+M, for example, argues: "those research scientists who really want to speed up the development of science nowadays are disillusioned, pen-pushing masterminds and people devoid of utopias." Artists believe that their work is characterized by a subjective attitude towards the world and a commitment to the elements of sensory perception: their isolation, their personal

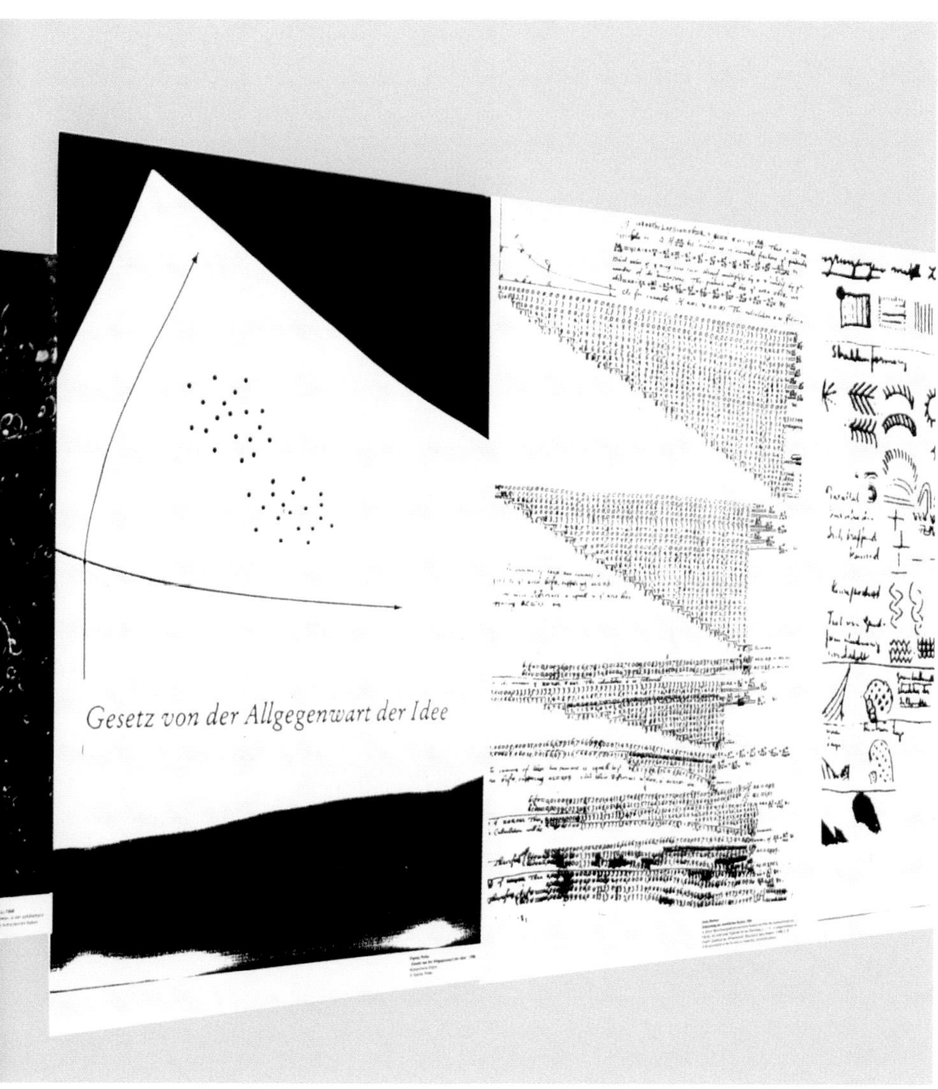

Wall installation with sketches from the worlds of art and science

subjective perception, the unconditional quality of their attitude, and, of course, their emotionality. Joep van Lieshout writes: "As an artist, I always try to follow my intuition, or rather my feelings or instincts…" And Christiane Dellbrügge states: "Artists are self-commissioned and have no obligations to any institute, discipline or scientific truth." The truth to which artists are committed is their personal truth, a truth they stand by with their statements and the results of their work. At this exhibition, the truths of the various sciences can be reconsidered and tested for a moment in an encounter between such positions, and discussed in relation to their preconditions and the problems they raise. As such, this encounter presents a great challenge to everyone interested in the arts and the sciences.

NOTES

1   Leibniz, Gottfried Wilhelm: "Drôle de Pensée, touchant une nouvelle sorte de Représentation" in: *Wunderkammer des Abendlandes. Museum und Sammlung im Spiegel der Zeit*. Bonn 1994, p. 122 f.

2   Ibid. p. 124.

MARTIN ROTH
SCIENCE AND ART – A FLIRTATIOUS RELATIONSHIP OR AN UNHAPPY LOVE AFFAIR?
A CONVERSATION WITH STEFAN IGLHAUT

STEFAN IGLHAUT: In numerous debates on the feasibility of representing science at exhibitions, it is widely believed that artists are needed as translators to render science intelligible. The translation work involves presentation, design and exhibition dramaturgy, without necessarily addressing art in the narrower sense. At the exhibition "science+fiction" we have a special situation. We've brought together art and science as equals in order to illuminate topics from different perspectives and break free of the tired formats "art exhibition" and "science exhibition". Given our experiment, what's your feeling about the necessity of presentation and translation?

MARTIN ROTH: I doubt whether we need the artist as a translator. Before content is translated, it must be made clear and understandable within its own context. An exhibition that imparts incomprehensible scientific discourse through incomprehensible artistic presentation cannot be good, because it leads to permanent misunderstanding. The message of a research project, discovery or object can only be translated into a different context, even an artistic one, if it is clear and comprehensible from the start. However, the flirtatious relationship between art and science goes back further than Trockel and Höller, whose documenta and EXPO exhibits did little to explain biological issues to a mass audience. And Trockel's exhibition on sex left one feeling that it was the most boring, prudish thing in the world.

STEFAN IGLHAUT: In my opinion, what's essential is the agreement reached with artists, and the relationship between artists and their curators or clients. Unfortunately, commissioned work has a negative ring these days. I believe it's wrong to think the ship will veer off course once artists climb aboard. There's just as much confusion when scientists have a say in the design of an exhibition, as science fairs like those in Leipzig during the late 1990s show.

MARTIN ROTH: Why did Oppenheimer want to use artists as mediators for his Exploratorium, with which he created the first science center? Because people no longer had any faith in science after the construction of the atom bomb. And why was art needed as a vehicle and medium to popularize science in the late 20th century? Because the complexity and opacity of scientific issues hampered their communicability. One question remains: is research still relevant if it is not communicable?

STEFAN IGLHAUT: In the end, that's a question of the relevance of fundamental research. Not all highly specialized fields are easily communicated to the public or appropriated by artists.

MARTIN ROTH: Where's the borderline? The public debate on genetic technology has shown that even the most extensive efforts to popularize a subject can make it sound harmless and trivial in comparison with reality. And one mustn't forget that this nature-versus-culture debate was conducted in the *FAZ* features section and even prompted ministers of culture to define the German government's position. Science's flirtatious relationship with art can only develop into a genuine marriage if the chances, limits and dangers of subjects such as genetic technology are made clear. The real potential of museums and exhibitions lies elsewhere. Politicians have missed chances too: why have PUSH funds been given to new institutions instead of going to truly experienced "translation" institutions? This would have made an effective large-scale campaign possible, with renowned and experienced educational institutions imparting new scientific methods.

STEFAN IGLHAUT: Indeed, not much remains of the initiative "Public Understanding of Science and Humanities". Surely the benefit to be had from a popular hands-on science show under a pyramidal roof would have been greatly exceeded by other forms – ex-

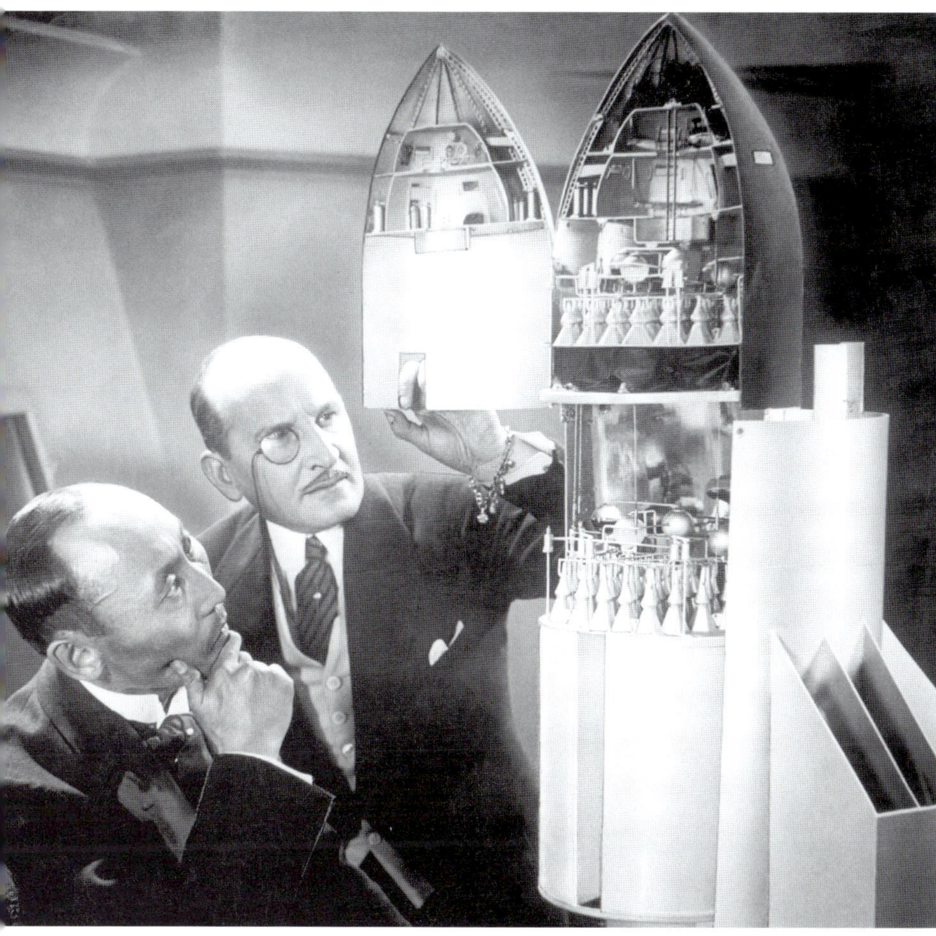

Scene from the film *By Rocket to the Moon* by Fritz Lang (1929); SCIENCE FICTION SATELLITE

hibition duels between artists and scientists at famous museums; Damien Hirst and Hubert Markl grappling with biotechnology; Fiona Tan and Bassam Tibi speaking out on culture in the globalization process. …

MARTIN ROTH: Nevertheless, if a message cannot be put across, there's no use turning to other disciplines for help. And if help is necessary, then I hope it's not always art that conveys and interprets science, but that it's a two-way process.

STEFAN IGLHAUT: I would put it like this: due to their proliferation, science fiction books and films are the art forms that transport science into society. Popular art forms such as these are the source of our images and expectations of the future, e.g. life in cyberspace, genetically optimized organisms, ending the ageing process, journeys to distant galaxies, teleportation, universal language comprehension and so on. Normally it's not the research community that articulates provocative positions that are relevant to the general public. Particularly in such flourishing fields as the biosciences, these positions are first defined through contact with the public. A scientist rarely gives a cultural and economic interpretation of his findings when he presents them. It's not his business – although there are a few charismatic individuals with PR talent who do that sort of thing. Thus a standpoint must be found, it must be established – all the more so in the case of an exhibition, by contrast to the features section of a newspaper, where standpoints can vary on a daily basis. The research community, like society in general, is not the place for clearly-defined positions that merely need to be translated into a popular medium.

MARTIN ROTH: Let's stay with the example of science fiction. If filmmakers succeed in conveying complex scientific discourses simply, if bestselling authors sketch out realistic visions of the future, if museum curators create exhibitions along the lines of "When Art Meets Science", well, I could relate to that. Science needs to be popularized in a comprehensible way.

STEFAN IGLHAUT: But then the uncertainties would also have to be popularized. After all, scientific subjects are full of contradictions. In professional circles, there are extremely controversial discussions on, say, the analyses and prognoses relating to climatic change. The issue of unemployment and society's response elicit very different reactions in political and scientific communities. And when they attempt to explain how the human brain functions, neurophysiologists, doctors and philosophers take different approaches. Research alone doesn't yield a comprehensive or easily communicable picture. And normally, exhibition-makers are not given a clear or easily understandable interpretation of a scientific discipline or a research project to use as a foundation for their work. Rather, they must establish their standpoint through the exhibition. This is always an act of selection and interpretation, even translation, which can naturally go wrong. Your proposal of an "Art Meets Science" exhibition doesn't target a mass market. Such a title implies that art and science retain their independence, and not that one interprets or illustrates the other. For this reason, I would agree with you. It is similar to our work on "science+fiction". Constructs from the domains of art and science do not necessarily have to be transferred back and forth.

MARTIN ROTH: We seem to be close in our outlooks, and yet different in approach. What interests me is how long people have believed that something complicated is necessarily more meaningful, profound, and intelligent – and why they hold this belief. Through her erotic performance in a miniaturized submarine in the human circulatory system, Raquel Welch did more for the acceptance of minimally invasive medicine and nanotechnology than could have been achieved by the programs of the Federal Center for Health Education, by medical conferences or the health insurance industry. That was in the 1966 film *The Fantastic Voyage.* And yet I'm convinced there would have been little societal support for nanotechnology if Gerhard Richter or Rosemarie Trockel had devoted their energies to it. With the sex exhibition at the German Hygiene Museum, Rosemarie Trockel achieved little in terms of "translation work", compared to what Oswald Kolle pulled off at an exhibition a few years earlier. It remains a matter of target group, exclusion, and elitist thinking. It's worth rereading what Pierre Bourdieu once wrote about the habits of museum visitors and curators.

STEFAN IGLHAUT: What we are talking about here is culture's power to interpret current scientific knowledge. And yet we must distinguish between popular films, the omnipresent "zero medium" of television (to quote Enzensberger), the highbrow feature-page debates with well-known figures like Sloterdijk or Craig Venter, and exhibitions and museums. An exhibition doesn't normally have to compete with Raquel Welch or Sloterdijk. As I've already said, it's no use merely illustrating science via art – even if people keep trying. I encountered the most absurd variation on this theme at Siemens. A PR manager thought he was being particularly artistic when he commissioned artists to interpret Siemens's corporate principles. No artist of stature would touch that sort of thing.

MARTIN ROTH: A scientist doesn't enter dangerous terrain if he has an artist interpret his work. On the contrary, it enhances his image and market value within his community, and of course the other way around. It's a classic win-win situation. An ambitious scientist needs the exhibition as a place to demonstrate his work to the public, since the age of major, impressive discoveries is long gone and the invisible can only be made visible – and fame acquired – with the help of translation media. Thus exhibitions must make provocative gestures, they must simplify and confront. Otherwise they're merely the continuation of the traditional bibliography by other means.

STEFAN IGLHAUT: And yet the specialization of disciplines and the variety of interests have hindered the general comprehensibility of science and its traceable link to our world. If an exhibition manages to illustrate individual research projects through comprehensible images and texts, it has achieved much. Institutions must respond quickly, but often they use their own sluggishness as an excuse. A new building has been built for the Science Museum in London, the Welcome Wing, and in the lobby there are changing

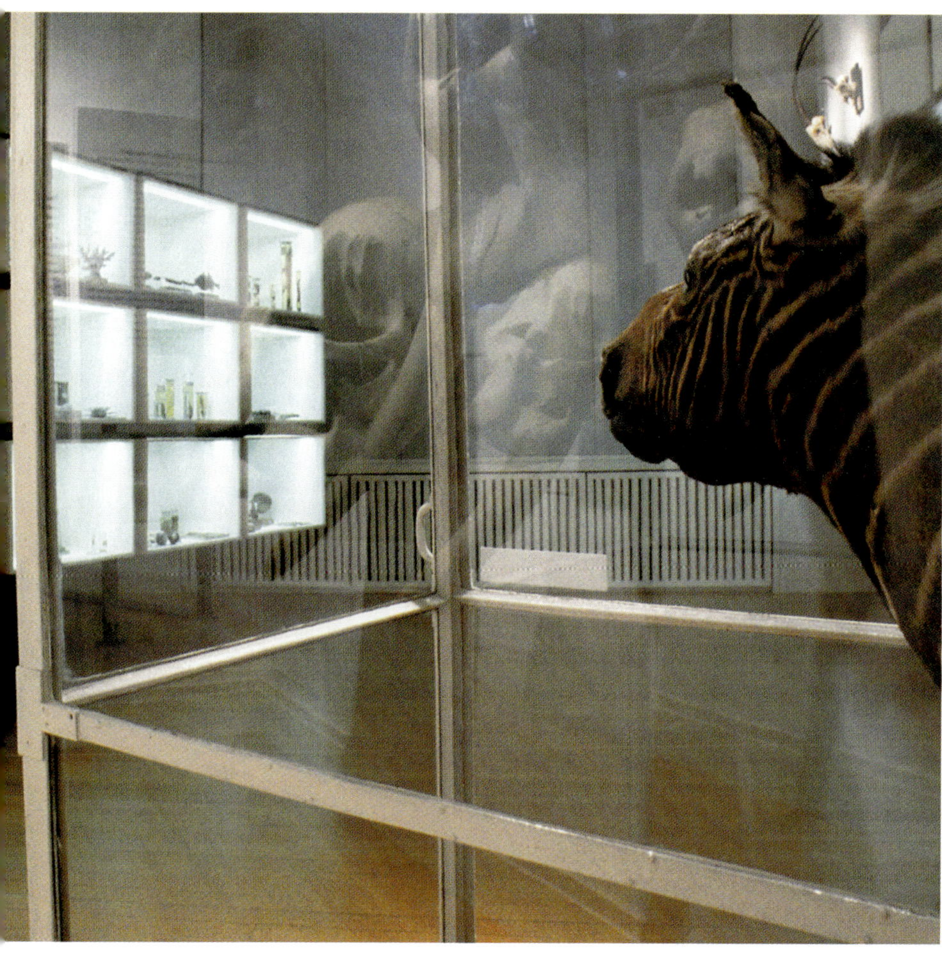

A view of the zoological section of the exhibition *Theatrum Naturae et Artis – Wunderkammern des Wissens,* which ran from December 2000 to March 2001 at the Martin-Gropius-Bau in Berlin and featured the collections of the Humboldt University Berlin.

exhibitions on topical issues such as BSE, foot-and-mouth disease, the birth control pill for men, embryonic research, and so forth. Artists have at times realized similar projects on their own, but for the most part they do not see themselves as mediators, since they believe in their own independence.

MARTIN ROTH: Why did you choose to work with artists if there was a danger of making matters even more complicated? It would certainly be more interesting to find someone willing to translate content as accurately as possible, on a one-to-one basis.

STEFAN IGLHAUT: We prepared for "science + fiction" by providing a thematic impetus, even setting out guidelines. We began with thematic briefing sessions for the artists in order to initiate a dialogue and moderate their first contact with scientific topics. Many in the art world smiled at us. The hard-liners even considered our approach impermissible. Imagine that! On the other hand, the scientists involved were worried that our guidelines were too vague and loosely defined to attain "adequate" results. It's surprising how timid people are. In Germany, artistic autonomy on the one hand and the communication of science on the other are bogeymen that block action. Even so, there are many possible solutions: documenta 11 provided many impressive examples of how to tackle a subject with documentary precision and aesthetic equanimity.

MARTIN ROTH: The equation "comprehensible = shallow" isn't valid either. Easily comprehensible exhibitions hold no appeal. They offer no meat for us to sink our teeth into. The disappointing exhibition on genetic technology at the German Hygiene Museum comes to mind. It was supposed to address the worries, fears and reservations of the populace and make the topic more accessible. Instead, it was an oversized schoolbook that left visitors cold. A little while later, the German Hygiene Museum put on an exhibition on the human brain. It was staged by Via Lewandovsky. He managed to portray

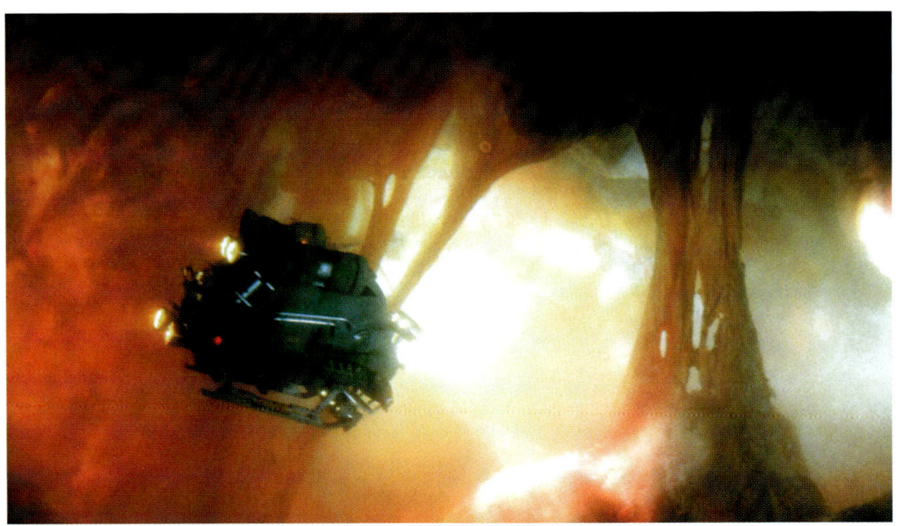

Submarine Kraken II, scene from *Innerspace* (1987). In the film a submarine is shrunk to molecular size and navigates the human body with its crew. NANOFICTION SATELLITE

the twilight zone of our thought processes, taking visitors through a kind of three-dimensional flashback of moods and knowledge, suspicions and recognition. However, I'm fairly certain that here, too, visitors left with little new knowledge, even if they were made curious. Exhibition-makers must be masters of the art of seduction and have a yearning for opulence. The *brut* quality of "Theatrum Naturae et Artis" at the Gropius-Bau in Berlin was like an exercise in ascetic reductionism that only the initiated could enjoy.

STEFAN IGLHAUT: Maybe one problem is that scientists and companies alike have suitable content, but do not present it to the public in a provocative, polarizing way for fear of damaging their image.

MARTIN ROTH: I'm reminded of Georg Frank's thesis that in our "attention economy" exhibitions have become a place where scientists demonstrate their work to the market for the purpose of self-legitimization and gratification vis-a-vis their colleagues. That might be true. I'm not in a position to judge.

STEFAN IGLHAUT: I feel that self-portrayal is a legitimate motive, and yet it doesn't necessarily result in comprehensible, impressive images of what moves the world. A recent program in the ZDF series "Abenteuer Wissen" (Knowledge as Adventure) showed genetic changes in living creatures that had been caused by chemical residues in the soil – even in remote regions like the Tirolean Alps or the Arctic Circle. Animals are being born as hermaphrodites and no longer reproducing. The documentary was memorable, not because of its research findings, but rather because of its narrative quality and powerful imagery. A storyteller is necessary, be it artist, exhibition-maker, documentary filmmaker or science fiction author.

MARTIN ROTH: I only want to point out that translations can make the results muddy. Do we really need a translator? I still insist – I'm trying to provoke you – that exhibitions can be informative, provocative and entertaining while retaining their captivating clarity. Wouldn't it be more effective to present science and research in their purest form, with all its aesthetic charm? Using nice colorful images, nanoscientists have made us believe that the smallest of all worlds is colorful and possesses graphic structures. When chaos research was experiencing its heyday, hitherto unheard-of fractal systems were presented to us as estuaries and frost patterns. These images have remained in our minds. The resourcefulness of the natural sciences is always underestimated. This is shown by the recent scandals involving falsified scientific research. The falsifiers need to be very imaginative performers.

STEFAN IGLHAUT: If every falsifier were a master of presentation, we surely wouldn't have to worry about how to present science at exhibitions. The goal of these fakes is rarely to influence the public's perception of science, but rather to gain professional recognition, funding and publicity. The topic is surely worthy of its own exhibition. It really is an interesting phenomenon.

MARTIN ROTH: All told, the relationship between art and science is fraught with jealousy and envy. It is one that has never been clearly defined. Despite years of hard work, Leibniz never managed to establish an academy of science in Dresden as an institute for research, presentation and education, even though the city was excellently suited to his needs, and the natural science and art collections were excellent. The Palais Royal des Sciences made no headway in this matter either. In the end, the arts and the sciences remained divided. Even if names now cause some confusion, since the boundaries used to be drawn differently.

STEFAN IGLHAUT: Leibniz, who crossed the boundary between science and art, had a tremendous influence on today's exhibition practices both as a patron and as a point of reference. Horst Bredekamp and Jochen Brüning were completely justified in pointing this out at "Theatrum Naturae et Artis". But I consider it extremely difficult to reunite cultures that have drifted so far apart. Today, science and art are areas of society with different organizational principles, and they can perhaps only be truly united in a medium such as science fiction. Even so, I think we took the right path with "science + fiction" in allowing representatives from both areas to speak on the same level. However, this must not mean that their statements are compatible at the end of the day.

MARTIN ROTH: Much would be achieved if their statements were understandable at the end of the day – clarity still being a high art, even in science.

STEFAN IGLHAUT / THOMAS SPRING / GEWERK
SCIENCE + FICTION: EXHIBITION SCENOGRAPHY

"Science + fiction" is a scenographic art exhibition that links artistic works with scientific topics and is scheduled to run at both art and science museums as a travelling exhibition. Its design and presentation aesthetics must blend well with the ambients of these different museum spaces (white cube and science museum). To meet this basic requirement, an architectural grid system was developed, presenting the entire exhibition as an experiment and requiring scientists and artists to integrate their themes and ideas into a kind of formal matrix.

As part of the architectural grid system, the individual parts of the exhibition are pieced together to form the overall installation. The system consists of recurring modular elements with which the different spatial objects can be built – a semantic allusion to the logical-conceptual methodology of scientific research, which first breaks down its ob-

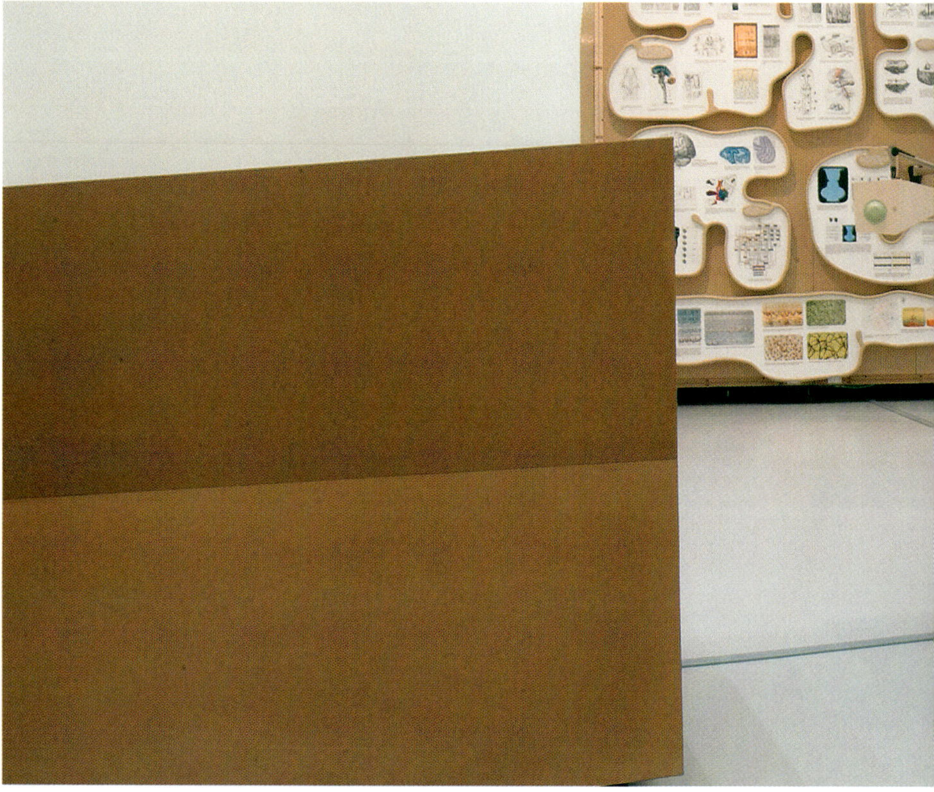

ject of study before reassembling it. In addition to creating a consistent presentation structure, the modular exhibition system gives producers the freedom to make their own thematic links and enables visitors to compare and trace artistic and scientific positions in a large range of combinations.

The modules also serve as display cases for the installation "Framework", an ensemble of satellites that provide background information on the large works of art, presenting a playful array of artifacts and images from the worlds of science and art. The satellites can be given new contents and rearranged at the different exhibition locations.

In accordance with *Arte Povera* principles, all materials and components are presented in their natural form. This emphasizes the temporary, transitory nature of the exhibition. Associations with archives, scientific collections, teaching/demonstration rooms, laboratories and art studios are intentional.

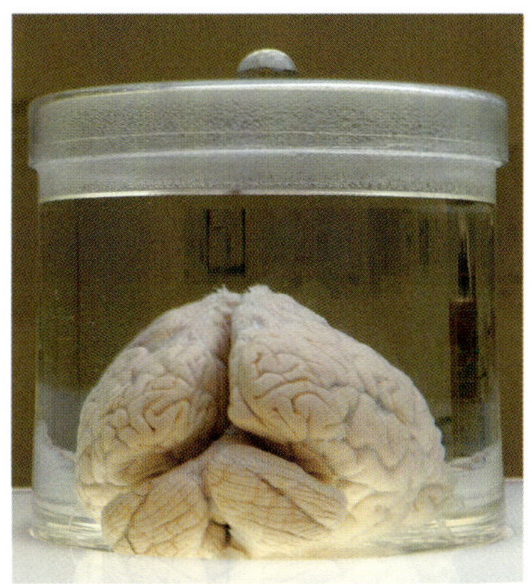

**Preserved brain, collection of
the Charité hospital in Berlin
Framework installation**
Framework guides visitors through the
exhibition's topics, providing background
information and presenting objects of art and
science on the same level. In the entrance
area, a preserved brain, a globe from the
project "Republic of Refugees" by the artist
Ingo Günther, and a model Bucky Ball introduce the central themes of the exhibition.
BRAIN RESEARCH SATELLITE

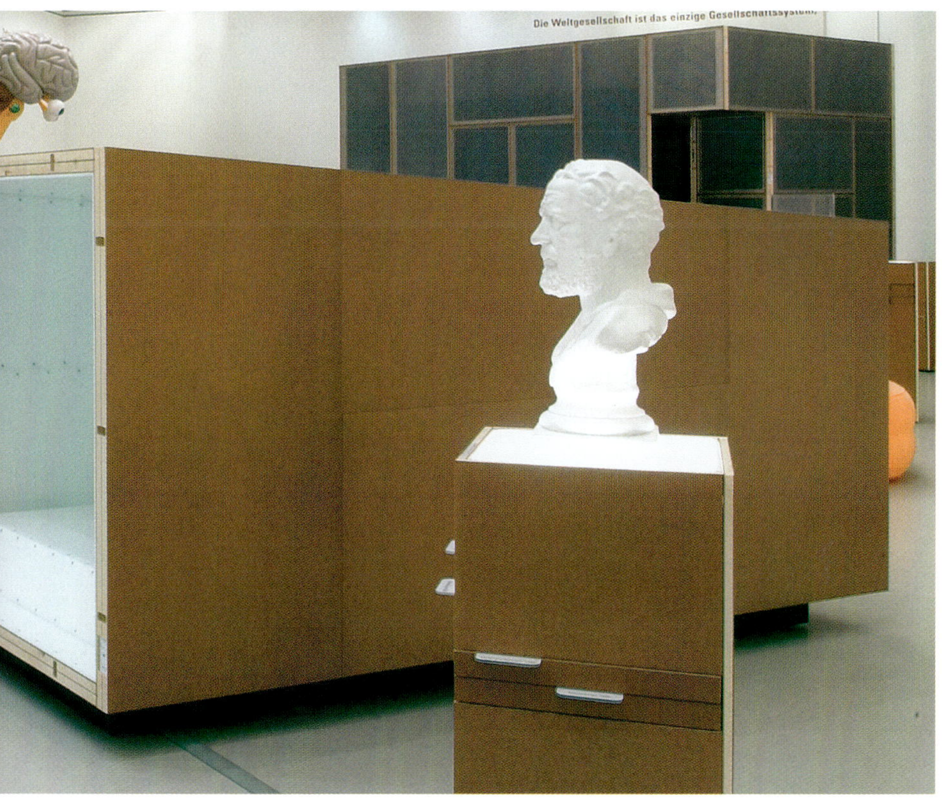

Model of a Bucky Ball
The leitmotif of the section dedicated to
nanotechnology is the Bucky Ball, an artificial
carbon molecule named after Richard Buckminster Fuller, the inventor of the geodesic
dome. The molecule has a tightly-knit
cell-like structure that consists of pentagons
and hexagons. The material is conductive,
extremely hard and yet flexible.
NANOSCIENCE SATELLITE
gewerk, Berlin

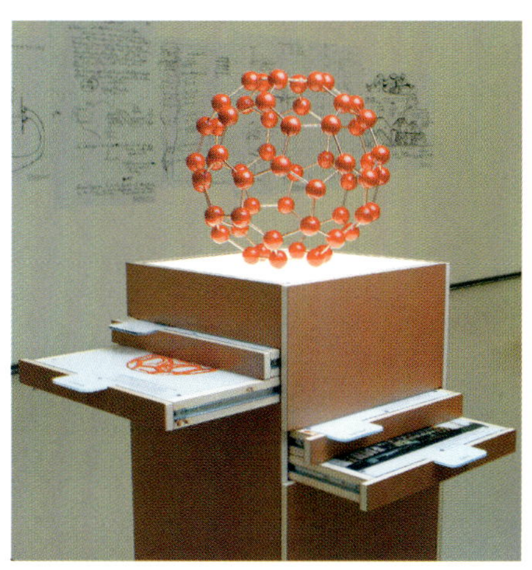

Bloodstream submarine Kraken II, film model from *Innerspace* (1986)

Long before the term "nanotechnology" was coined, the motif of micro- and nano-cosmos appeared in works of science fiction. The concept of microscopic surgery was showcased in the 1966 film *The Fantastic Voyage*, which Isaac Asimov later turned into a novel. However, the film characters do not use molecular machinery made of real atoms, but rather a large, scientific-looking apparatus that magically shrinks people and machines to a microscopic size by miniaturizing the atoms themselves – in violation of numerous laws of physics.
NANOFICTION SATELLITE
Stiftung Deutsche Kinemathek / Filmmuseum Berlin

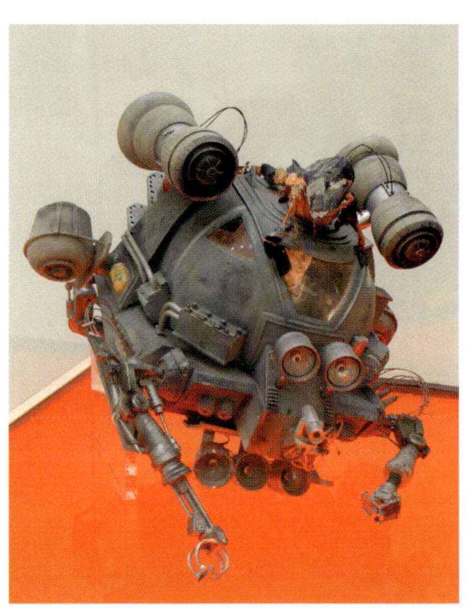

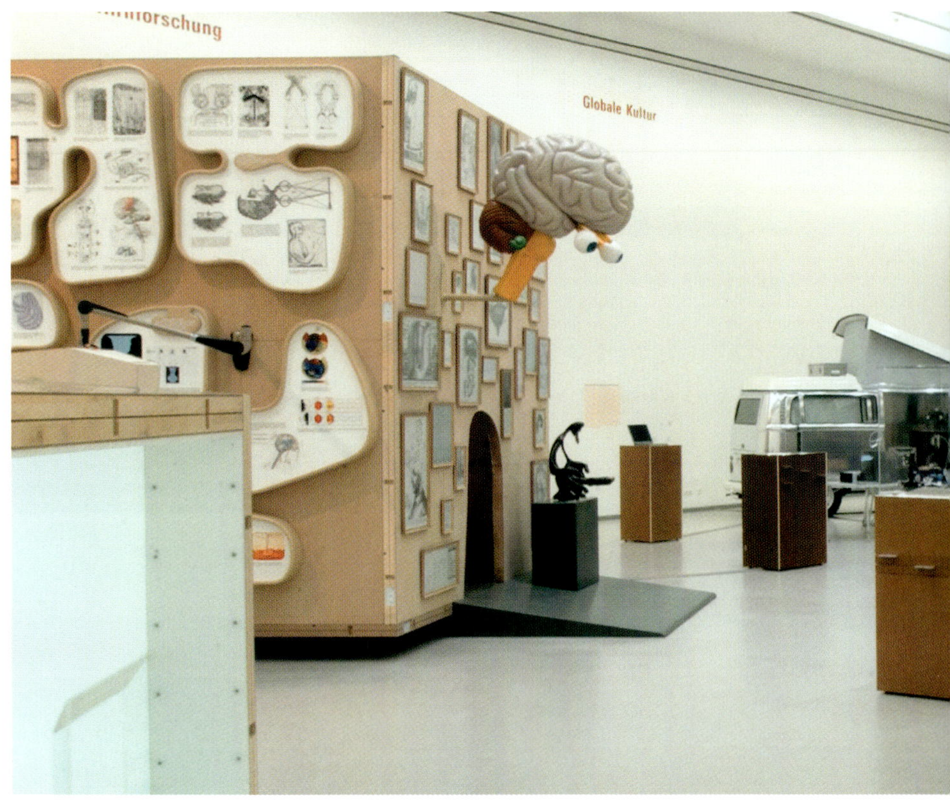

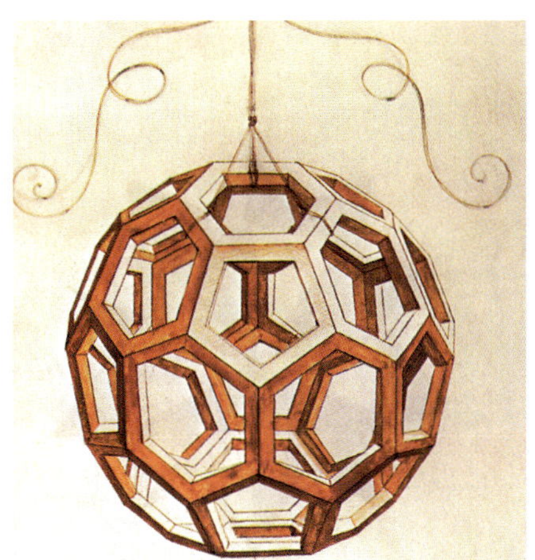

Leonardo da Vinci, illustration from *De Divina Proportione* by Luca Pacioli (1501)

The form of the Bucky Ball has been known to mankind for a long time. It is based on the icosahedron, a highly symmetrical body composed of 20 equilateral triangles. The icosahedron was studied by the ancient Greeks and is one of the five platonic bodies, which also include the tetrahedron, octahedron, cube and dodecahedron.
The Bucky Ball is formed by cutting the edges off an icosahedron. The first known drawings of this kind were done by Leonardo da Vinci within the framework of his studies of geometry.
NANOSCIENCE SATELLITE

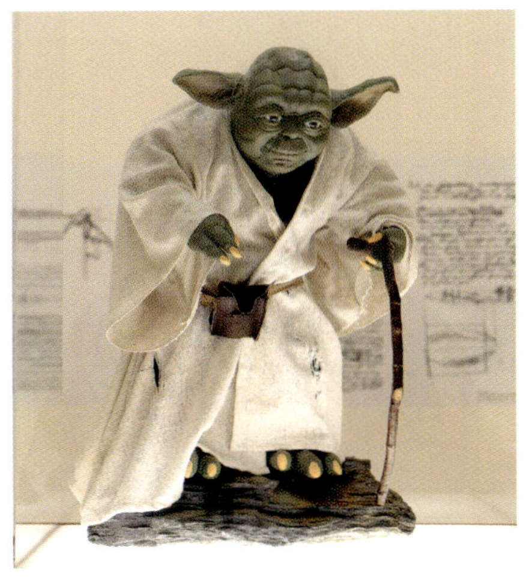

Model of Master Yoda from *Star Wars*
Science fiction stories and characters express profound societal myths via science. They often provide society with role models and guiding principles for future scientific study, influencing research goals and interests.
SCIENCE FICTION SATELLITE
Sylvia Mörtel, Taunusstein

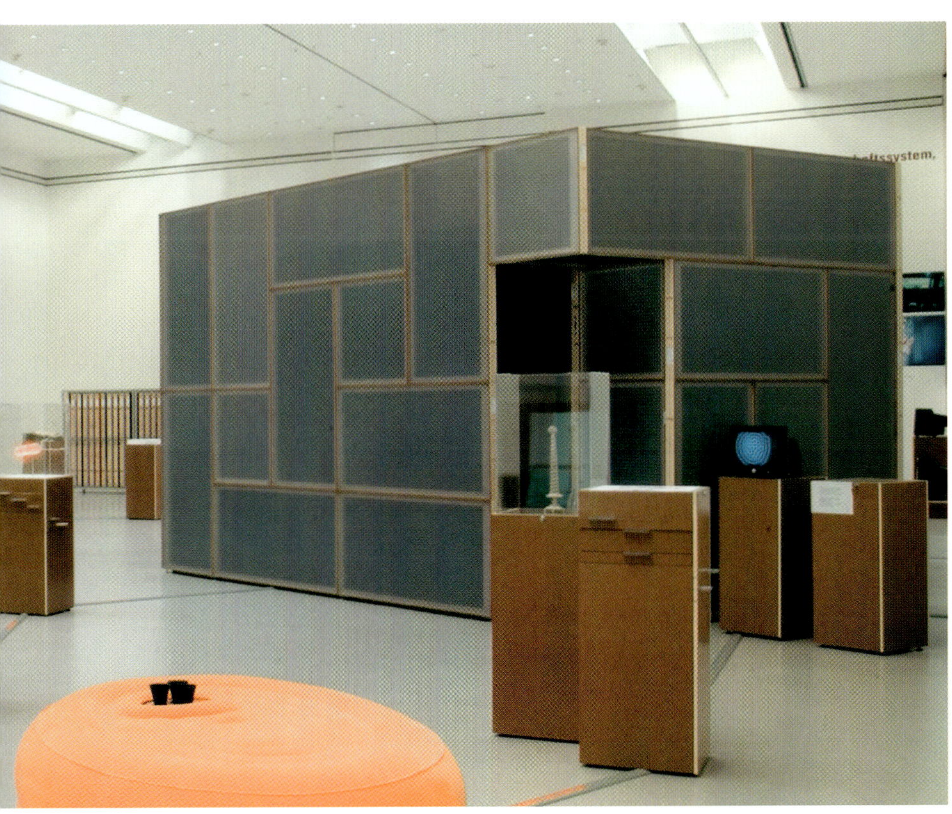

Richard Buckminster Fuller: American Pavilion at the 1967 World Fair in Montreal
Buckminster Fuller – architect, inventor and visionary – developed and patented the construction principle of his geodesic domes. These are based on the triangle and the polygons formed by it. The triangle's sides economically stabilize the opposite angles. "Structure is triangle. There is no other cosmic case that can be combined sixfold with so little effort and formed by a minimal series."
NANOSCIENCE SATELLITE

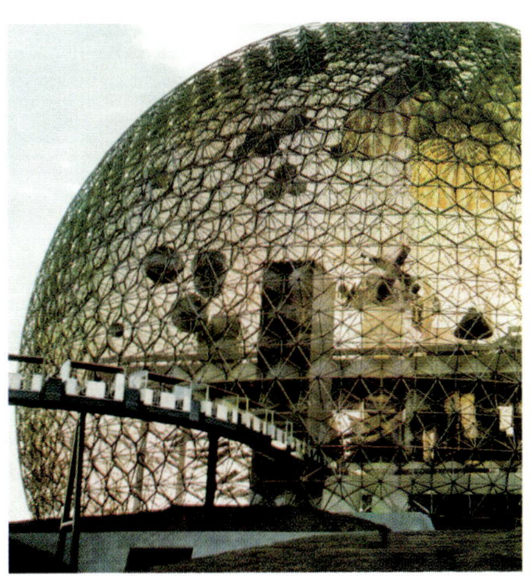

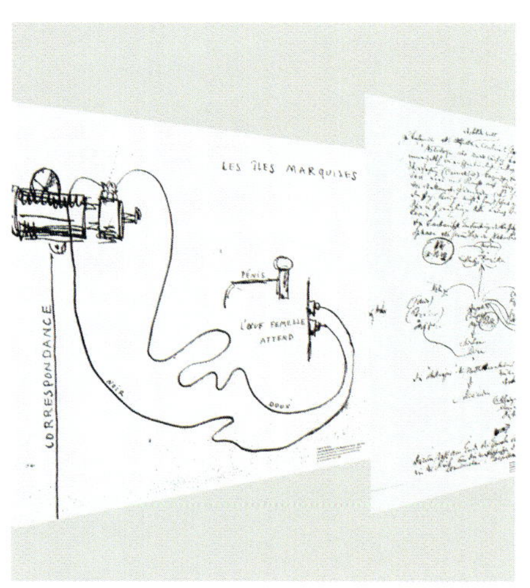

Exhibition Displays

This wall installation, featuring sketches by scientists and artists, focuses on the moment of creation and discovery. Conversely, a wall collage with current press and TV images reveals the societal background of art/knowledge production as well as its subject matter. On seats equipped with audiophones, visitors can listen to statements on the exhibition's main concepts.

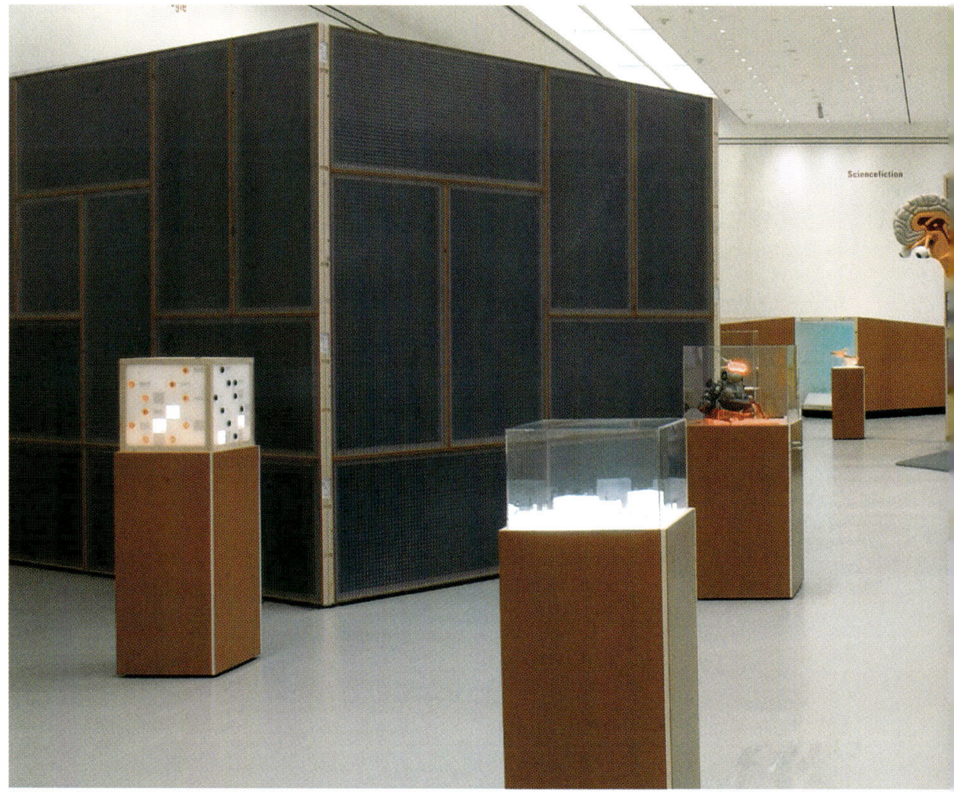

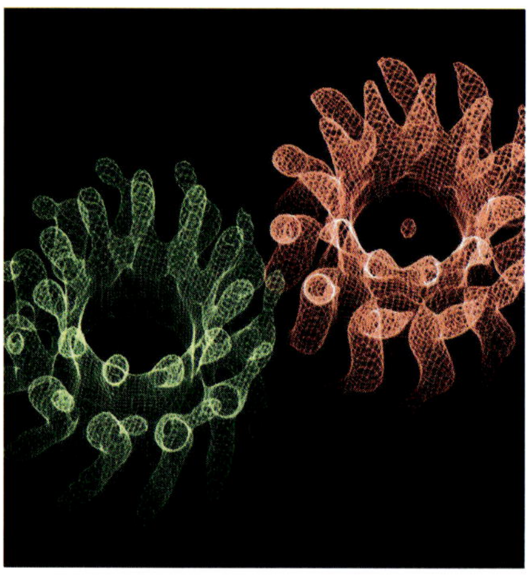

Biological Engine

A biological rotor was discovered in the cell membrane of the bacteria *Ilyobacter tartaricus*. Its three-dimensional structure is depicted here. When the smallest of biological rotors turns, it supplies energy for the molecule ATP, the fuel for all living cells.
NANOMOTOR SATELLITE
© Max-Planck-Institut für Biophysik, Strukturbiologie, Frankfurt am Main; Janet Vonck, Tassilo Krug v. Nidda, Werner Kühlbrandt, Thomas Meier, Ulrich Mathey, Peter Dimroth, ETH Zürich

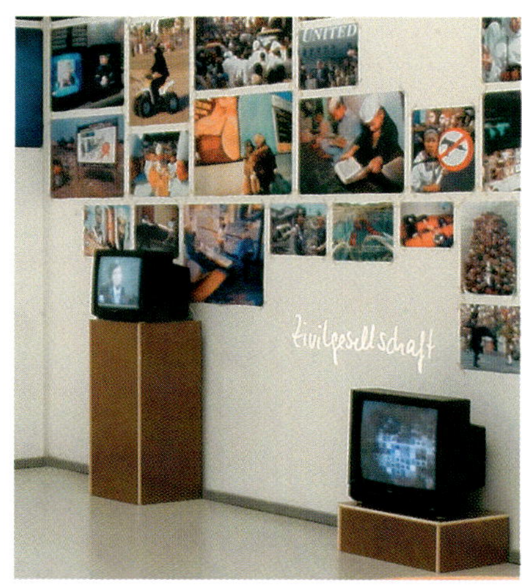

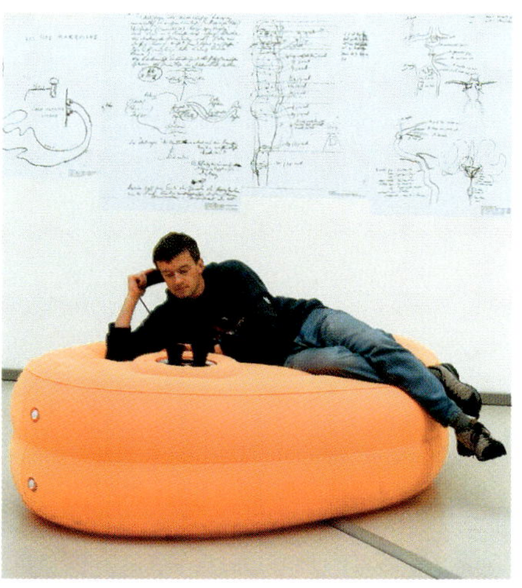

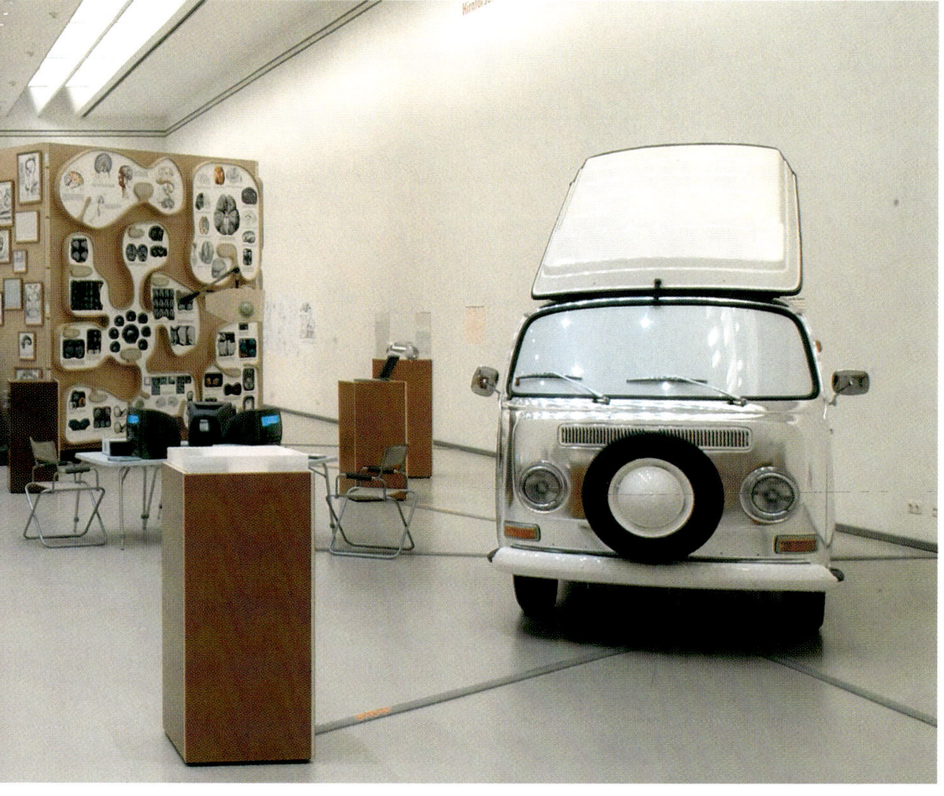

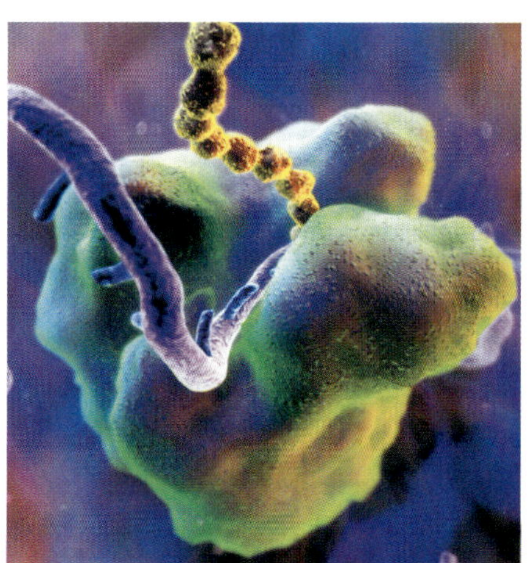

Ribosome
A ribosome reads a DNA strip (purple) in order to obtain information on how to assemble the amino acids that a protein (yellow) is made of.
NANOMOTOR SATELLITE

STEFAN IGLHAUT: Your work often contains references to popular science fiction books and films. At times you make use of science fiction strategies yourselves. What is it about them that interests you?

M + M: What interests us most about science fiction is the scientist and his work. He anticipates and influences efforts to alter space and time. He compresses time by making it possible for people to travel at the speed of light *(Event Horizon)* or to use systematized telepathy *(Minority Report).* He overcomes spatial boundaries by penetrating the human body *(Fantastic Voyage)* and discovering new beauty there *(Dead Ringers).* Through experiments and the use of special chemicals, he gives physical form to unconscious, genetically conditioned dream worlds *(Dr. Jekyll and Mr. Hyde, Altered States).* Maybe he's only with us for an evening, but it's better than sitting through an entire semester of a tedious introductory course. In the best-case scenario, his "work" lives on as an autonomous creation *(Mr. Stitch, Blade Runner).* There are a lot of reasons why an artist might envy him. What artist doesn't have a bit of the mad scientist inside?

STEFAN IGLHAUT: You portray the mad scientist as a kind of renegade who flies in the face of social norms and codices as he attempts to transcend reality. Would you describe the attempt to define oneself by deviation and difference as an aesthetic principle?

M + M: As far as the mad scientist goes, yes. For him, reality can only play a minor role as a yardstick for the results he wants to achieve. It is the impossible, or what seems to be, that guides him: the desire for eternal life, the desire for never-ending sexual gratification, the attempt to break free of the constraints of space and time. As Victor Frankenstein says, "If I were given the chance to conduct research into just one of these things – for instance, the meaning of eternity – I wouldn't care if the world thought me mad." Naturally, deviation holds a large amount of aesthetic potential. By contrast, the scientists of today who are responsible for accelerating developments in their fields are disillusioned paper-pushers with no belief in utopias. They aren't socially acceptable either, but cynical empiricists who routinely conduct their experiments on elementary particles, straining and modifying nature with the tricks and detailed knowledge of their colleagues.

STEFAN IGLHAUT: You reject the idea that scientists are capable of utopian thought, and yet biomedical attempts to optimize the human body are at least based on a vision, if not a utopian plan. This issue cropped up in your early work – for instance, in your ironic documentation of the use of a hip prosthesis with the M+M logo. Are utopias more of an artistic format than a scientific one?

M + M: The signed hip prosthesis is part of our work "Abgabe/Eingabe" (Output/Input), for which we also donated blood and sperm. In fact, in connection with the biomedical work you mentioned, many of these works were interpreted in a predictable way in the 1990s. The stereotypical criticism voiced by one French curator was that our work could only have emerged in Germany. And yet what was crucial to us was the penetration of the anonymous system of the human body. We were inspired by the concept of inner beauty in Cronenberg's film *Dead Ringers*. One might see a utopian element in the fact that a generally inaccessible place was made artistically utilizable, through arbitrary change, with no consideration for the functionality of the respective systems. Of course this is only possible with the assistance of bribed specialists, in this case doctors, who are willing to grant us entry into one of their guarded domains. The system doesn't condition us; rather, we freely intervene in the system. We proceeded in a similar fashion when working on "Autobahnschleife" (Highway Ring) and "Duftwolke" (Fragrant Cloud): we were able to enlist the support of structural engineers and meteorologists

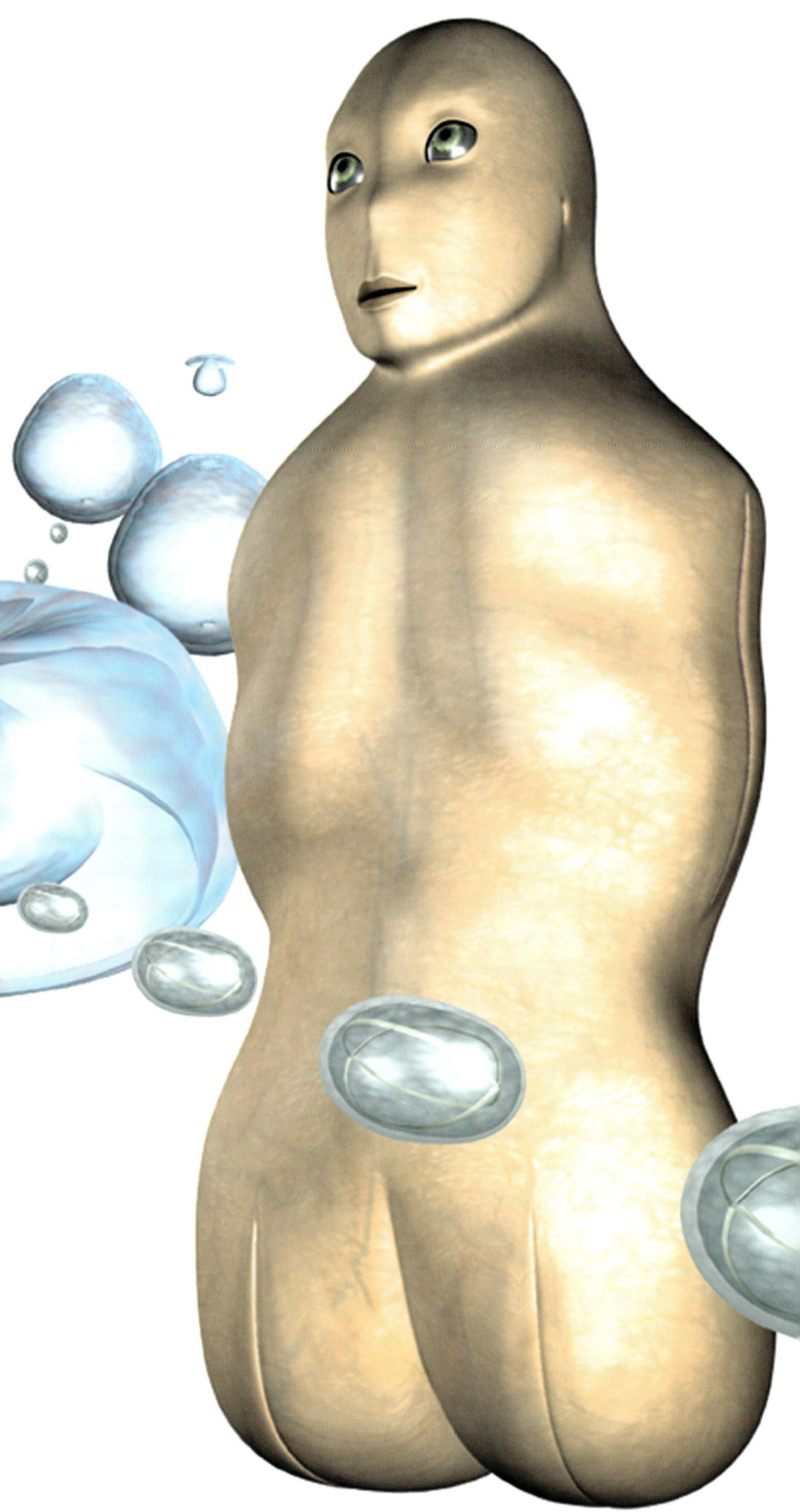

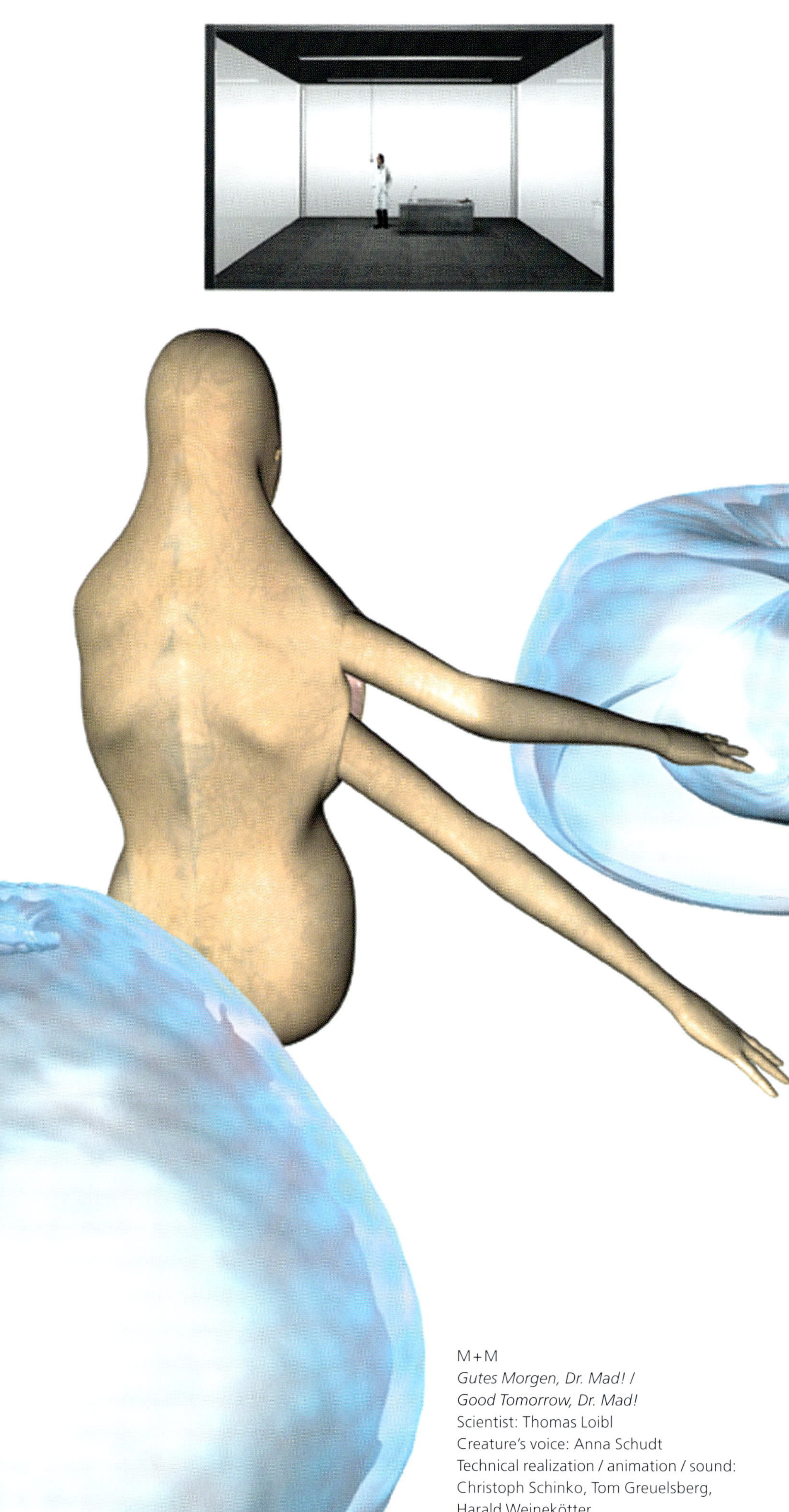

M + M
Gutes Morgen, Dr. Mad! /
Good Tomorrow, Dr. Mad!
Scientist: Thomas Loibl
Creature's voice: Anna Schudt
Technical realization / animation / sound:
Christoph Schinko, Tom Greuelsberg,
Harald Weinekötter

for these projects. Once again, the focus is on the individual modification of determinant organisms and networks as a highly personalized form of artistic intervention. Science, on the other hand, seeks to optimize a generally valid model or book of rules.

 What systems do you explore in your work for "science+fiction"?

M + M: In "Gutes Morgen, Dr. Mad!" (Good Tomorrow, Dr. Mad!), we do not concern ourselves with the concept of a system in the narrow sense. Nevertheless, the visitor is followed by the scientist's extended eye, his surveillance camera, which is located in the middle of the experiment. Bizarrely enough, visitors can look back out at the researcher behind his layer of protective glass. When you're no longer sure whether you haven't been miniaturized yourself, whether you aren't perhaps in the frustrated biologist's scrotum – that's when this fatal, inextricable combination of observer, scientist, lab and creature becomes most intense.

STEFAN IGLHAUT: Where does this malice come from? Do you experience modern science as threatening? Or are you also fascinated and beguiled by fantasies of what is possible?

M + M: What is possible surpassed fantasy a long time ago. And the daily array of revolutionary scientific innovations has sated our curiosity. More fascinating is the question of whether our ethics can keep up, whether they will prove superfluous, whether they can stabilize values, slowing down time and scientific progress or even reversing them. The natural sciences are not menacing these days, since in their complexity – and without a clear ringleader à la Oppenheimer or Frankenstein – they no longer have a distinctive profile. Increasingly, we respond to science as a kind of nature with evolutionary forms and developments that we can accept coolly and without fear. In addition, as with unrequited love, science appears to be the best cure for its own dangers. The cinema – thank God – helps us out of this dilemma, since science and morals are firm fixtures of cinematic discourse and have their traditional place there.

STEFAN IGLHAUT: But reality is much more complicated than a Hollywood script. Current research is rarely presented to the general public with the clarity and emotionality of a film. Do you regard the counter-worlds created by the Hollywood dream factory as more appealing realities than those offered by science, since they present clear images and a clear world order?

M + M: It is precisely the correlation between both worlds that interest us. Let's assume that science, as a producer of reality, creates a new system of life and a new natural world in, around and out of us. Then the scientist will have the most intimate relationship with this new world. In films he is presented romantically as a kind of demigod who is wrapped up in his own field. In our work we latch onto scientists like parasites in order to penetrate more deeply into their world. By intervening artistically in the scientifically researched, mechanically optimized human body, our work "Abgabe/Eingabe" resembles Land Art, which leaves its mark on the original natural environment.

STEFAN IGLHAUT: You mentioned ethics earlier, suggesting they might not be able to keep up with scientific developments. Do you see the discussion of values as a response to modern research?

M + M: If we accept the sciences and their findings as a natural fact, then values become problematic, not least because Darwin is always in the wings with his model of evolution and the culture of the Erlenmeyer flask seems to reign supreme. We have to try to work parallel to this second nature.

STEFAN IGLHAUT: Would this work aim at aligning art more closely with science, instead of drawing borders and maintaining distances, as suggested earlier? Or do you mean the creation of a parallel aesthetic world?

M + M: By "parallel" we mean an independent model that reflects similarities but places different emphases. In "Gutes Morgen, Dr. Mad!" we focus on the border between science in film and our understanding of the natural sciences in everyday life. The work is based on the traditional protagonists of the genre: the scientist and his creation. However, one must see our homunculus as a happy creature. He is genetically optimized and

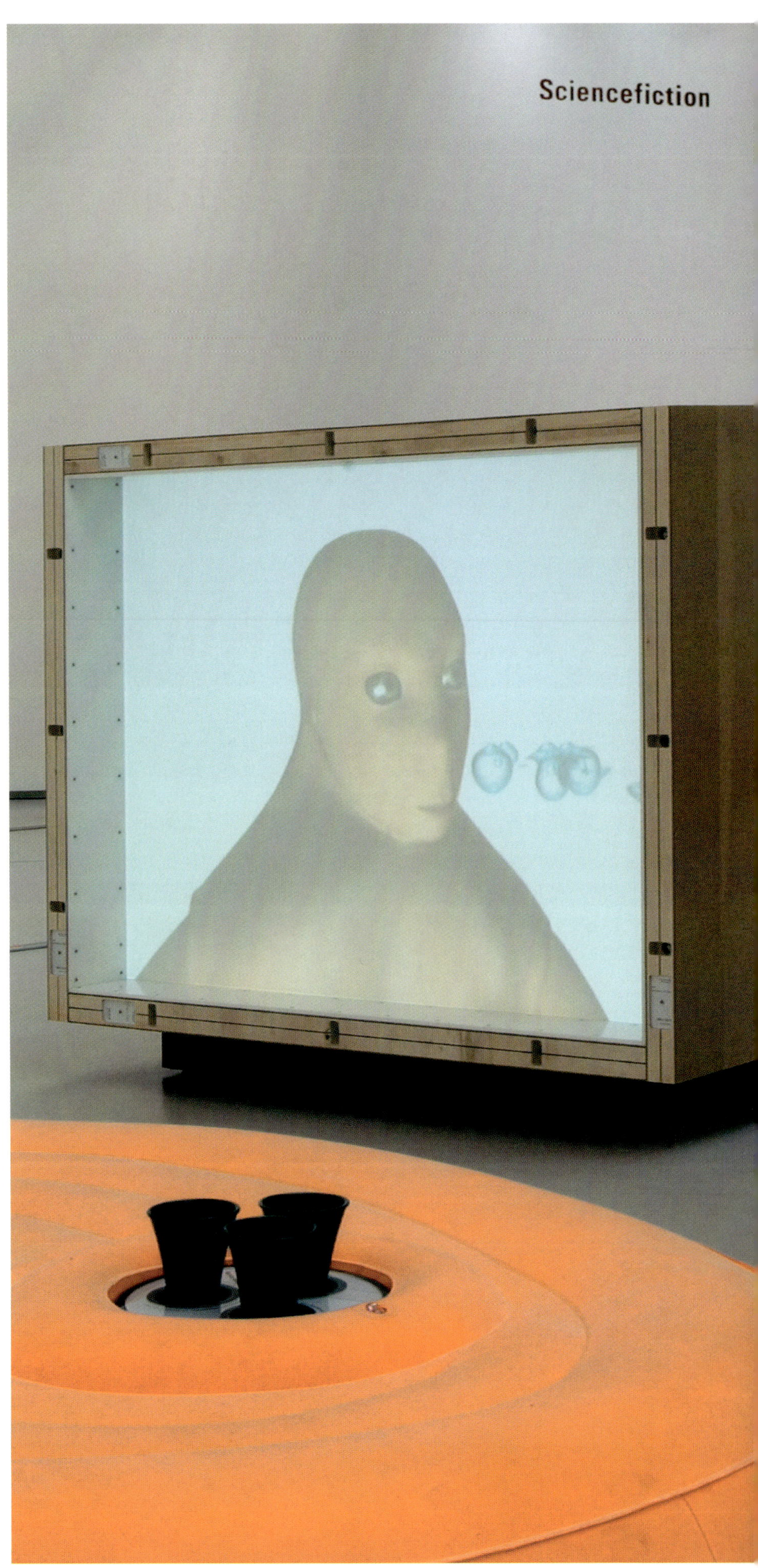

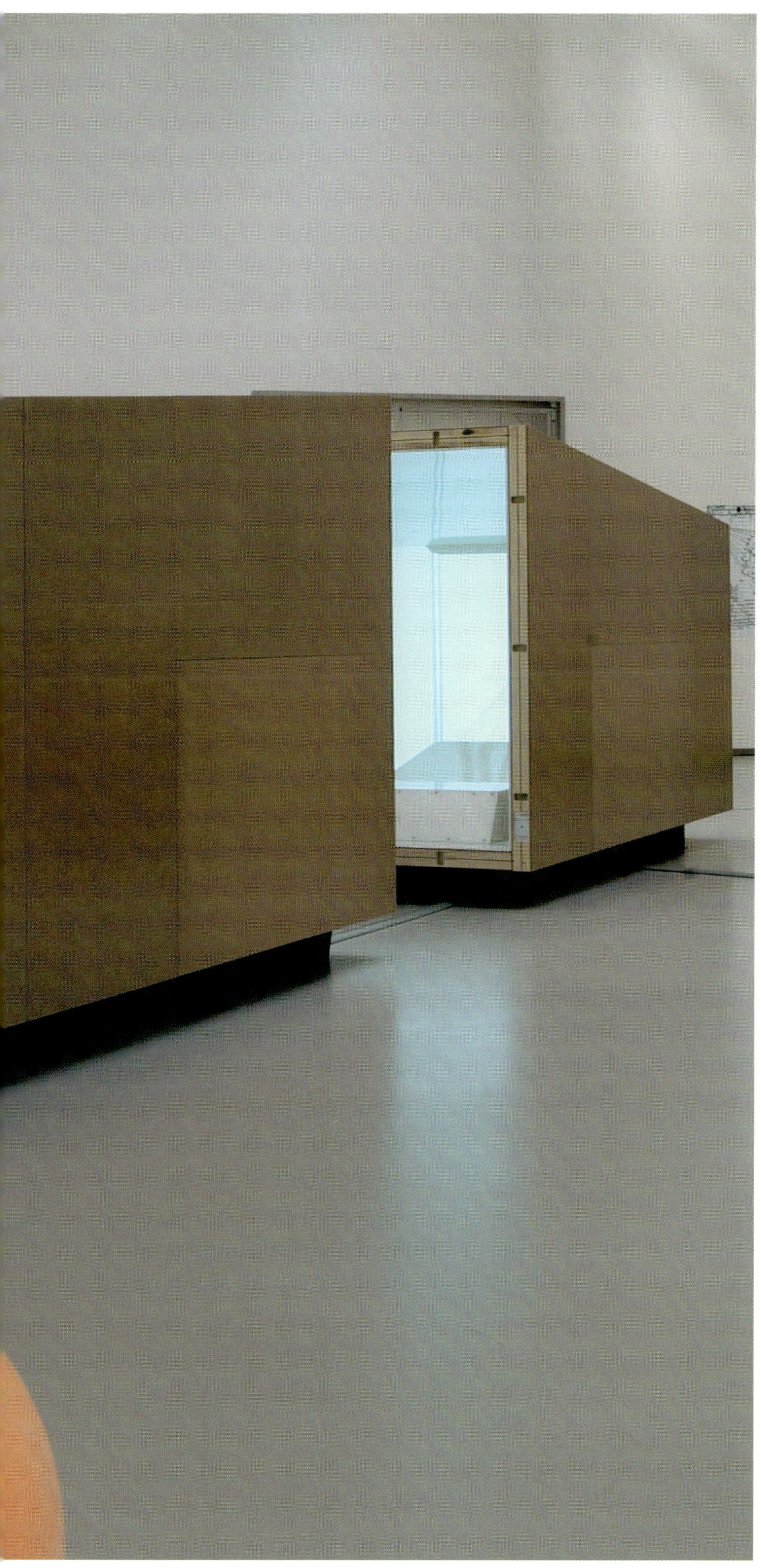

M + M *Gutes Morgen, Dr. Mad! Good Tomorrow, Dr. Mad!*

has lost his fear of death, and he hovers in a room without gravity. Once the scientist achieves his goal, he becomes obsolete. However, our scientist is a mixed bag. Basically he is the above-mentioned, stoic laboratory technician who stares bleakly at his work from behind his desk. But then he jumps up, spouting wildly enthusiastic aphorisms from his infamous film predecessors. Sexuality gains an added meaning in the relationship between the two. Apparently the researcher perceives his creation differently from the way it perceives itself. The doctor projects much onto his creation that can unhinge an experiment in the lab.

STEFAN IGLHAUT: To what extent does "Gutes Morgen, Dr. Mad!" make science fiction the theme of a reflection process? Or is it better described as a work of science fiction itself?

M + M: Naturally the installation is a work of science fiction. You could almost describe it as an epic 3D animation in abbreviated form. If you work with 3D animation, science fiction as a topic quickly becomes science fiction itself. And if you see a dream creature emerge from its shell, you become one with your own personal science for a moment.

STEFAN IGLHAUT: That sounds as if it is not only the mad scientist, but you as artists who create a "work" that takes on a life of its own. Is this more likely to happen with computer-animation technology than with other artistic media?

M + M: Yes, there's much truth in that. At the very least, the process isn't entirely controllable, particularly the momentum that develops with 3D animation techniques and a humanoid creature. It's like painting by numbers. A new figure is given form, movement and a spatial environment. The results constantly exceed the framework of previous ideas and begin to take on a life of their own. Just when you think you've found a bright, childlike voice that suits your creation, its appearance changes almost autonomously, and it now requires a more mature, more mysterious voice. Likewise, there's no plot that doesn't change in the process of realization. It's more extreme than work with actors, who also like to influence the overall product. At least they have "finished" faces and bodies. If the computer-generated figure then starts to lead its own life, like a growing child, it becomes more difficult to maintain an objective distance, even when it doesn't correspond to your original ideas. This was also true of Mary Shelley's Frankenstein, and who knows, maybe it will be true of subsequent generations of "creative" genetic technicians.

STEFAN IGLHAUT: Science fiction serves not only as a source of content for you, but also as an aesthetic reservoir. The major science fiction films have ever-larger budgets, with special effects and international stars. How do you compete with such powerful images, which are familiar to everyone?

M + M: Everyone knows the famous scenes from film history. We like to start off with this field of reference. We stimulate the stored images in the viewer's mind using key motifs. This can be done with sound, text or image fragments, or with similar plot lines. Once the mental images have been prodded, we exploit them for our personal version by employing breaks and shifts. We used to start with quoted material, but that's become boring now, and we prefer to stage the stories right off, like independent film productions with a film crew, 3D specialists and actors whom we can interest in our project. But even here the works live from a tensile relationship with the cinema images.

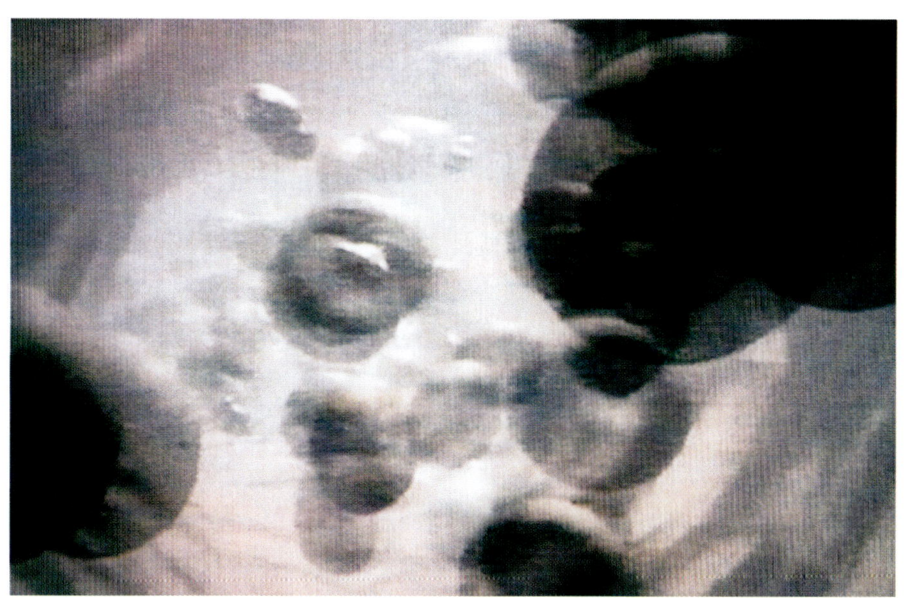

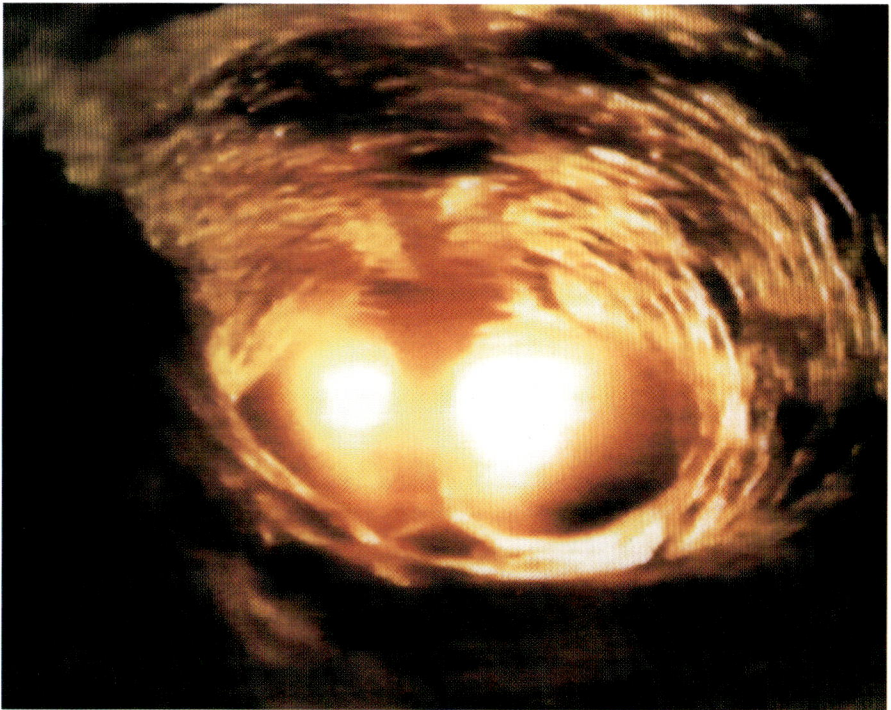

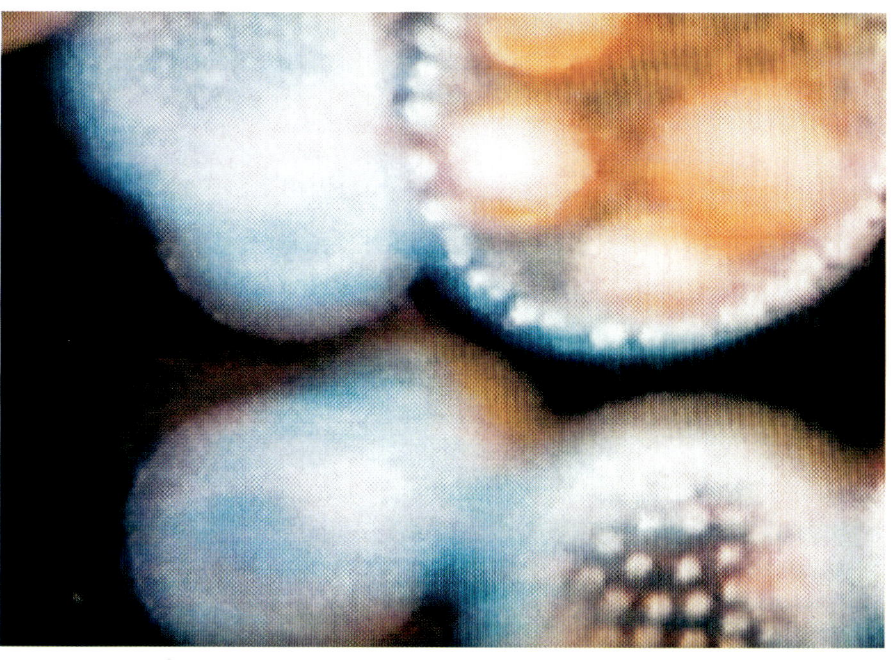

EVA KIMMINICH
IDENTITY AND SOCIETY – CULTURE AND VIOLENCE
REFLECTIONS ON THE POWER AND DYNAMICS OF SIGNS

Critical engagement with the processes of identity formation requires holistic hypotheses and a semiotic approach, because identities are constructs that are primarily brought forth by sign systems. Whereas traditional, closed social systems establish binding descriptions and meanings on the basis of ethical-aesthetic criteria, since the last third of the 20th century an open system has developed and corroded established realities. This process of dissolution releases the social subject into a semantic diversity which not only causes confusion, but also creates unique opportunities.

Identity numbers among the key concepts of our age, such as post-colonialism, globalization, multiculturalism and hybridism, all of which are closely interwoven. Identity forms the focal point of a variety of different processes running along the interface between subject or individual, social and/or ethnic group, and national/cultural community and political leadership. These are frictional processes involving appropriation and delimitation, in the context of which emotional energy is released and violence exercised to a high degree. Within the framework of the politics of identity characteristic of our post-colonial and globalized society, these processes are being increasingly stimulated. Globalization is also propagating a simplified, unitary culture, the spread of which appears to be dissolving traditional identities. However, the social transformations connected with this process are at the same time eluding the control of any steering mechanism. The dynamics released generate new spaces permitting a free construction of individual and collective identities and realities.

Critical engagement with the processes of identity formation therefore entails focusing on the elementary questions which will assume socio-political explosiveness in the near future. In light of the urgency of these problems, researchers from the humanities, social sciences and media studies have been collaborating in some 180 interdisciplinary projects based around two central strands of inquiry and sponsored by the Volkswagen foundation since 1990. Identity formation entails not only being at one with oneself, but also an engagement with alterity, i.e. the experience of others and oneself as alien. Identity is an experience linked with at least one other person whose similarity or dissimilarity is simultaneously the cause of this identity's existence and the possibility of its extension or alteration. Identity requires difference, but above all the recognition of its dissimilarity, and this is only possible through a process involving more than one individual.

In contemporary scholarly discourse, identity is thus no longer observed as a developmental process concluded at a particular point in time. Within the framework of the "risk society" that has been emerging above all since the 1980s, radical social changes have proven the unsuitability of identity models relying on continuity, consistency and coherence, and have triggered the search for alternatives in theory and in practice.

Identity as Dynamic Construct and Self-Organizing System

At a theoretical level, the integration of key discoveries in the natural sciences into the humanities and social sciences contributed to the constructivist turn during the 1970s. With the aid of the models generated in this context, the guidelines for a new concept of identity were traced, taking societal shifts into account. Since this time, identity has been comprehended as the constant production and reshaping of a mental structure. This dynamic is manifested in changeable self-representations, since its changing mental conceptualizations must prove themselves empirically.

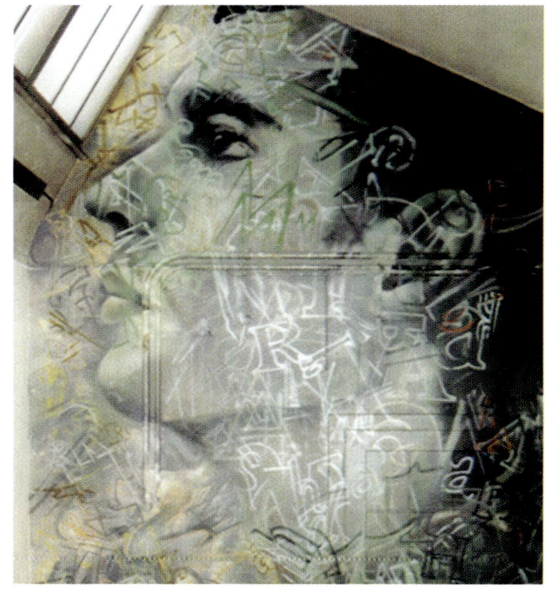

Self-portrait by the Palestinian spray artist Tarek Abu Hageb. For the artist, letters have their own life. Put together correctly, he says, they possess character and melody. – It is the creative use of signs that generates the difference and identity of a human being.

Whereas in traditional societies the forums and fronts for these processes were outlined distinctively, the post-colonial individual has been confronted with an unstable "here and now", primarily since the advent of globalization. As a result, we can more readily refer to a "here and there", a "before", "now" and "afterwards". The resulting breaks in continuity and coherence are linked with a multiplication of potential orientation points, a sudden diversity that shifts the initial socio-political and/or ethnic orientation of development into the field of vision of what are now self-constitutive ego entities.

Identity, Body and Social Body

The resulting fracturing of the unidimensionality of traditional identity formation also exerts an effect on the body, which plays an important role in this process. The disciplined body of socially integrated subjects becomes the governor of a self-forming individual. His disposition, appearance and gestures must be extended to make use of different symbolic paths of formation and forms of expression; the individual must learn to put these into practice and interpret them, whereby, however, his perceptual spectrum is altered.

The conservative or neo-conservative politics of identity comprehend identity formation as taking place predominantly via identification, i.e. via an uncritical adoption of traditions, norms and inherited values. In this way the subject is included in what are, for the most part, national and thus racially based mental constructs and body concepts. These form a social body, which affords the individual recognition and self-assurance. The price of this protective armor – which is also a constricting corset – is the loss of a differentiated and differentiating ego identity. The step out of such a collective pathos to an individuality which is self-determining by way of delimitation is a difficult one. However, the identity formation processes undergone by the post-colonial individual are constantly impacted on by new perceptions of self and other. It is a fractal experience, constraining the individual to relocate the self repeatedly in different situations. This form of identity production creates new, singular paths of self-experience and representation, since it occurs empirically, i.e. in time and space, and takes place intersubjectively. This gives rise to patchwork identities, whose conceptualizations are closely linked with the concepts of multiculturalism and hybridism, which remain controversial because of their openness to instrumentalization. They point to a distinctive type of self-formation which occurs under unstable conditions. As a consequence, the differing experiences guiding them must constantly be brought into accord with one another and be rendered visible in flexible forms.

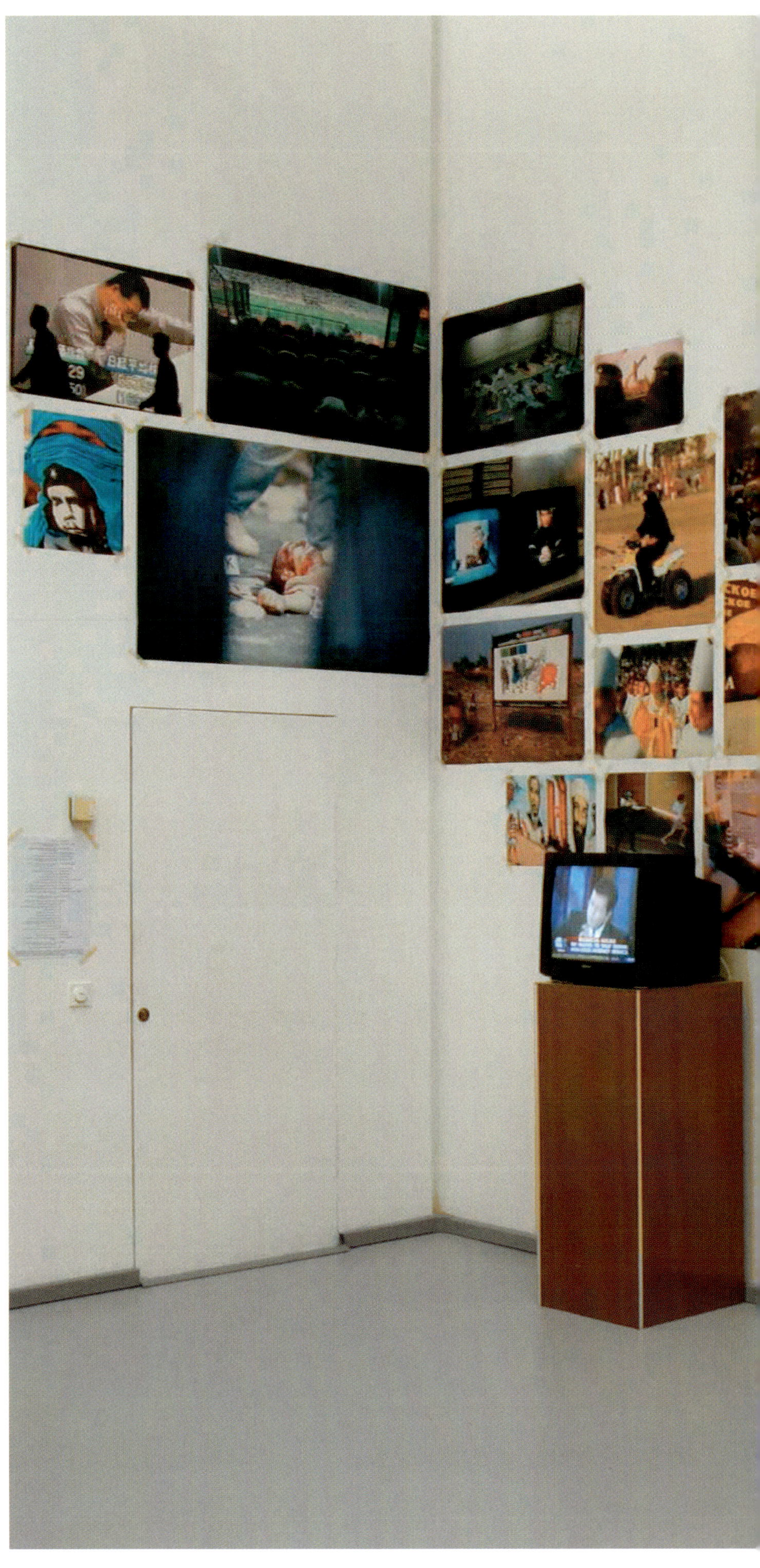

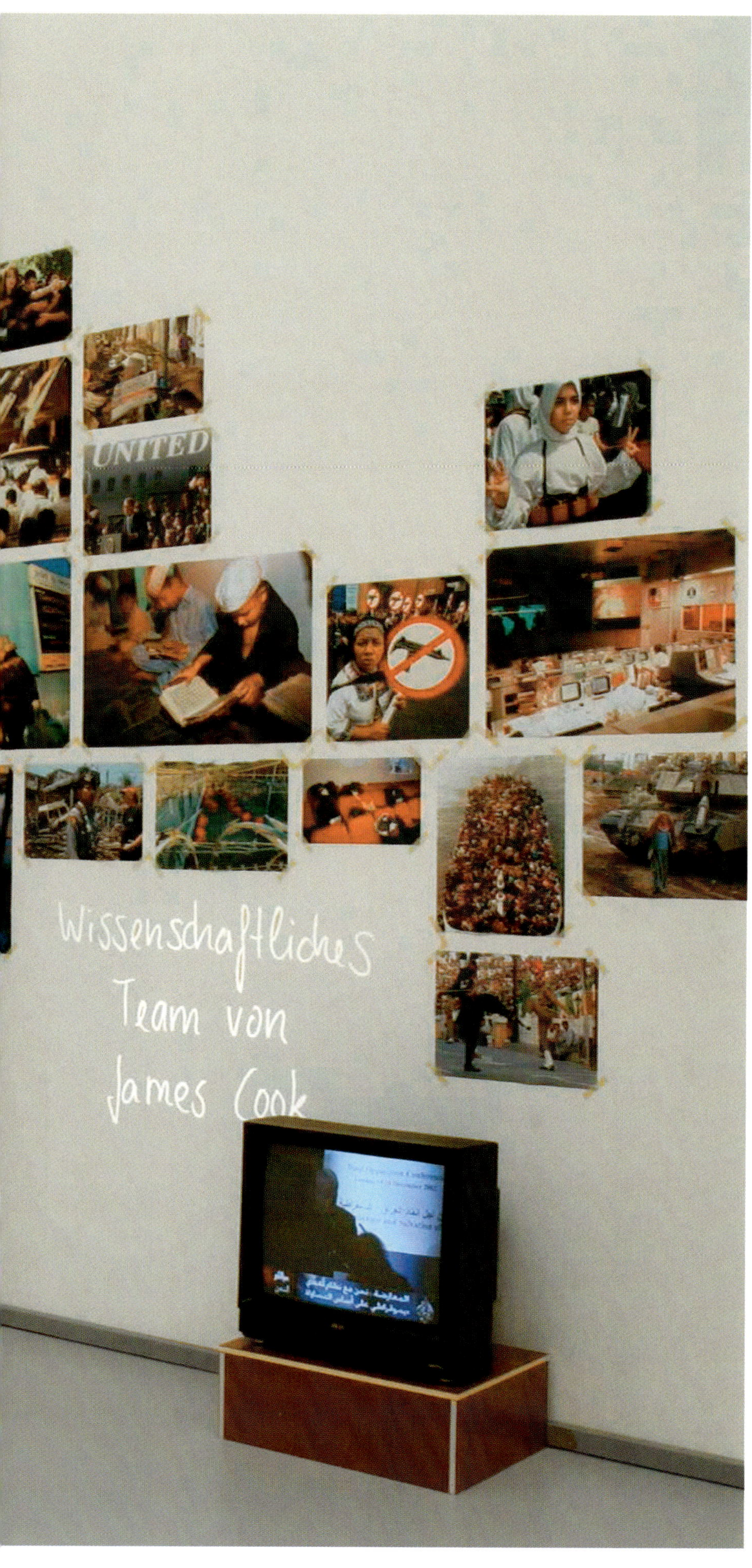

Globalization Installation: Press photos, TV news from Al Jazeera and Fox, projection of scientific concepts: gewerk, Berlin

This internal and external coordination takes place above all via the narration of stories and/or in the structure of the generative establishment of history in the form of so-called story and history-telling. Stories and history are starting points for human thought, activity and speaking. They are to be seen as linguistic realizations by which events are represented and referred to other stories and other actions. This means that with the help of stories, actions are positioned within a relational chain of actions, which are in turn embedded within stories. Their interconnections should be seen as the construction site of collective and individual action models and thus as the blueprints of identity formation. Therefore each rivalry on the basis of which hegemonic claims can be derived, asserted and defended is rooted within their discourses.

Hence identity is a priori narrative; it is cultural and determined politically and aesthetically. In order to uncover its determinants, the concepts upon which it rests must be illuminated, since what is concealed behind the catchwords of multiculturalism and hybridism – which are for the most part employed merely syntagmatically for postmodernism in a euphemistic sense – also has a paradigmatic and historical dimension. It is transmitted in stories which are readily faded out of history, and its discourses bring to light argumentation strategies and examples of application in social practice. Thus, the concept of multiculturalism exposes, in contrastive terms, an unspoken, neo-conservative monoculturalism which levels differences; the concept of hybridism sheds light on the colonial-racist praxis of past hybridization theories, which retain a latent efficacy.

Consequently, cultural identity is closely linked to ethnicity. The capacity to cultivate and maintain it is decisive for the continued existence of an ethnic group. It is for this reason that the concept of cultural identity has been linked to the political aspirations of ethnic minorities since the 20th century. In North America, Africa and Asia a liberation struggle developed against the pressure to assimilate exerted by colonial administrations and against a cultural patronizing which is still subtly practiced in European immigration countries today, and which is accompanied by economic, social and cultural exclusion via western, capitalist-influenced structures. This struggle for recognition and equality of one's own identities – i.e. identities regarded as exotic from the viewpoint of the others – has still not been concluded. Cultural identity therefore remains a central concept for the future. It denotes the emotionally laden self-conception of an ego within a collective defined nationally, socially and/or ethnically. Should this self-conception uncritically accommodate itself to the collective's prescriptions, it remains a subject; the price is the implicit external determination of a second-hand identity.

Cultural Identity, Body Concepts and Conflicts

One of the most elementary and distinctive aspects of cultural affiliation – and thus the basis of identity development – is the body of the individual. It's constitution, physical nature, movement patterns, gestures and facial expressions are decisive for the initial classification by the other in terms of experiences of identity and alterity. Under National Socialism the bodies of different races were measured and placed in aesthetic-ethical categories based on socio-biological criteria. Such constructs, combined with political goals, provided the evolutionary legitimation for a self-creating Aryan race, and the basis for its claim to superiority over all other races. In this context, skin color played and still plays a decisive role. It still gives visibility to a struggle between cultures, that is, to a struggle of standards and symbols. It still plays a decisive role in determining insider and outsider status in relation to a society or group. Often the outsiders independently create new guidelines based on the characteristics of their rejection within the framework of alternative conceptualizations, and, under certain circumstances, we thus see an interplay between recognition and rejection. Blackness, for example, has in some cases taken the place of the aspiration to the kind of adaptation that resulted in countless black women and men following the example of, among others, pop star Michael Jackson by lightening their skin with chemical tinctures and straightening their hair – procedures which seldom brought the desired recognition and in most cases resulted in financial and health problems. It was the following generation that, in full awareness of its own injuries and deformations, first began to accept, live and celebrate its blackness by reappropriating the black culture which had been taken from it and devalued, and by reappraising black history in opposition to white history.

Subject, Subversion and the Individual

Recognition or rejection of the body as an empirical representative of identity is a fundamental experience which must be repeatedly negotiated, asserted and defended. Thus the existence and development of an identity or a culture is always linked to violence. Just as identity draws its mental foundations from a culture in order to embody itself, every culture needs bodies which incarnate, defend or alter it. The smaller the scope a society gives its members for identity development and for difference, the greater the likelihood that subcultures will form. Subjected to increasing pressure, these become charged on the one hand with aggression; yet at the same time new spaces for the production and representation of identity emerge within them. Political subversion models use the metaphor of the rhizome to illustrate such processes. A rhizome is a subterranean root-like stem which spreads aimlessly, emitting stems and nodules which develop in an anarchic way. The rhizome thus provides an image of a form of self-development that not only detaches itself from discursive prescriptions, but exposes them as discursive strategies of identity absorption.

Dealing with identity formation means focusing on construction processes which find expression in different sign systems as well as in interactive and media representations, and which manifest themselves in both creative and destructive acts. They define the victim as well as motivating and legitimizing the executioner. Individual, group and society are caught in an incessant struggle to control the signs and symbols with which hierarchical orders are arbitrarily enforced and maintained. The noble symbolic treasure of a culture, which is still readily excluded from the seamy violence of socio-political action, is thus the real locus of power-political confrontations; at issue is the power of the definition. Opposing (but not evading) this process is only possible for those who recognize the effective power of ideas and are capable of extracting these ideas from cultural-hegemonic contexts and ideological concepts, reinvesting them in semantic terms and embedding them in their own stories, which are based on empirical experience. Only when history-telling becomes history-re-telling via story-telling does a form of access to symbols become possible through which a fundamental redistribution can be initiated.

REFERENCES: Barkhaus, Annette; Mayer, Matthias; Roughley, Neil and Thürau, Donatus (eds.): *Identität, Leiblichkeit, Normativität. Neue Horizonte anthropologischen Denkens*. Frankfurt a.M.: Suhrkamp 1996. Beck, Ulrich: *Was ist Globalisierung?* Frankfurt a.M.: Suhrkamp 1997. Elias, Norbert: *Die Gesellschaft der Individuen*. Frankfurt a.M.: Suhrkamp 1987. Frank, Manfred and Haverkamp, Anselm (eds.): *Individualität*. Munich: Fink 1988. Nghi Ha, Kien: *Ethnizität und Migration*. Münster: Westfälisches Dampfboot 1999. Mühlmann, Heiner: *Die Natur der Kulturen. Entwurf einer kulturgenetischen Theorie*. Vienna/New York: Springer 1996. Kimminich, Eva (ed.): *Kulturelle Identität, Konstruktionen und Krisen*. Frankfurt a.M.: Peter Lang 2002. Posner, Roland: *Der Mensch als Zeichen*. In: ZfS 16/3–4. Tübingen: Stauffenburg 1994, p. 195–216. Schmidt, Siegfried J.: *Kalte Faszination. Medien Kultur Wissenschaft in der Mediengesellschaft*. Weilerswist: Velbrück Wissenschaft 2000. Shusterman, Richard: *Philosophie als Lebenspraxis*. Berlin: Akademie Verlag 2001.

CHRISTOPH KELLER
EVERYTHING BEGAN SO HARMLESSLY … –
THE PERSPECTIVE OF THE ETHNOGRAPHIC VIEWPOINT
A CONVERSATION WITH THOMAS SPRING

THOMAS SPRING: Christoph Keller, the key element of your project for "science+fiction" is a camping van covered in reflective material. In the van there is a video installation that presents scientific films on shamanism which you have revised. You have also set up a kind of camping or fieldwork situation near the van where visitors can look at videos from an ethnographic film archive. In this project you have made a scientific topic the starting point for an artistic statement. How is this done?

CHRISTOPH KELLER: The situation is such that I have often dealt with scientific content in my work. This has to do, among other things, with my biography. Before becoming an artist, I studied hydrology, combined with mathematics and physics. Of course, my experiences from this period have influenced my work. In recent years, a number of my projects have explicitly explored scientific topics. However, when I examine or analyze a topic from an artistic perspective, I have a completely different approach and can arrive at entirely different results from those of a scientist. I do something like straddling the border between the sciences and the arts, and perhaps other areas too. I have a certain possibility of leaping back and forth between these spheres.

THOMAS SPRING: Is this possibility more of a personal matter, or do you believe these spheres are themselves in motion?

CHRISTOPH KELLER: Sure, something is in motion. The rigid structures which people had until the late 60s, when faculties were bound to strict traditions, no longer exist today. A lot has happened since then. Nowadays people have come to realize that scientific correspondences have always been a component of artistic approaches; and, conversely, that scientific projects have at all times pursued an aesthetic-philosophical or a socio-political project as well and thus, to a certain extent, also a religious one. Today it is obvious that certain things converge, and that the arts and the sciences are taking on new roles – though this does not occur according to any clear set of rules. It is undoubtedly a process which will go on for longer and be accompanied by a shift in society.

THOMAS SPRING: The starting point of your project for "science+fiction" involved an intense exchange about the phenomena of globalization, and the constructs of "foreign" and "native" cultural identities. How did you get from there to shamanism?

CHRISTOPH KELLER: What I found so interesting was the possibility of being able to see an artistic project simultaneously as a research project. In fact, that was my initial idea. But then, while I was contemplating globalization, and the relationship of the foreign and the native as a scientific topic, the field of shamanic studies emerged. There are an astonishing number of ethnographic films addressing magic and shamanism in primitive or simple cultures. This was what interested me. I wanted to investigate the relationship between western ethnographers and shamans as "scientists" of other cultures. This interested me and was the research task which I went on to set myself. The outcome is the video installation seen in the van.

This project is one in a series dealing with pseudo sciences and charlatanism, and it fits very well into the topic of the foreign and the native, of the self and the other in science, because it actually deals with the other, to be precise with the cultural other on a level which is not directly describable, but only by way of misunderstandings.

THOMAS SPRING: Your reflective van seems conceived as a fairly strong metaphor. But is the van actually an image making a statement about science, or is the whole thing rather a kind of experimental set-up for dealing with the visitor, one in which he becomes involved in a reflective world where it is not a matter of interpreting the van as a statement, but rather of perceiving himself and the films he sees in this situation from a new perspective?

 In my video works I often create situations that enable the visitor to arrive at a certain way of seeing the material, a way he would not have done so otherwise. As far as this goes, I see here a continuity with my other works, for instance with "Encyclopaedia Cinematographica": through the arrangement of the monitors in a space, the films can be understood not just via their surfaces, but also as conceptual units, in other words, in a completely different way than would be the case if they were merely projections, like those probably familiar from the cinema or other installations. With regard to such works, it is the form of the spatial or physical relationship into which the visitor enters that is important.

There is a kind of field study situation outside the van, where the visitors themselves are given the opportunity to research into ethnographic film material and, if they want and have the time, to watch the films in their entirety. In part, these are videos of the films I used in the installation. I have made my research material available to the visitor so as to give him the possibility of discovering something completely different in it, and of assuming the role of the researcher instead of remaining just a passive user.

In "Expedition Van", the central topic of my installation is the "shamanic journey". The outstanding feature of shamanism is that the shaman can go into an ecstatic state or trance and then travel to another world or level. It may be an underworld or a kingdom of heaven – this differs from culture to culture or from mythology to mythology. Nevertheless, there is always the motif of a journey and the fact that forms of shamanism have existed in nearly all cultures. In the case of ethnographic film material, the shaman's journey is accompanied by a second one, and this is the journey of the ethnographer who has also set off to other regions. And when the visitor takes a seat in the van and watches the material, a third traveler, so to speak, joins in.

THOMAS SPRING: What interested you in particular about ethnographic films? These are not the most recent scientific films to investigate shamanism. What picture do they give of shamanism?

CHRISTOPH KELLER: Many of the ethnographic films which I have used are from the 60s and 70s, that means from the period in which I was born. I am able to work on this material as I do because it has attained a certain distance from the present – as was also the case in other archive projects of mine, where I dealt with materials that belong to an intermediate stage of history.

No classical figure of the shaman is portrayed in the films. What is interesting about this project is that everything which is to be filmed, namely magic or what the shaman does – shamans travel to underworlds, speak with spirits and alter things there or go into ecstatic states and ascend the tree of life, and so on – is not filmable. So from the very start, it is rather impossible to document it on film. And this was what made the work so very appealing to me.

I did not go to the jungle myself and I did not report as an ethnographer would about other cultures, instead I simply look at the products of my own culture and then take them as the starting point for my own explorations; I discover specific patterns there and try to understand them.

THOMAS SPRING: Are you making a statement about science with your project, or does it operate more like a kind of fragment of reality which you integrate into your work?

CHRISTOPH KELLER: I would find it presumptuous to say I was making a statement about science. Certainly, my own ideas about science enter into it all. But as to whether I am making a general statement, I would have to answer in the negative. For this would mean giving a definition of science in or through art. Instead, what you can do is give a description or a translation, but not a definition. In fact you must question to what extent you are in the position to criticize science at all with your own language and background, since the words you use and the insights you draw on have the same foundations as what you would like to criticize.

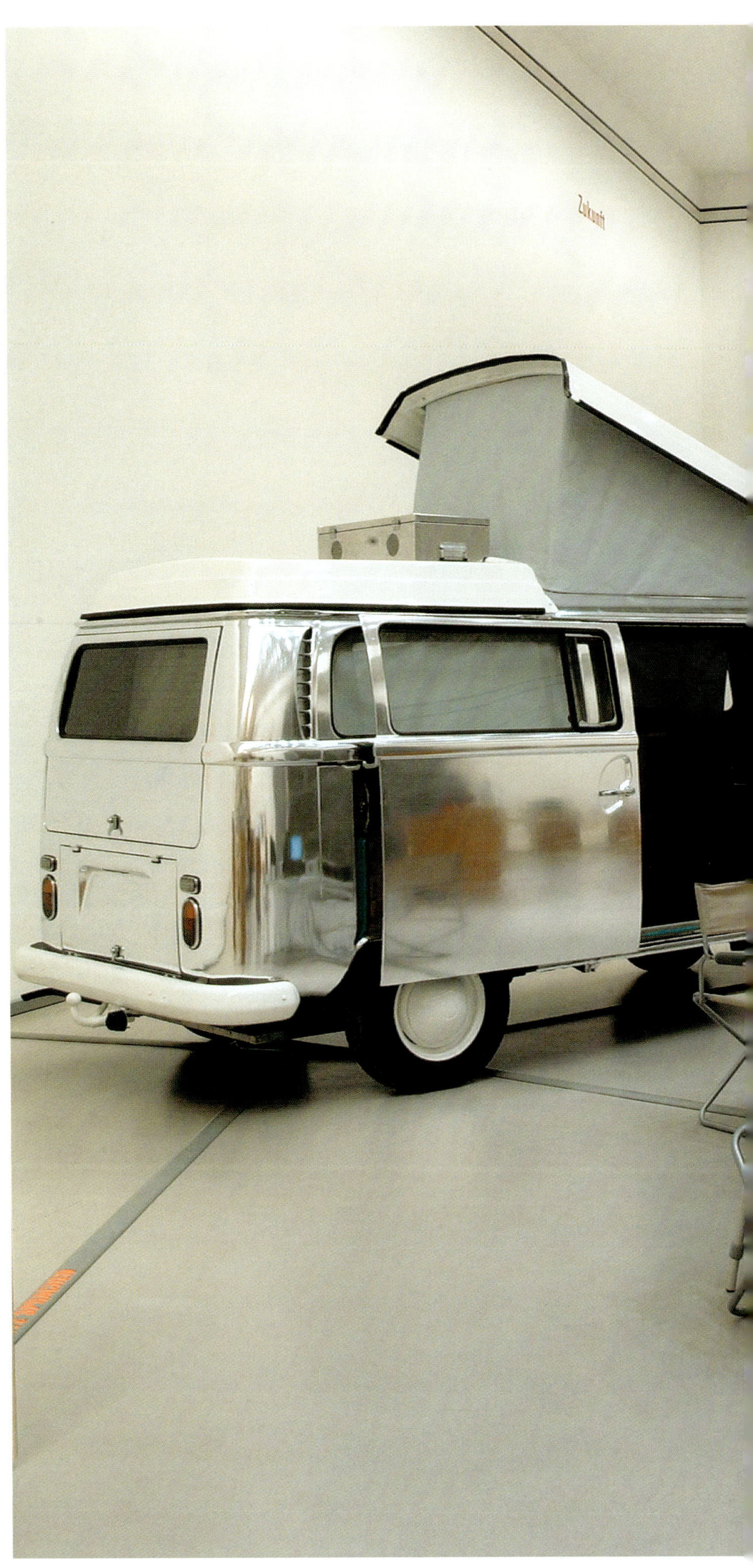

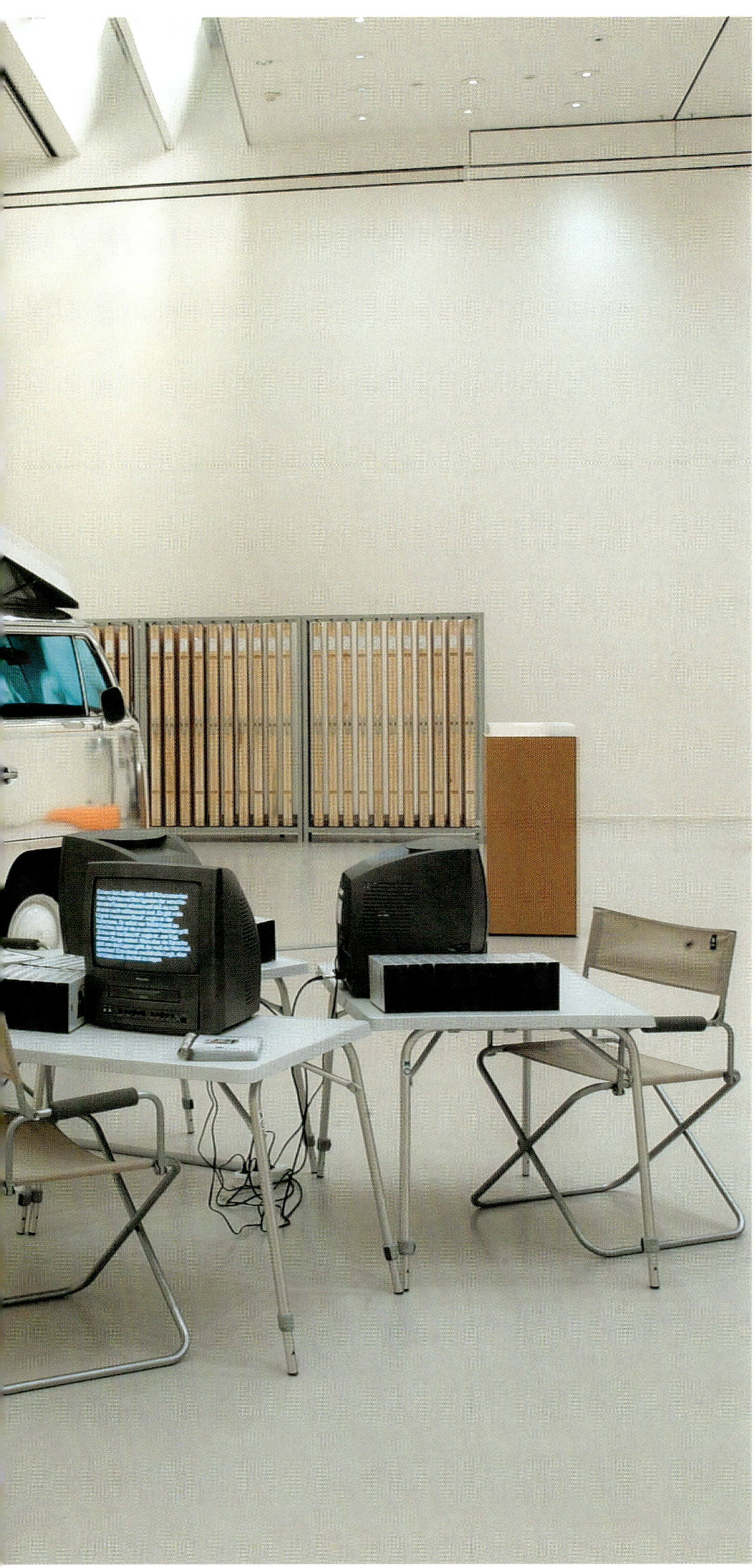

Christoph Keller *Expedition Van*

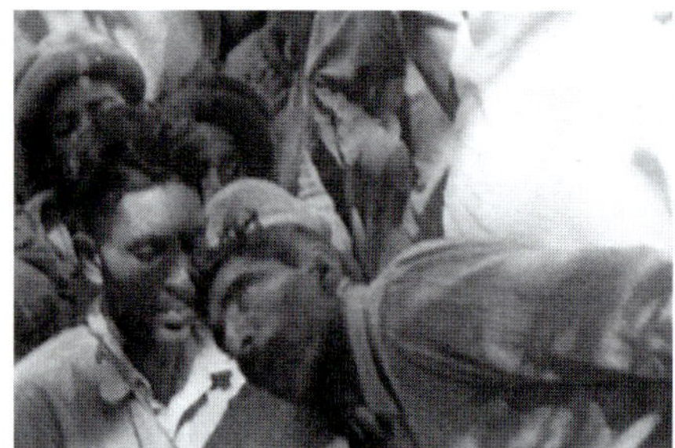
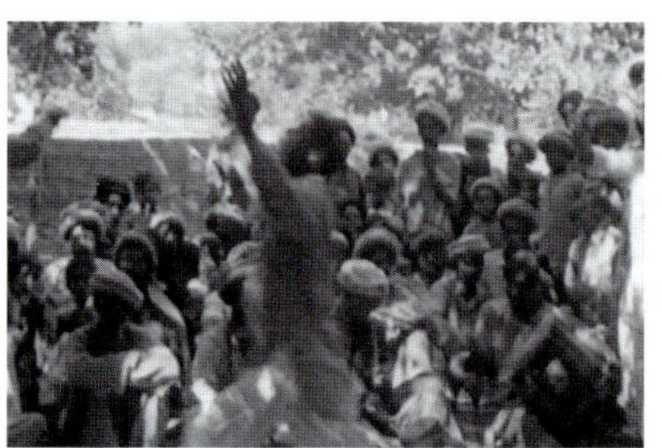

"In 1939 Åke Ohlmarks, who studied the peoples of Siberia, diagnosed shamanism as 'arctic hysteria', caused by the icy cold, long darkness and solitude in the Arctic. He even differentiated between a southern and a northern form of this illness. Elsewhere people believed that all shamans suffered from epilepsy – due to their convulsions during trances. Insanity and psychosis are also associated with shamanism. Even today such biases probably resonate in evaluations of shamanism."

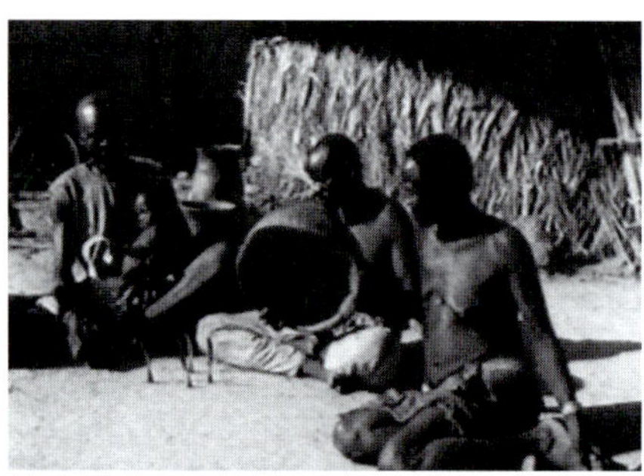
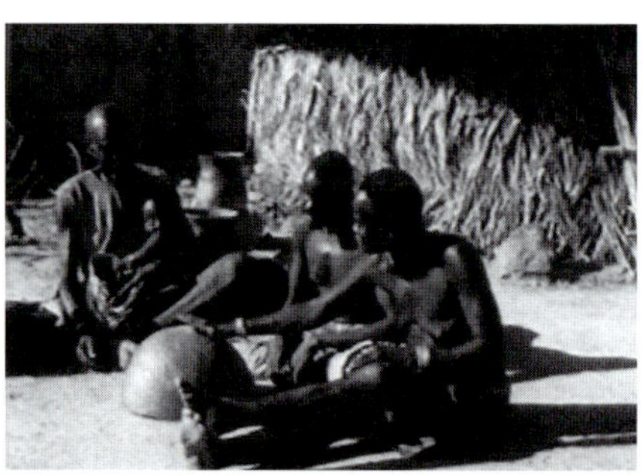

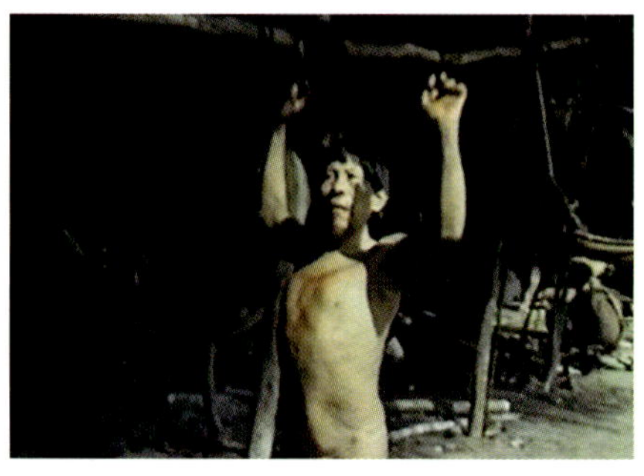
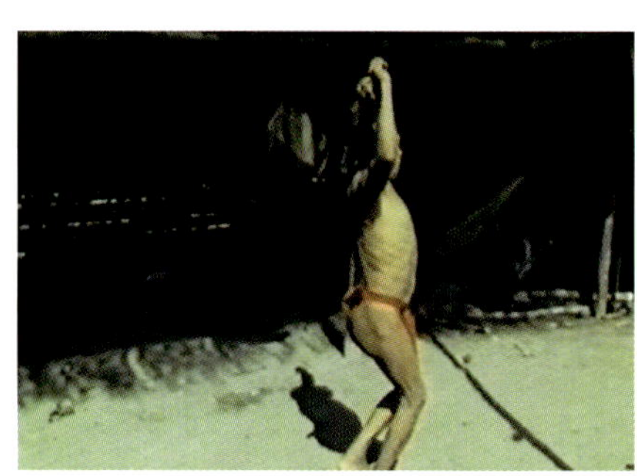

"The shaman becomes a cosmic traveler because he commands the techniques of ecstasy – that is, because his soul can safely abandon his body and roam at vast distances, can penetrate the underworld and rise to the sky. Through his own ecstatic experience he knows the roads of the extraterrestrial regions."

"At a certain point in time and without me noticing it, my task mysteriously changed from just collecting anthropological data to internalizing cognitive processes in the shamanic world."

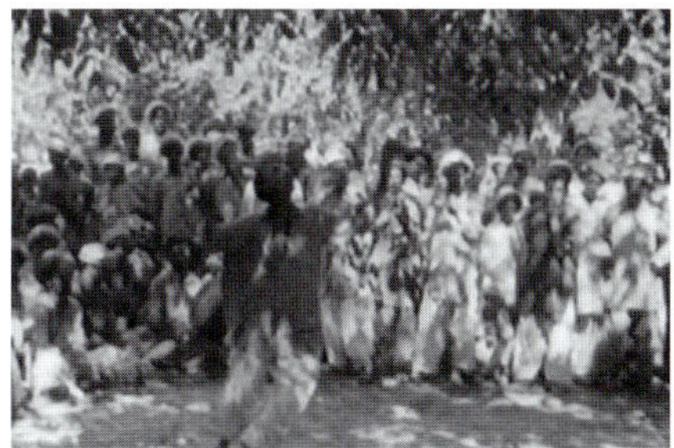 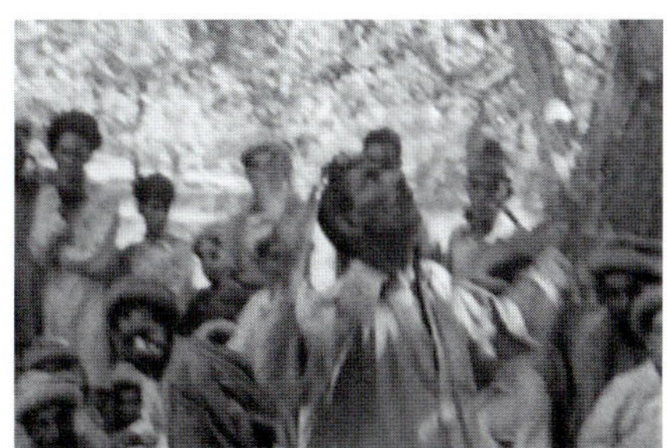

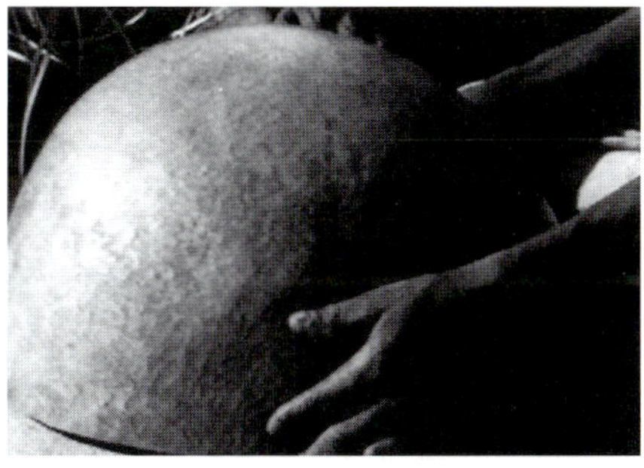 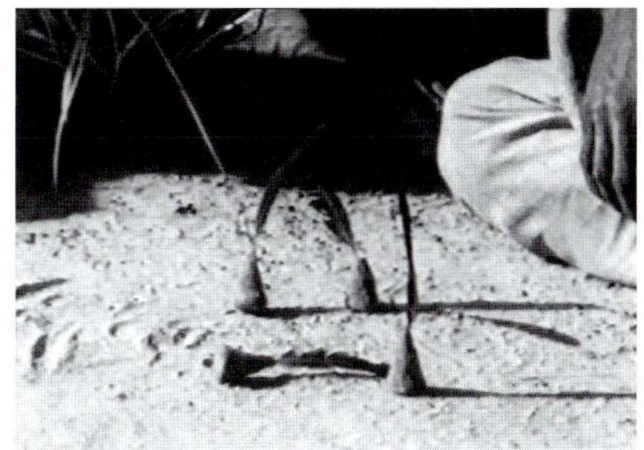

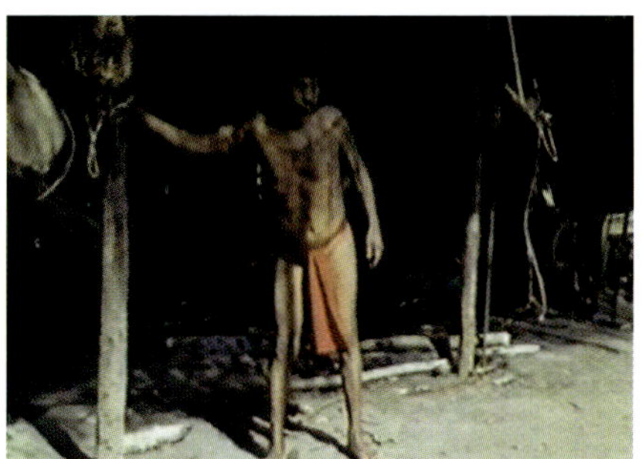 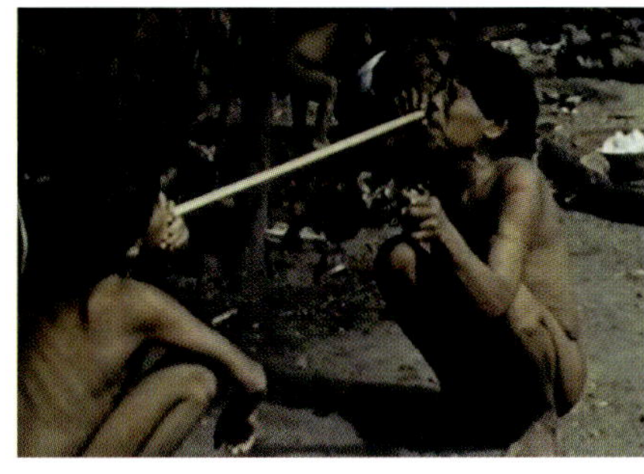

"The shamanic journey involves three phases: a prior period of preparation and purification, induction of an altered state of consciousness, and the actual journey. The initial phase of preparation and purification may involve a period of isolation, fasting and celibacy, perhaps alone in the wilderness or in a solitary hut."

Christoph Keller *Expedition Van*.
The van reflects images from all the countries and situations through which it has been driven, reporting on an expedition into uncharted zones while mirroring the viewers' own cultural notions. The film material has been selected from the scientific-ethno-graphic films on magic, shamanism and shamanic journeys from the Institute for Scientific Film, Göttingen.

"Eliade discovered that the shaman's most distinctive feature was that he travelled to other worlds. This is the cornerstone of shamanism for its serious practice. Through such journeys, the shaman or the apprentice learns how to contact spirits: he learns directly from the spirits and receives their help."

"When he came in, he stated that the shaman who had been out with him had been unable to hold the evil spirit, but he, Saraq, had grasped it and stabbed it, inflicting a deep wound. It had then made its escape, but the wound was so deep that he could not conceive of the possibility of it surviving. All believed his report, all believed that he had driven away the evil spirit which had been troubling the village, and no one was afraid any longer."

THOMAS SPRING: Science was supposed to be a topic of this work, so why, as an artist, did you become interested in shamanism of all things? Are you searching along a border so as to identify it? We are dealing here with cultural systems that construct reality, it is through them that the world is experienced. When one operates within one single system, this experience may be very limited. If one has several perspectives, one has a greater choice and something may become evident that is not at all discernible when one has only one perspective. Is that how it works?

CHRISTOPH KELLER: First of all, art is not a system for me, otherwise it would be predictable and would function. But that is not how art works. There are people who would like to see art as a system, but it is probably something more like a field, and no matter how vaguely one has to formulate it, art is part of our reality and active within it. I believe a very important aspect is that one cannot instrumentalize art as a system or as an "external observer", since this would simply not correlate with reality. At all times art can only deal with descriptive patterns and these are in part also based on what it explores, what it describes. Ultimately, it repeatedly describes its own function in what it describes. So art will never be a tool.

THOMAS SPRING: A tool? You mean, like science is a tool?

CHRISTOPH KELLER: The difference is that the sciences are founded on a clear definition of objectivity in terms of an objectifiability based on the principles of logic – I am now talking about the kind of science that quotes Newtonian mechanics, and here a clear definition exists.

In the case of art I believe there is a much greater possibility to make a statement while simultaneously questioning its very framework; and this creates a certain relationship between the person making the statement and the surrounding world, and they cannot be completely separated from one another. But this is also just an attempt to give a description. In the end, I believe all attempts to give an exact definition of what art is in relation to science are bound to fail.

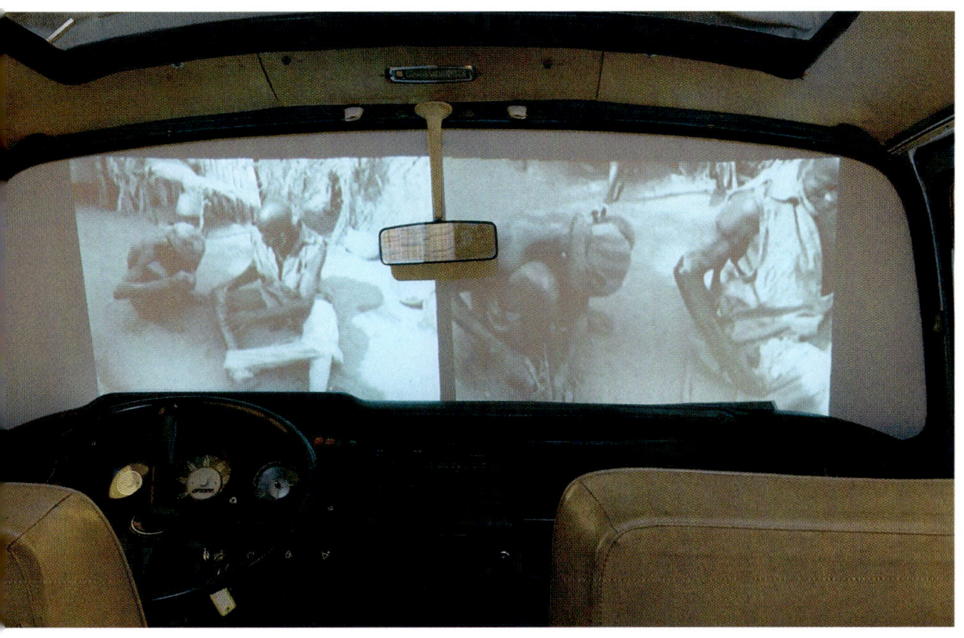

A double projection of sequences from ethnographic films about shamanism can be seen on the inside of the windshield.

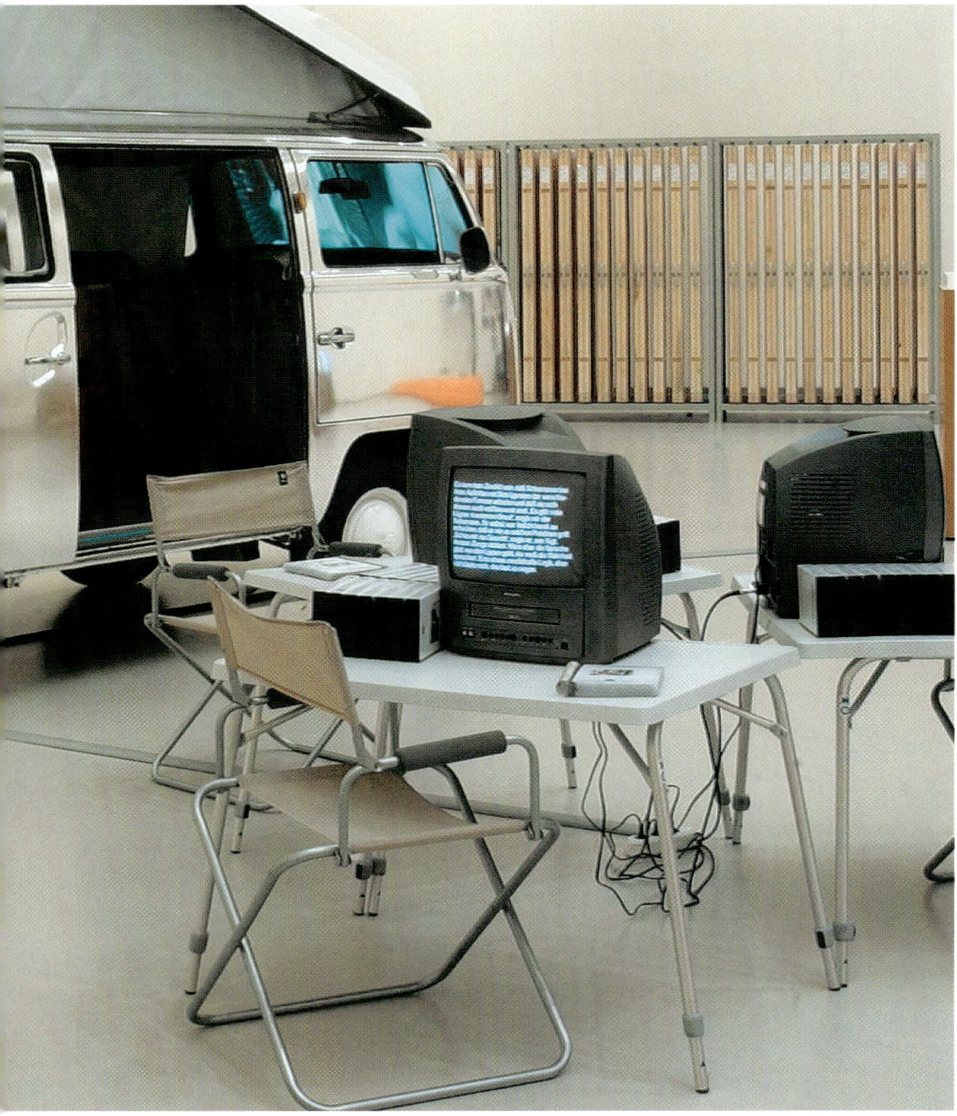

The van has been placed in juxtaposition to a field study situation, a mobile scientific film archive set up on several camping tables. Visitors can use it to create their own filmic pathways through the worlds of shamans and ethnographers.

JÖRG P. KOTTHAUS
"TOP-DOWN MEETS BOTTOM-UP." FROM NANOSCIENCES TO NANOTECHNOLOGIES

From Nanosciences to Nanotechnologies

The interdisciplinary field of nanosciences has developed over the last two decades at the interface between physics, chemistry, molecular biology and material sciences; its subject is research into and the tailoring of properties and functions on the nanometer scale. This scale ranges from about one nanometer (1nm = one billionth of a meter), the equivalent of the diameter of just a few atoms, to the minimum feature sizes of electronic components on highly integrated chips used in state-of-the-art microelectronics – typically 100 nm. Based on this a wide range of nanotechnologies are developing which utilize the control of matter on the nanometer scale in order to realize new, functional materials and systems for a wide diversity of products and applications.

Research evolved from the continual sophistication of predominantly physics-based methods of fabrication in a "top-down strategy" in the area of microelectronics, which today uses lithographic processes to pattern very different materials with precision of a few nanometers. On the other hand, research into chemical synthesis is making it increasingly possible to create complex molecules up to macromolecular units, giving us "bottom-up" access to nanoscale systems. This involves combining methods of molecular recognition and self-assembly developed from biochemistry with classic strategies of chemical synthesis, so that today it is possible to buy both tailored inorganic nanoparticles and specific DNA molecules. What has made such fabrication at all possible is almost unbelievably precise measuring and characterization technologies, enabling us to make visible and manipulate nanoscale units down to individual molecules and atoms. A broad spectrum of scanning probe techniques capable of scanning surfaces based on the revolutionary invention of the scanning tunneling microscope by Gerd Binnig and Heini Rohrer (winners of the 1986 Nobel Prize for Physics) can today reveal surface structures with details under one nanometer. Additionally, we can use light, X-rays and electrons to perform microscopy showing details down to the nanometer scale or to examine molecular structure by diffraction methods. The use of individual atoms or molecules as local probes in, for example, fluorescence spectroscopy, nuclear magnetic resonance spectroscopy, and spectroscopy of radioactive tracers gives us an insight into their nanoscale environment, as the physical properties of such probes are measurably influenced by their spatialsurrounding. The combination of all these fabrication and investigation methods increasingly allows us to understand the atomic structure of complex materials including complex biological molecular systems such as the human genome. These methods also provide us with an insight into the function of nanoscale systems such as minute electronic or magnetic memory cells used in information technology, as well as nanoscale biological systems. This means that today we can, for example, research the mechanisms of individual ion channels in biological cell walls that control vital functions in our bodies or molecular motors in muscle fiber enabling our movement. Particularly our understanding of the smallest functional units in biological systems is still in the infancy of an exciting phase of exploration. As physical, chemical, and biological interactions are hardly distinguishable on the nanoscale, this is where the natural sciences are bound to converge. In other words, nanoscience is more than just research into the world of the minute, but by its nature provides a link between the traditional natural science disciplines and can ultimately only be successful as such.

Following on from what initially were nanosciences intended to extend the horizons of knowledge, a broad spectrum of nanotechnologies is developing through a combination of top-down and bottom-up approaches. However, it cannot be denied that many of these various nanotechnologies are still in their infancy, their true potential is barely visible at present. They will probably be the key technologies of the next few decades and could well influence our lives far more than microelectronics, which dates from the nineteen-sixties, does today. The following is intended to be a detailed but certainly not full exploration of the possibilities this mosaic opens up.

Nanomaterials

A comparably mature branch of nanotechnology develops composite materials in which tailored nanoscale subunits produce materials with exceptional properties. "Nanomaterials" filled with nanoparticles are classic examples of this. Such materials are in everyday use as paints, inks, cosmetics, polishing pastes, ceramics, fluorescents, adhesives and protective coatings, using the special optical, mechanical or chemical properties of a wide diversity of materials filled with nanoparticles. Nanoporous materials such as zeolites or metallic foams with a network of minute cavities are, for example, widely used as catalysts in chemical processes, as well as in detergents. Other nanocomposites take the form of metallic alloys with a mechanical memory, carbon fiber compound materials, which as lightweight and resilient materials have become a feature of our daily life in many different ways, or semiconductor structures consisting of layers just nanometer thick and having special electronic and optoelectronic properties.
Examples of recent results of research into properties based on nanostructure include the self-cleaning effect of the lotus flower arising from its nanoscale water-repelling surface structure. This serves as a basis for development of biomimetic products – i.e. ones that imitate nature – such as paints and l coating techniques with highly dirt-repelling properties. Similarly studies of the nanoscale structure of shells and bone material provide important insights for the development of extremely robust layered materials. New areas of research include carbon nanotubes made of rolled-up graphite sheets, which might be used as electron emitters in flat screens or as light hydrogen storage materials, as well as colloidal nanocrystals that can be employed as artificial fluorescents in lighting technology or as fluorescent tracers in biochemical analysis. There is also great interest in molecular clusters such as the football-like fullerenes made up, for example, of 60 carbon atoms or metal clusters with a characteristic atom structure, as well as more complex, chemically synthesized clusters often with a shell-like structure. In all cases, mastery of the nanoscale structure results in new combinations of properties virtually unknown in natural materials and essentially characterized by the surface and interfacial properties of the nanostructures. This means that nanotechnology will play a key role in the development of complex synthetic materials, ranging from clothing and construction materials that adapt to environmental conditions to new kinds of storage and transfer media in the field of information technology.

Nanosystems in Information Technologies

A major branch of nanosciences is development of innovative functional elements for information technologies. The aim is to develop electronic, optical and magnetic switching and memory units capable of processing information with greater speed and reliability than existing technologies. The semiconductor lasers used in CD drives and laser printers are already based on nanoscale-layered semiconductors, known as quantum wells, as are highly-sensitive input amplifiers for cellular telephones. The development of these devices is based on broad research into the principles of layered semiconductor materials since the beginning of the nineteen-seventies – research that was awarded the Nobel Prize for Physics in 2000. Given this background, there are reasons to expect that what are known as semiconductor quantum dots, which have been researched and produced using a number of different processes for around ten years, will eventually result in technological innovations in data storage and communication. However, as yet no breakthrough has been achieved either here or in the related area of the one-electron transistor making it possible to switch a current using just a single electron. At present it is still not certain whether and how we will be able to develop future "nanoelectronics" superior to scaled down silicon microelectronics. When the latter reaches maturity in around ten years it will be using components reduced to dimensions of just a few ten nanometers and produce silicon chips containing eacharound 100 billion components. In addition to electronic information technology, it is to be expected that photonic, light-based information processing will gain in significance. So far no conclusive answers to some fundamental questions of photonic switching have been found. At present, light signals in data transfer using optical fibers are either switched by micromechanical elements or first converted into electronic signals, processed electronically and then using lasers reconverted into light signals. Here, it is hoped that nanoscience and nanotechnology will make it possible to develop faster and highly integrable photonic devices to serve as the basis for computers using photonics. This expectation is, on the one hand, based on further development of photonic switches based on semiconductor nanostructures and, on the other hand, on the optical properties of what are known as photonic crystals, which at present are the subject of intensive research. These crystals use the spatial modulation of the optical constants by way of three-dimensional nanostructuring. For example, it is now possible to fabricate controlled defects in such photonic crystals to divert light within a wavelength of light (typically 500 nm). The processes of fabricating photonic crystals are steadily being improved and their use in relevant technological applications can be expected in the next ten years.

Semiconductor research has made possible the precise fabrication of artificial crystalline stacks with layer thicknesses on the nanoscale. This also lead to the development of new kinds of layered magnetic devices with electric resistance that changes substantially in small magnetic fields. These devices are already in daily use as read heads for magnetic hard disc memories. Nanotechnology-based fabrication processes have also led to the ever-greater storage capacity of computer hard discs. Nanotechnology also develops new display media such as the "electronic paper", which on demand reproduces texts and images transmitted via cellular phone on a thin film, and is expected to be launched on the market shortly. The production processes for such innovative media increasingly use the techniques of what is known as "soft lithography", a process based on the chemistry of molecular recognition and self-assembly. This will eventually make possible more efficient and lower-cost production of electronic and electrooptical integrated circuits – at present they can only be made with elaborate classic lithographic processes – using an ink jet printer or a stamping technique based on intelligent ink from organic semiconductors. Here it is to be expected that the increasing use of nanoscale molecular recognition combined with the present rapid development of new organic semiconductor systems – pure research in this field was awarded the 2000 Nobel Prize for Chemistry – will give rise to completely new branches of industry producing a wide diversity of displays and more effective means of lighting in the not too distant future. To put it another way, the light bulb, now over 100 years old, could well be just as obsolete as the bulky picture tube of today's television sets ten years from now.

Processes in silicon microelectronics are already today in a position to produce new, extremely miniaturized sensoric and actoric devices with dimensions no greater than those of a computer chip the size of a thumbnail and contain structures of no more than a few micrometers (1 micrometer = 1/1000 millimeter = 1000 nanometer). Examples of

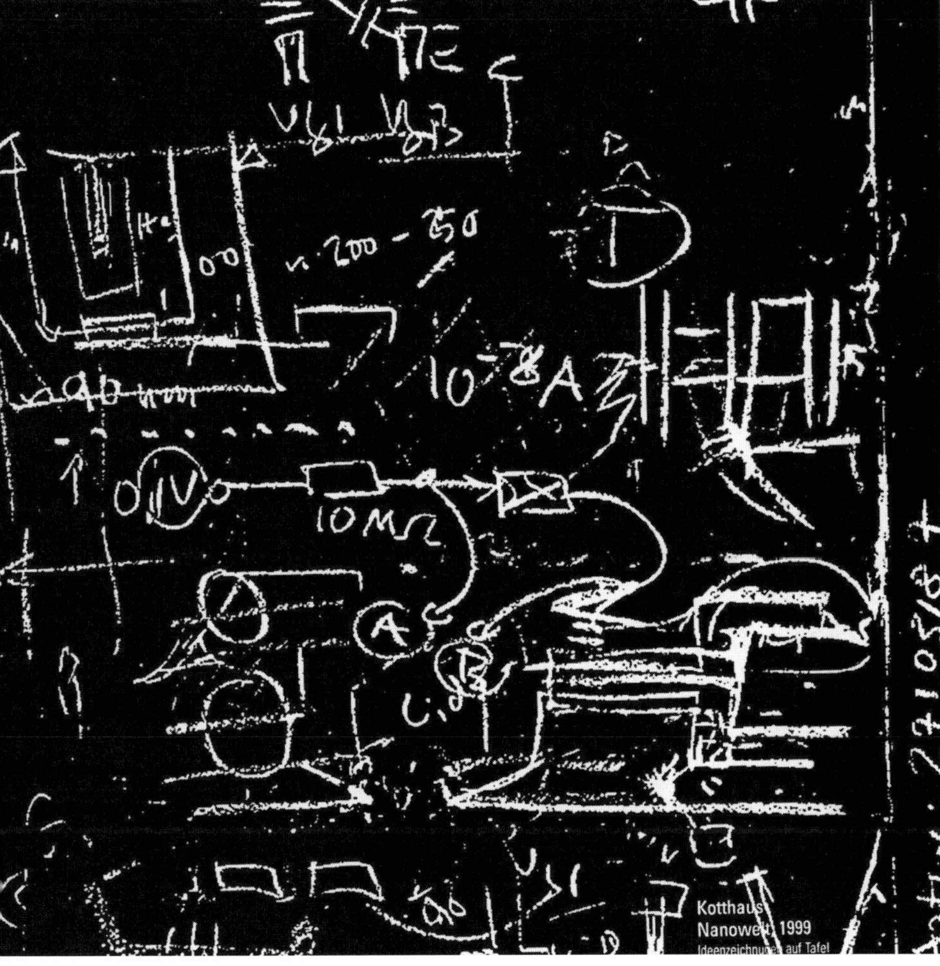

Outlines of scientific ideas presented on a board. Talk and discussion on the subject of electrodynamics, Jörg Kotthaus, 1999. WALL INSTALLATION SKETCHES SCIENCE/ART

this are MicroElectroMechanical Systems (known as MEMS); their present use includes making acceleration sensors which enable inflation of an airbag within a fraction of a second when a vehicle collides with an obstacle. Such MEMS components are increasingly used in the automotive industry and industrial robot technology. For example, greatly miniaturized mirror arrays based on MEMS are now used to rapidly switch light signals from different inputs to different outputs or to enable the large-scale projection of images using laser. Research into NanoElectroMechanical Systems (NEMS) is now underway with the aim of developing even smaller and more sensitive sensoric and actoric devices.

For example, it is now possible to make nano-strings of silicon that exhibit mechanical resonances similar to guitar strings but thanks to their minute dimension in the typically million times higher radio frequency regime. Combined with appropriate chemical sensitivation, research is today underway with the aim of developing such nano-strings to act as highly sensitive gas sensors. In other words, it is quite conceivable that within ten years NEMS systems based on this technology could serve as artificial noses to establish the presence of harmful substances; such noses being sufficiently sensitive to register absorption of minute quantities of harmful substances by a change in the resonance frequency of specifically sensitized nano-strings. It is equally possible to envisage such NEMS systems as electronic frequency filters that can be integrated into silicon and are based on mechanical movement; elements needed, for instance, in cellular phone technology to separate channels. Even use in highly miniaturized mechanical computers may well be more than just fiction. Similar to the area of MEMS with its steadily growing technological significance research in NEMS is anticipated to result in new technologies that as yet cannot be envisioned in detail. A combination of such nanoelectromechanical systems with nanoporous or nanocrystalline and chemically sensitive sensors, or with biochemically active molecules may eventually lead to minute sensory devices which could be used in chemical and medical technology, and environment analysis. Robot-like tools to process matter and move it with nanometer precision are needed to enable specific manipulation of matter on the nanoscale. Tools already in existence are based on the principle of the scanning probe microscope, which is able to move a fine tip across a surface producing images with resolution down to individual atoms. With scanning probe microscopes one can move precisely selected individual atoms on a surface and in this way assemble artificial nanoscale aggregates. Using suitable tips, it is also possible to modify objects on the nanometer scale, plough near-surface layers and steer locally electrochemical processes such as oxidation. A number of research groups is currently concentrating on accelerating the relatively slow process of scanning probe manipulation by parallelization of a large number of tips that can be addressed independently. IBM as part of its Millipede Project recently used such tip arrays to demonstrate the storage capacity of ten DVDs on the area of a postage stamp – a volume equivalent to 25 million pages of printed text. Other research groups are endeavoring to further miniaturize the lever-like tips of scanning probe microscopes and, in consequence, substantially increase working speed owing to reduced mechanical inertia. Chemical functionalization of the tips has made it possible to use them as selective chemical tools that, for example, can ensure that only certain molecules are addressed. This way it is today possible to measure binding forces in individual molecules and use them as identification characteristics of the molecules. Nanorobots based on such scanning probe techniques are now considered to be perfectly feasible.

Another method of nanomanipulation, known as laser tweezers, uses the fine focus of a laser beam to capture and move molecules. By placing electric voltages on nanoelectrodes it is now also possible to capture larger, individual molecules on surfaces and to transport them. Binding magnetic nanoparticles to molecules chemically also makes it possible to control their movements on the nanometer scale with the help of magnetic fields. Even though development of such nanorobotic systems is still in its infancy, research in this field can be expected to produce a wide diversity of technological applications on a scale presently hardly conceivable.

Nanoscale Functional Systems in Chemistry, Medicine and Environment Analysis

Understanding and targeted influencing of structures on the nanometer scale is of prime importance for new technologies at the interface between physics, chemistry, biology and medicine. This is where nanoscale research is creating the foundations for progress in medicine, pharmacy, biotechnology and environmental analysis. Innovations in biotechnology are already today being taken forward by the synergies provided by interdisciplinary research. Parallelization and miniaturization of biochemical techniques combined with modern physical measurement techniques led to the breakthrough in genome research. An answer has been found to a problem considered to be insoluble only a few years ago. The human genome has to a great extent been decoded. However, it will not be possible to make any meaningful use of this information until the function and regulation of complex biological systems has been understood. Just as in information technology, progress will here, too, depend on miniaturization of biochemical processes of analysis. Both the pharmaceuticals industry and companies that have shaped the semiconductor industry (e.g. Intel, Motorola) have recognized the trend and are today investing time and money in DNA technologies. This is a perfect example showing that the combination of information technology with modern methods available in chemistry, molecular biology and semiconductor physics is developing a new interdisciplinary field with excellent potential for innovative technologies capable of creating smallest sensors and manipulating minute quantities of matter down to individual molecules. Nanotechnological processes will play an increasingly more important role in the exchange of information between living things and machines. An example that could be utilized for medical patients is local and rapid biochemical analysis employing miniaturized laboratory systems on a biochip the size of a thumbnail – a technique just as dependent on nanotechnological developments as is active prosthetics. The latter attempts to link nerve cells directly with artificial sensoric and motoric elements. Looking still further ahead, it seems conceivable that by imitating natural viruses and molecular motors nanotechnology will be able to develop small vesicles and probes to transport pharmacological substances precisely to the place intended. Here, too, this is still, on the whole, early days for nanosciences and nanotechnologies. However, particularly in the area of medicine and pharmacology there is great demand for techniques to detect biological malfunctions at an early stage via minute quantities of foreign substances. Similarly one is searching for methods to transport minimal amounts of drugs to the place they are intended to be effective without, as far as possible, disrupting other biological functions. Nanotechnology techniques would be desirable to screen new drugs and make it possible to analyze a broad spectrum of potential new drugs for their specific effect in a way that is extensively parallel but using only small quantities of what are often very expensive reagents. This is where nanosciences and nanotechnologies will in the long term unfold enormous economic benefits in combating disease as well as in prosthetics, in particular in the replacement of sense organs. Needless to say, this is an area that gives rise to many ethical questions and adequate answers will certainly not always be easy to find. However, the nightmare scenarios of small "nanobots" that unstoppably take over our world and ultimately destroy it appear scarcely realistic. The evolution of the abundance of natural "nanomachines", which control the most important vital functions and combat disease in the bodies of all living beings shows us that on the nanometer scale malfunctions can in most cases be controlled by suitable regulatory mechanisms. As is the case in all new technologies, we should not be tempted to play down the potential dangers associated with nanotechnologies and need to adopt a responsible approach to the wide diversity of possibilities that such technologies offer.

CHRISTA SOMMERER & LAURENT MIGNONNEAU
IF WE KNEW WHAT IT WAS WE WERE DOING, IT WOULD NOT BE CALLED RESEARCH, WOULD IT?
A CONVERSATION WITH STEFAN IGLHAUT

STEFAN IGLHAUT: An important element in your previous work was the creation of environments for artificial life and life-like processes in virtual space. This work, which employed specially developed interfaces, was principally concerned with making things visible, with a visual staging. You're now approaching the theme of nanotechnology using an invisible sculpture. Is this a reaction to the stream of images created by the micro and nanosciences, or does this decision have more to do with your own development as media artists?

CHRISTA SOMMERER & LAURENT MIGNONNEAU: Our interactive works are always concerned with the establishment of a close link between content and realization. Many of our works deal with artificial life and seek to illustrate the principles of life, evolution and the emergence and interaction of individual entities, and such themes are best presented in visual terms. But in the case of nanotechnology, a visual realization seems contra-intuitive and a tactile realization more appropriate. With the Nano-Scape installation we were particularly interested in capturing the obduracy of nanotechnology, which is not accessible to our five senses, and translating this in artistic terms. In the broader context of media art and our position within it, this step can be understood in terms of our interest in development and in researching fresh, new themes. For example, ten years ago we already began to develop generative systems at a time when hardly any other artists were showing an interest in this topic, and it is only in the last two to four years that many artists have discovered it. For us this is a sign that we have to continue moving forward. Put another way, our central concern is researching thematic fields which have not yet been opened up, where new ideas – coupled with new technology – can facilitate new artistic realizations and interpretations. In this sense, the Nano-Scape installation constitutes an artistic/scientific experiment which aims to open the thematic field of nanotechnology to intuitive experience.

STEFAN IGLHAUT: Nevertheless, I would like to ask whether you are more interested in the idea of nanotechnology with its construction and manipulation of atomic and molecular structures or in the technique of tactile representation without images. Is your invisible sculpture conceived and constructed in such a way that it really imparts a deeper understanding of the subject of nanotechnology?

CHRISTA SOMMERER & LAURENT MIGNONNEAU: As we said, our interactive works are always concerned with establishing a congruence between the content of the work and the technology employed. Real plants can be used as an interface in an exploration of biological growth (Interactive Plant Growing, 1992), water can function as an interface in the case of artificial life (A-Volve, 1994/95), and in the case of a journey through the Internet, the train window becomes the interface (Riding the Net, 1999/2000). In the case of Nano-Scape, the question of how to open up nanotechnology to intuitive experience took priority. While all our works are concerned with the mediation of knowledge as opposed to pure facts, we also enjoy making this knowledge perceptible through intuitive experience. This process takes place on what is probably the border between art and science, an area that we find particularly inspiring, since it still offers a great deal of conceptual freedom.

STEFAN IGLHAUT: You have continued the process of evolution in cyberspace with virtual plants and artificial life-forms which can reproduce. In this context a significant concept is that of self-organization, which also has a central role in the nanosciences. In Nano-Scape, what role is played by the concept of self-organization, that is, in simple terms, by the concept of regular events in a suitable environment devoid of any command hierarchy?

 Self-organization and the creation of "open systems" always play a central role in our artistic works. We're interested in the creation of flexible and self-generating image and/or tonal structures which first develop via the interaction of the visitor within the systemic structures. For this purpose, we have developed, for instance, algorithms which make possible the development of new generative image and tonal elements, through which internal self-organization, image evolution, growth and emergence then come into being. The visitor to this system always provides the decisive impetus and is part of the image evolution; it is the visitor who, as it were, breathes "artificial life" into the system. In the case of the Nano-Scape installation, the principle of self-organization is integrated insofar as the invisible sculpture only develops fully through the interaction of the visitor and gradually organizes its amorphous surface only as a result of the interactive event. What is decisive here is how powerfully, how often and where the visitor touches the invisible sculpture and how the different visitors react to the sculpture in relation to one another. The principle of self-organization or the principle of "Autocatalytic Sets" is based on the idea that once interaction between several individual elements reaches a certain level of complexity new events and new qualities develop which can no longer be traced back to the qualities of the original individual elements. This process thus involves emergence, and it is generally assumed that complexity and innovation can develop in this way in natural, social and artificial systems.

STEFAN IGLHAUT: How is Nano-Scape constructed and what does the visitor experience?

CHRISTA SOMMERER & LAURENT MIGNONNEAU: The Nano-Scape installation consists of four tables with an invisible sculpture on each. When the visitor moves his hands over the table, he will sense a certain resistance, but due to the force of repulsion will not be able to touch the table itself. This nanosculpture feels like an invisible, solid surface. Only when the visitor attempts, as it were, to soften the surface with his hands do the finer details of that surface become detectable – different force fields can be detected as elevations, hollows, and as soft and hard parts, which in turn facilitate the recognition of individual forms. Since nothing is visible, the visitor must discern the sculpture using his sense of touch. However, every time it is touched the sculpture changes because it reacts to every individual movement and gesture. It is in a constant state of flux, so to speak, and continually reorganizes itself. In terms of form it cannot be definitively described; it is more an expression of the interaction, interference and also the intention of the visitor. Quantum physics has given us the principle of the observer influencing the result of his observation. In Nano-Scape the behavior of the nanosculpture becomes an invisible and incomprehensible yet tactile and experiential entity, the qualities of which, like those of nanoparticles, nevertheless elude the field of our daily experience.

STEFAN IGLHAUT: Avant-garde media art or techno art has blossomed during the last 20 years and produced whole buildings, exhibitions and festivals devoted to the genre. Mobile images and computer-controlled installations have now been integrated into all areas of contemporary art, and science centers work exclusively with interactive media. Does this general dissemination mean that the genre of media art is disappearing?

CHRISTA SOMMERER & LAURENT MIGNONNEAU: No, on the contrary, the fact that the genre is growing in significance is the result of the avant-garde media art of the 80s and 90s that made this development possible in the first place. Centers, exhibitions and festivals during the 90s, supported by a strong response in the media, performed an explanatory and educational function which allowed a very small, almost familial media art scene to emerge, one which incidentally was seen as abstruse, bizarre and not really acceptable by the wider art scene. Artists who are seen today as pioneers of media art were already developing concepts and works ten or fifteen years ago which still provide a conceptual resource today, not only for young media students, but also for more traditional artists who have now discovered media art. To say that this art form is now disappearing would make about as much sense as saying that book authors are no longer needed because there is online publishing. The question is not ultimately which

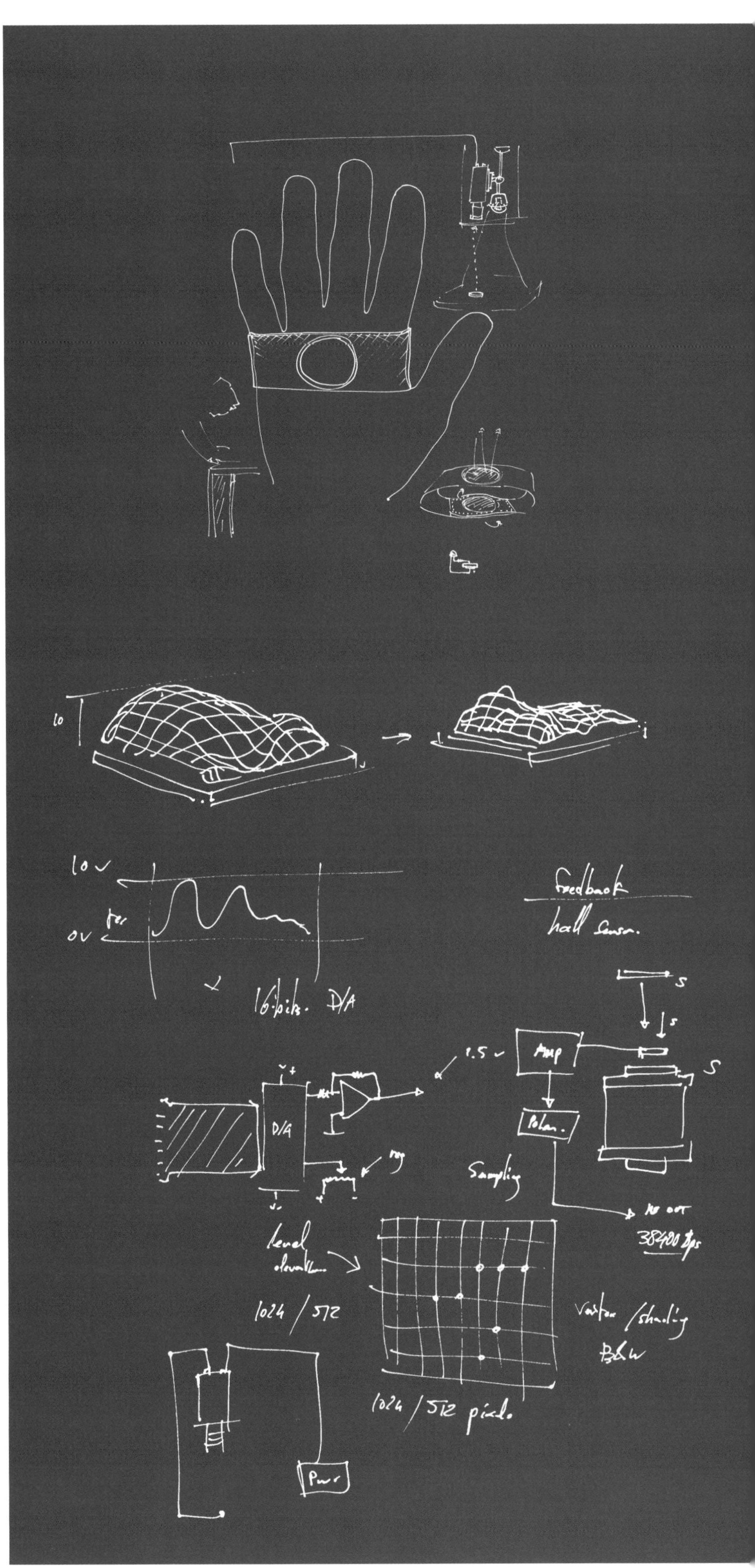

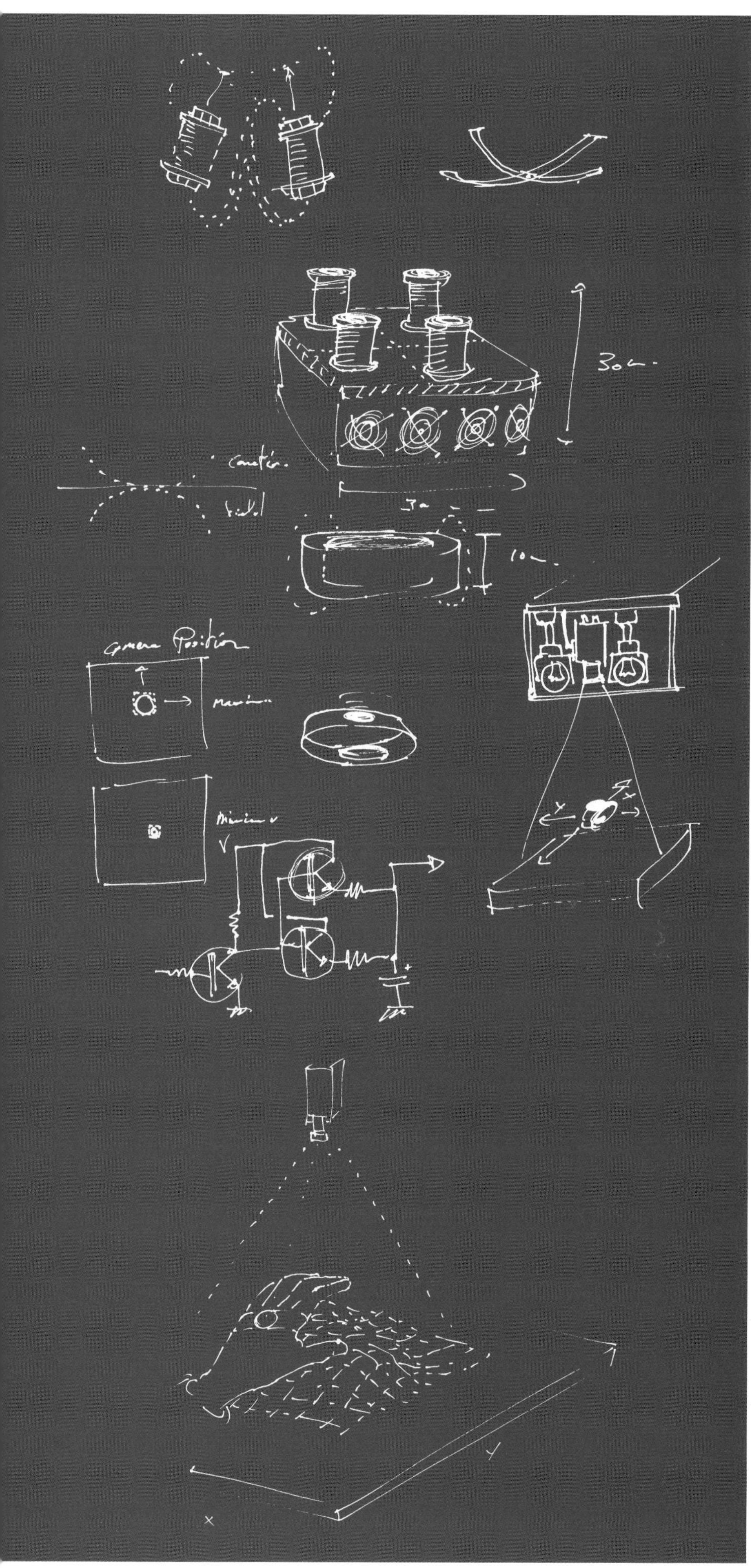

Christa Sommerer & Laurent Mignonneau *Nano-Scape*, design sketches

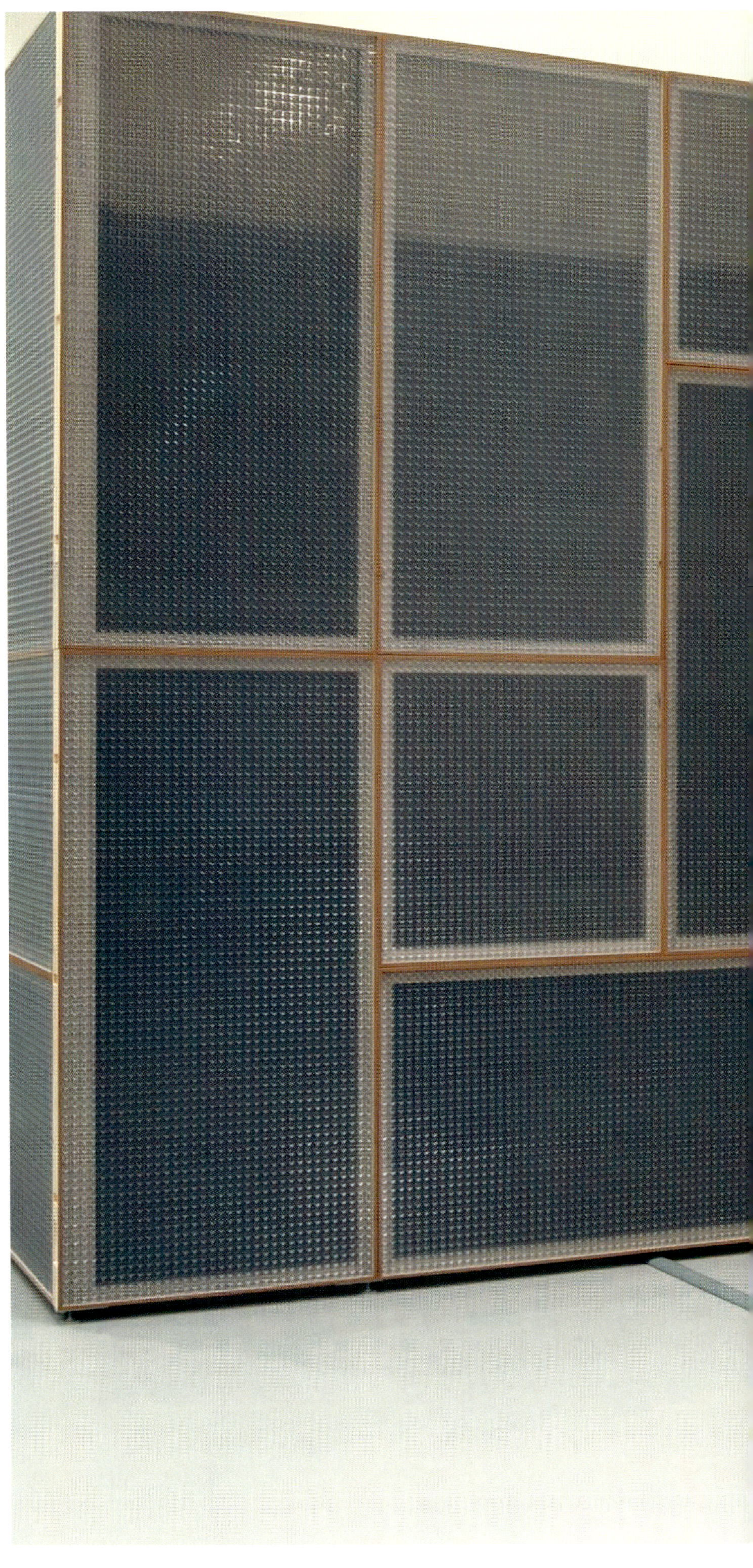

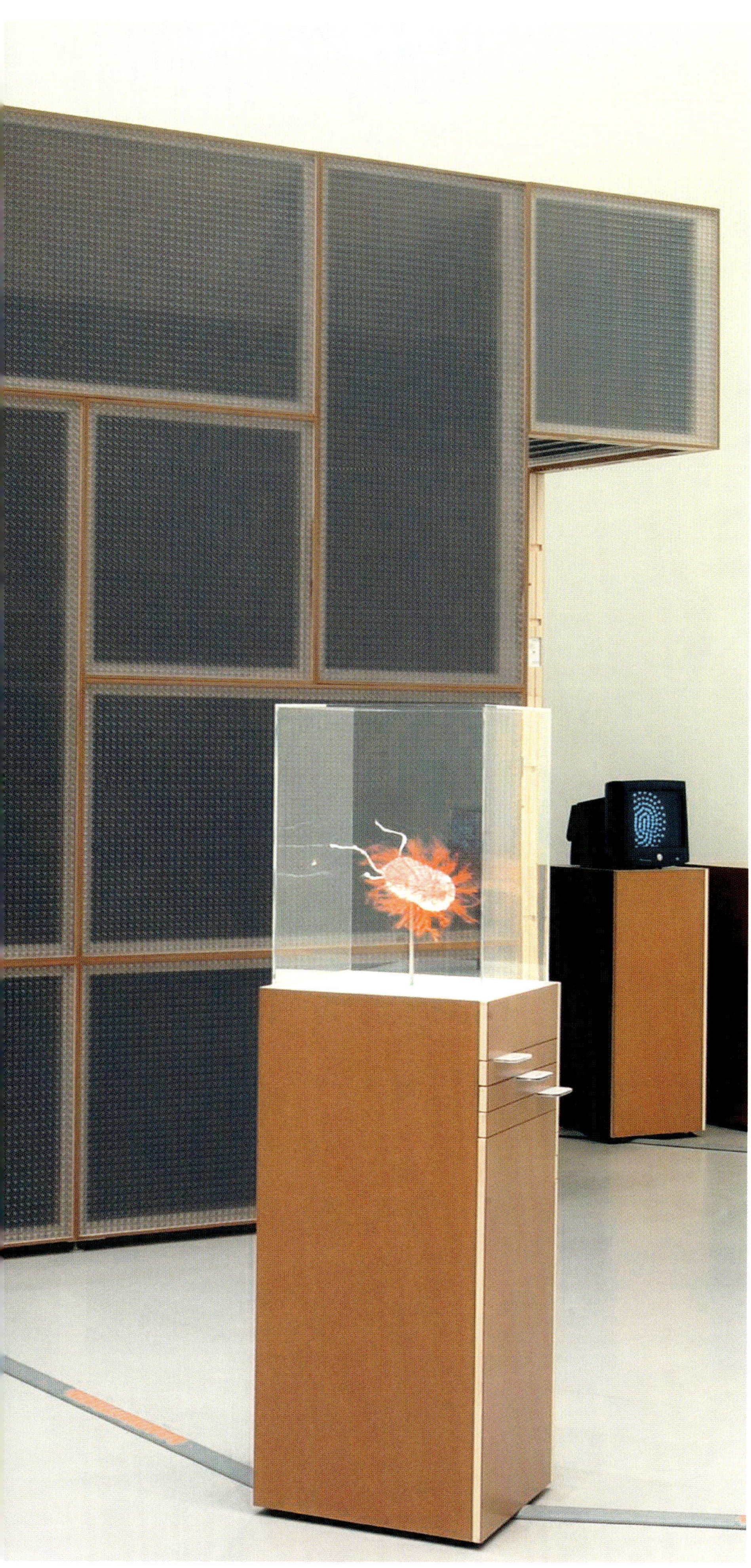

Christa Sommerer & Laurent Mignonneau *Nano-Scape*

media you use as an artist, but rather what you express with that media. In the case of avant-garde media art, expression, concept and material are closely connected. It is an art form that has developed many new forms of expression which are supported in their turn by new processes in the area of image and sound production. The fact that so many media artworks are being exhibited today is a positive effect, since media art is now generally more accepted, the hype of the 90s has blown over and there is a level of normalization and familiarization. However, you cannot expect ten to fifteen years of avant-garde media art, media critique and media philosophy to be understood suddenly, just because everyone now has access to cheaper computers and the Internet.

STEFAN IGLHAUT: Leaving aside a few sensationalist debates, the scientifically avant-garde theme of nanotechnology is still largely beyond the general comprehension of the public. Is your concept of an invisible nanosculpture also a reaction to the appropriation of the artistic avant-garde by the wider market?

CHRISTA SOMMERER & LAURENT MIGNONNEAU: Not directly. If you understand the wider market as including the general public, then it was precisely the general art public rather than the elite who first supported and accepted avant-garde media art. It was due to the enormous public interest during the 90s that these works were first discovered; after all it was for this wider public that they were created, and the feedback from the public was consciously integrated in terms of concepts and their realization. Indeed, so-called interactive art lives from this interaction with the general public. The fact that there is now a wider market for it is a very positive thing. It means more exhibitions, larger budgets and above all a young media art scene that can now move forward and expand the field as a whole. Nevertheless, the avant-garde artist must keep one eye on his own development if he is to avoid merely repeating what has proven itself in the past. For this reason we see ourselves more as researchers who, when they reach a goal or solve a problem, are already setting themselves the next goal or formulating the next problem, even if now and again this means the risk of plunging into the unknown. As Einstein put it so well, "If we knew what we were doing, it would not be called research, would it?"

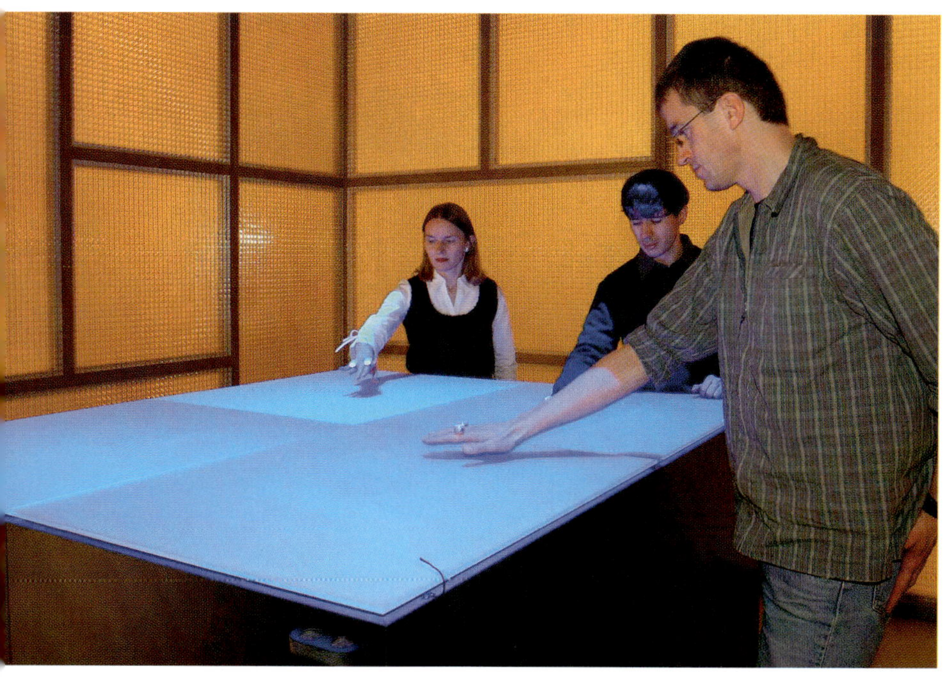

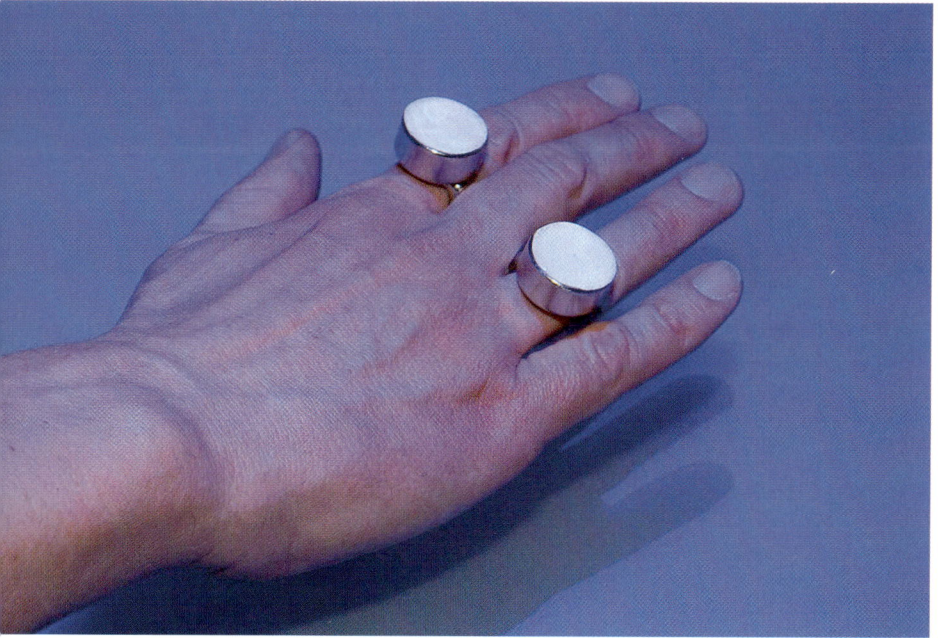

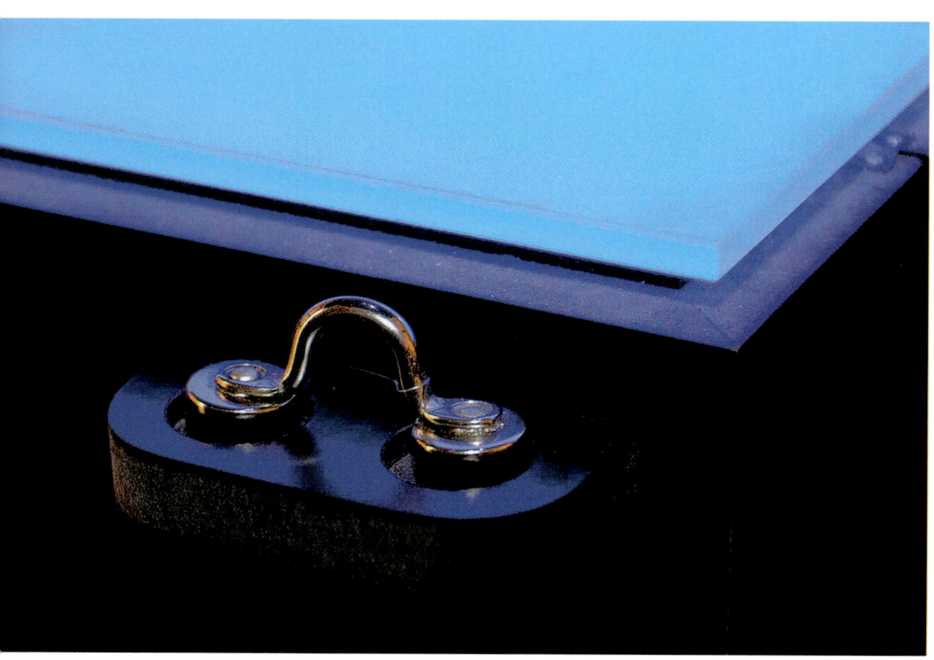

ANDREAS K. ENGEL
EMBODIED MINDS – THE CHALLENGE OF MODERN NEUROSCIENCE

Contemporary neuroscience is boldly approaching one of the most challenging problems that natural science can possibly face: the biological foundations of intelligence. Obviously, intelligent behavior emerges from the activity of the central nervous system. By providing massive resources for information processing and storage, our brains enable us to perceive the environment and our own bodies, to acquire new events and remember the past, to make plans and to solve problems. In particular, intelligent behavior is grounded in the capacities of generalization and abstraction, which liberate the individual from constraints imposed by the current situation and allow him the generation of strategies for problem-solving that apply to a multitude of contexts.
For the most part, the neural mechanisms underlying intelligent behavior are still unresolved, and it is still far from clear which features of neural networks are essential for the emergence of the intelligent mind. The search for the biological roots of the intellect is closely linked to the quest for artificial intelligence: Why are current computers or robots not even remotely capable of genuine intelligent action? What are the crucial differences between biological brains and information processing machines? Are these two classes of systems fundamentally distinct, or might it become feasible to transfer the operating principles of the brain – if properly understood – to artifacts? The rapidly expanding field of neuroscience seems to provide new and exciting answers to these questions. Breathtaking progress is being instigated, on the one hand, by new research tools that allow the monitoring of information processing in the living brain, and by new concepts and paradigms leading to the development of new research strategies on the other. The neuroscientific section of the exhibition is designed to illustrate both aspects to the visitor.

Powerful Brains

As demonstrated by recent findings in neuroscience, a number of factors contribute to the enormous processing capacities of nervous systems in higher vertebrates. Interestingly, implementation in artifacts is, at present, hardly conceivable for the majority of these features. Yet it seems likely that complex cognitive processes will emerge in artificial systems only if they ever share some of these key features with their biological counterparts.
As we know today, parallel distributed processing is one of the key architectonic principles in natural intelligent systems. This principle implies that information processing is not carried out by a single unit, but rather by a set of parallel subsystems or modules, leading to a tremendous increase in the performance and robustness of the overall system. A paradigmatic example of this design is provided by the visual system of advanced vertebrates, where more than 30 cortical areas have been discovered that process different types of visual information. This demonstrates that the representation and storage of sensory information rely on large networks of neurons. No central executive can be found in such parallel architectures. Coherent behavior of the system as a whole emerges from processes of self-organization, which produce global structure from locally acting rules that control the interaction between the network elements.
Another distinctive feature of natural cognizers is their activity and selectivity. Rather than just passively receiving information from the environment, they permanently generate hypotheses about the outer world which are then tested by a highly selective search for appropriate sensory input. Classical models typically assumed that cognitive

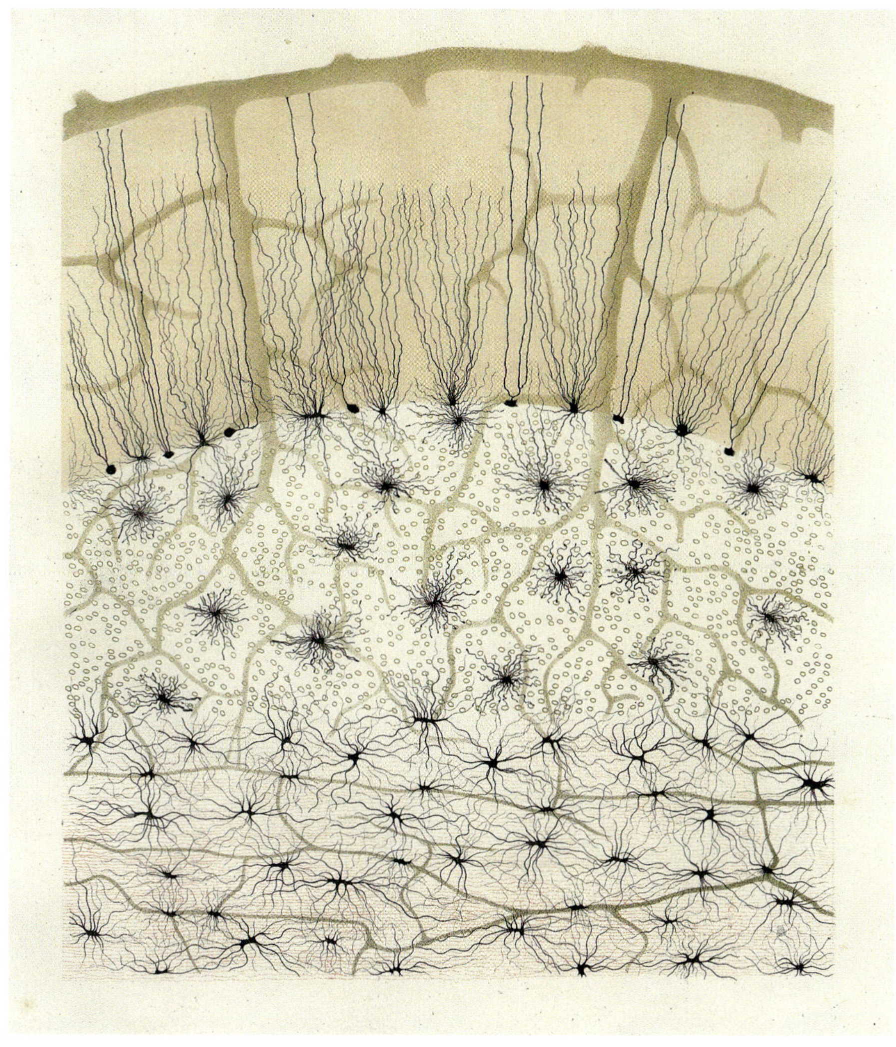

Neural network in the human cerebellum, drawn by Camillo Golgi 1894

systems could be described as serial input-output machines. Current approaches, by contrast, emphasize the role of rich system dynamics which generate intrinsically driven activity and lead to processes such as anticipation and expectation. Based on these, perceptual processing can be much more rapid and efficient. Important factors that determine such intrinsically driven activation patterns are, first of all, memory systems, but also neural systems that control emotional and motivational states. The latter are highly relevant for evaluating the significance of environmental events in terms of reward and punishment. Reflecting vital interests of the organism, they have a crucial influence on sensorimotor selection processes.

One of the most rapidly growing areas within neuroscience is the investigation of neural plasticity and its underlying mechanisms, which permit the malleability of neural nets under the influence of information exchange with the environment. The fact that nervous systems are able to change their network structure constitutes a hallmark that fundamentally distinguishes natural organisms from all currently existing man-made computing machines. While the influence of "function" on "structure" is a canonical feature of biological organization, technical systems do not yet allow a direct modifying influence of "software" over "hardware". Most importantly, plastic changes in the nervous system are experience- and activity-dependent and reflect meaningful interactions with the stimuli encountered in the environment. It is probable that intelligence and conscious mental life could not have evolved without these tremendous learning capacities of the nervous system. This type of plasticity endows the brain with an adaptive capacity on a time scale of hours, days and years. Adaptivity on shorter time scales is granted by the dynamics of signal flow in the brain. On the one hand, the pattern of signal flow in the respective local circuits is redirected in highly context-sensitive ways, depending on previous activation states and the current input pattern into the network. On the other hand, temporal dynamics itself can be employed as a coding dimension in information processing, since it is known that timing relations between signals of different neurons can serve to compose representational states in a highly adaptive manner (see below).

Finally, intelligence is grounded in the capacity of brains to interact with each other, to communicate and, thus, to become part of a social community. Embeddedness in social context is, beyond doubt, one of the most important prerequisites for normal cognitive functioning, for the emergence of intelligence and for the formation of conscious mental states. In particular, the development of self-awareness (or "self-model") depends on interaction and the functional "coupling" of brain states between different individuals, leading to the mutual representation of agents in a given social context. This, in turn, is what psychologists refer to as "theory of mind", i.e. the ability to internally "simulate" the intentions and possible future actions of other "co-subjects".

These key features of intelligent systems, which are beginning to be unravelled by current research in cognitive science, are the focus of an interdisciplinary research program that the Volkswagen Stiftung has established under the heading "Dynamics and adaptivity of neural systems". The neuroscientific part of this exhibition addresses these topics on three different levels which are methodologically distinct, but closely related in conceptual terms: first, the domain of structural and functional imaging, where projects investigate the localization and modularity of neural functions; second, the cellular and molecular level, on which the structure and plasticity of individual nerve cells are uncovered; and third, the level of neural networks, which mediates between the other two levels of observation and describes the dynamics of distributed cell assemblies.

Modules of Mind

The modern approach of structural and functional imaging is about to yield new and spectacular insights into the material foundations of the human mind. Using new techniques, neuroscientists are approaching specifically human capacities that had largely escaped rigorous scientific investigation before. Inevitably, the results obtained in this field will profoundly alter the conception we have of ourselves, both in everyday life and in the realm of scientific discourse.

In recent years, a large variety of tools for brain imaging have become available to the researcher, which deliver different but complementary types of data. Positron-Emission-Tomography (PET) requires the injection of radioactively labelled substances into the bloodstream, which are then used to construct an image of neural activation. A much better spatial resolution can be achieved with a technique more recently developed, Magnetic Resonance Imaging (MRI), which uses excitation by strong magnetic fields to differentiate different types of brain tissue, such as the grey and white matter in the cerebral hemispheres. A particular version of this method, called functional MRI (fMRI), allows researchers to monitor regional changes of blood flow in the brain which occur as a consequence of enhanced neural activation. Using the techniques of electro- or magnetoencephalography (EEG, MEG), finally, permits the recording of electric or magnetic fields from the scalp which reflect activity in the underlying neural tissue. The two latter methods complement PET and fMRI with their superb temporal resolution, which is in the millisecond range.

About two decades ago, the PET technique was already used to localize mental capacities to specific brain regions, thus reviving the classical battle between the two standpoints of localizationism vs. holism. While advocates of the former believe that specific

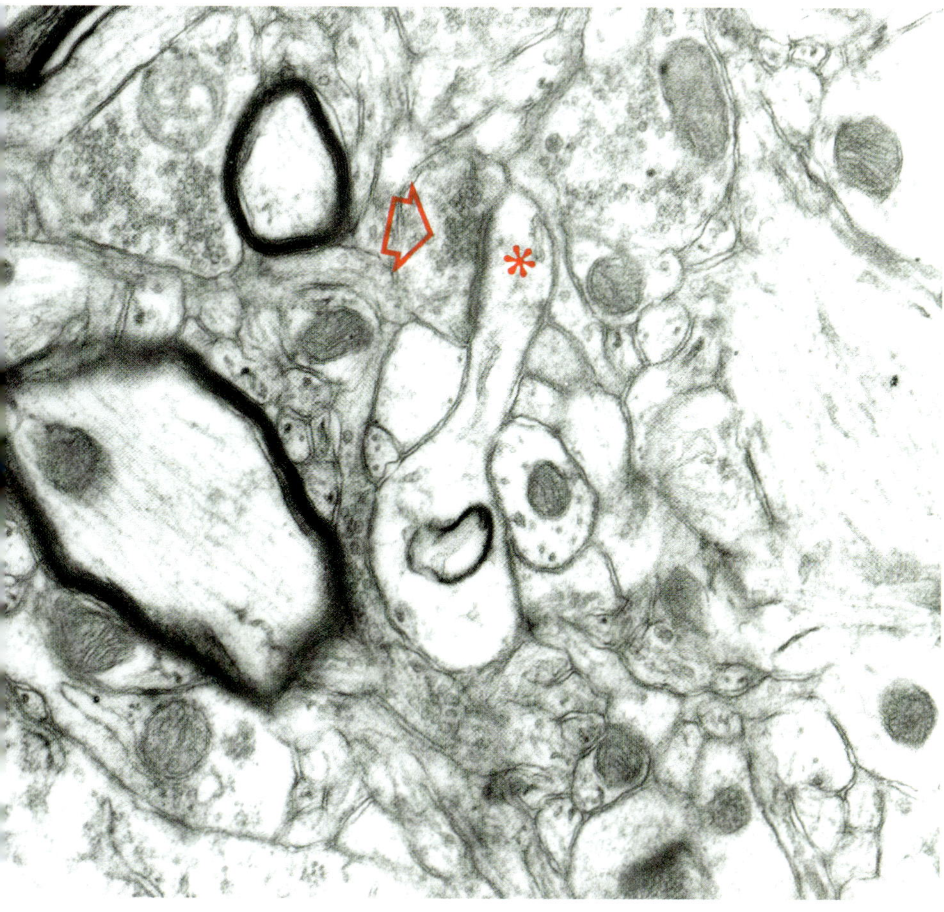

Cross-section of brain tissue. Arrow and asterisk indicate a synaptic gap. In the terminal button of the synapse it is possible to see vesicles containing the molecules known as neurotransmitters. Picture by Wolfgang Schlote.

cognitive functions can be ascribed to specific brain regions in a strict topographic manner, the defenders of the latter argue that all mental capacities make use of more or less the entire brain. The data obtained with the new imaging tools suggest a compromise between these two extremes. Indeed, most brain regions seem to participate in a circumscribed set of cognitive functions. However, complex mental processes typically require the activation of a large set of interacting neural modules. This is particularly true of processes like perception, emotion, language or consciousness, which have moved into the focus of current research. The exhibition does not only illustrate data from experimental studies, but simultaneously visualizes the "pictorial culture" that shapes the scientific discourse in this domain.

Malleable Building Blocks

Nerve cells (neurons) are the building blocks of nervous systems and serve signal generation and exchange. Thus, their function gives rise to all mental life and its behavioral manifestations in animals and humans. The structure of nerve cells reflects their operation. Two different types of processes extend from the cell body. The tree-shaped array of dendrites corresponds to the input region where the cell receives signals from other neurons. The output of the neuron, in turn, is transmitted to other network elements via the axon. Different nerve cells are linked through contact points, so-called synapses, where chemical substances (neurotransmitters) are released to exert an excitatory or inhibitory effect on the respective other cell. Each of the 100 billion cells of the nervous system has something in the order of 10000 synapses. The fine, detailed structure of the nerve cell branches and their contacts is shaped by learning and thus different from cell to cell. This results in the enormous complexity of natural information processing that way outpaces that of current technical systems.

The plasticity of neural networks results from the fact that synapses between neurons can change their functional efficacy depending on the intensity and timing of signal flow between the cells connected. As mentioned already, plasticity is fundamental to learning, memory and the emergence of individuality. Importantly, both the mechanisms and the degree of plasticity change in different developmental stages. During fetal life and early childhood, new fiber tracts grow and unused pathways are selectively dismantled. During adulthood, by contrast, mainly functional parameters can be modified, but no further major constructive structural changes occur. The strength of synaptic activation depends on the pattern of incoming signals. If several impulses arrive in immediate succession along the same fiber or simultaneously across different axons, much larger amounts of neurotransmitter are liberated than with more diffuse input patterns. Repetitive strong activation of a synapse leads to a phenomenon called long-term potentiation (LTP), corresponding to a long-lasting enhancement of synaptic transmission strength. In addition to an enhancement of transmitter output, LTP is associated with structural changes of the synapse, leading to an enlargement of the area that serves for signal transmission. This was discovered only recently in studies employing two-photon laser microscopy, a method by which even individual synapses can be imaged in the living brain.

Dynamic Nets

On the network level, neuroscientists establish models that try to account for how cognition and action arise from the interplay of individual nerve cells. As mentioned above, most neural subsystems show a highly parallel and distributed architecture in which numerous modules are linked into a complex network. This raises the question of how signals processed by parallel channels can be reintegrated into unitary representational states – a problem which was first identified in the domain of perception by the Gestalt psychologists and has now come to be dubbed the "binding problem". This issue exemplifies current approaches in network-oriented neuroscientific research.

One model that has been developed to solve this problem predicts that the dynamics of neural signals may bear the key to understanding integration in distributed networks. This hypothesis assumes that related information is integrated by synchronization of the respective neurons, leading to the formation of a coherently active cell assembly. If this prediction turned out to be correct, synchronized firing of cortical cells would be causally responsible for the Gestalt character of perceptual experience. Since temporal correlations would serve to encode dynamic relations between neurons responding to the same object, this would be of critical importance for the generation of coherent percepts.

Indeed, numerous studies have provided evidence that neurons in sensory and motor systems can precisely synchronize their discharges. A large body of data indicates that such temporal patterns are important for perceptual integration and the linkage of sensory with motor signals. In humans, such synchronization phenomena have been demonstrated with both EEG and MEG. As shown by these studies, perceptual processing, attention and consciousness are accompanied by enhanced neural synchrony. For instance, fast brain waves (so-called gamma-oscillations), which are known to reflect precise neural synchronization, disappear under deep anesthesia. Additional investigations have demonstrated that these fast signals occur prominently during states of enhanced arousal and attentiveness, and they show a striking correlation with the build-up of conscious percepts. Together, these results make it likely that synchrony is an important prerequisite for dynamic integrative processes in neural networks.

These and other recent results in neuroscience and the rapid growth of knowledge in cognitive science raise the question as to the potency and limits of neurobiological explanations. By definition, cognitive science aims at a naturalist account of mental processes, trying to identify their neural basis. It seems very conceivable that neuroscience might reveal biological prerequisites of intelligent behavior. However, it is less clear whether the same approaches will lead to valid explanations of consciousness, self and subjectivity. It might turn out to be impossible to bridge the famous "explanatory gap" between the objective and subjective, as a result of the incompatibility between the experiental 1st-person perspective and the 3rd-person perspective inevitably bound to the scientific approach.

For various reasons, it appears unlikely that neuroscience *per se* might deliver a comprehensive theory of cognition and that anything relevant about the mind could be formulated in a neurophysiological vocabulary. First, there seems to be a "context problem". Even complete knowledge of a person's brain states would not allow us to predict the subject's current thoughts or feelings. This is due to the fact that the contents of neural states can only be defined relative to the person's environment and to the situation he/she is involved in. Neural states as such have no meaning, since they can be individuated only with respect to a current situational context. This also implies that mental states cannot be explained by an "individualistic" approach, i.e., not by exclusive reference to inner states of a cognitive system. Secondly, it may be argued that cognitive processes cannot adequately be captured by descriptions at the sub-personal level. The fact that cognitive acts are performed by persons, rather than some of their parts, has frequently been overlooked by neuroscientists who like to point out, e.g, that the visual system is "recognizing objects" or "interpreting scenes". This seems to be inadequate terminology (sometimes referred to as the "homunculus fallacy") that suggests pseudo-solutions due to category mistakes. Finally, the well-known "qualia-problem" constitutes a notorious obstacle to reductionism. From the mere knowledge of brain states that accompany the sensation of pain it is impossible to deduct how "it feels to have pain". There may be some irreducible residue of subjective experience, therefore, that cannot be embedded in a naturalistic neurobiological framework.

Although both methodological and conceptual progress in cognitive science lend support to an optimistic view, neuroscience should restrain from rash chauvinist attitudes. Nonetheless, the famous "Ignorabimus" proclaimed by the German neurophysiologist Emil Du Bois-Reymond at the end of the 19th century can certainly be questioned. Natural sciences alone will perhaps not be able to fully account for the intellect, but this does not imply that consciousness and self will, in principle, escape the challenge of scientific theorizing.

THOMAS SPRING: Joep van Lieshout, your artistic works lie at the boundary between art, architecture and design. Do you have certain topics and motifs which you pursue over and over again?

JOEP VAN LIESHOUT: As an artist, I always try to follow my intuition, or rather my emotions or instinct – after all, that is what is most important. As for the actual form which a work then takes, whether it is a work of architecture, design, art or something else, that is not so important. As a rule, the topic involves a confrontation between the rational and the irrational, between realism and surrealism, between folly and good sense. These two things, these two poles and two directions are always very significant in my work.

THOMAS SPRING: You normally have a very intuitive approach, so what interested you in particular about this project on science?

JOEP VAN LIESHOUT: First of all, science has always fascinated me personally. Once I even wanted to study nuclear physics, but then I realized I could use my creative energies much better as an artist. I would have been less talented as a scientist than I am as an artist, and it would certainly have been much more difficult for me to exert myself. Today science interests me, because it represents the rational component in my works. I believe one should try to make out the truth and become familiar with the unknown, which is why I am interested in science. At the same time, science and art have a lot in common, because both of them are about discovering something which does not exist as such. And you can use creativity to discover something.

THOMAS SPRING: In this project, you examined the plasticity of the brain in workshops with scientists, in other words, how the brain transforms itself organically when environmental conditions change. Did this topic particularly rouse your interest?

JOEP VAN LIESHOUT: Yes, absolutely. But then when I actually contemplated the brain, what struck me most was that all people on earth have more or less the same brain and that it always, or almost always, functions equally well. And yet each brain is quite individual. I find this remarkable and exciting. But as an artist, what especially fascinates me is the human body. It is a subject which has interested me greatly in my own work and I have often studied how everything functions, all the organs in the body and how they interact. For me this is extremely important and so this project really came at the right moment.

THOMAS SPRING: Does your interest in the body and organs have anything to do with a specific plastic component which can be found in your work?

JOEP VAN LIESHOUT: Yes, perhaps it does. The beauty of human organs lies in their being so complicated. How everything functions and the complexity of simple metabolic processes, how sugar is taken from blood and vice-versa, how everything is controlled by the brain via nerves and hormones, how nerve cells change when we think and feel, how entire regions change when new tasks have to be carried out – that is really very, very complicated and very, very fascinating. And what interests me about it all is the appearance of things. Why does a kidney or a lung or a heart look like it does? This is certainly an accomplishment of millions of years of evolution – the same is true of the brain, which constantly reacts to its environment. For most people, who have no idea what the body is and how it functions, the complexity of the organs and their appearance is something tremendously interesting and mysterious.

THOMAS SPRING: How did you proceed in your work? How does an artist come to handle the topic of brain research as you have?

JOEP VAN LIESHOUT: There are two things that caught my attention. One is the anatomy of the brain, and so the question: What does it look like, how does it function and how

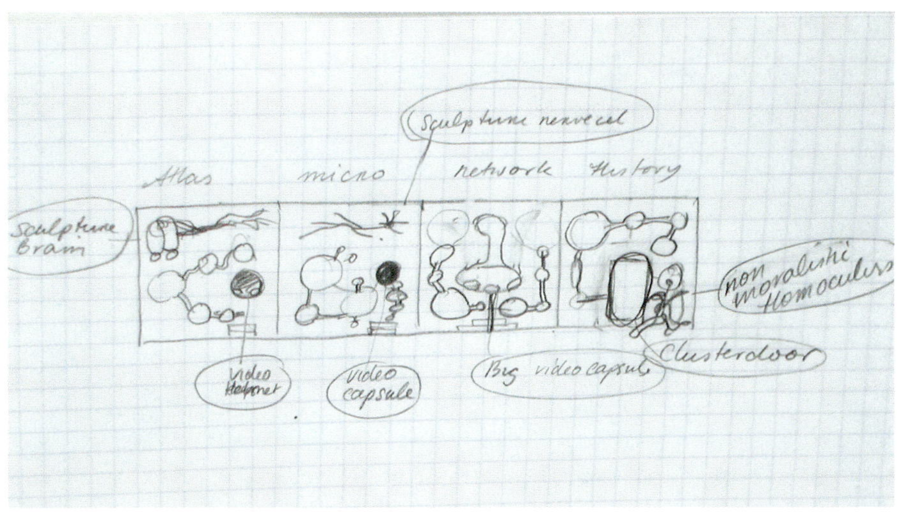

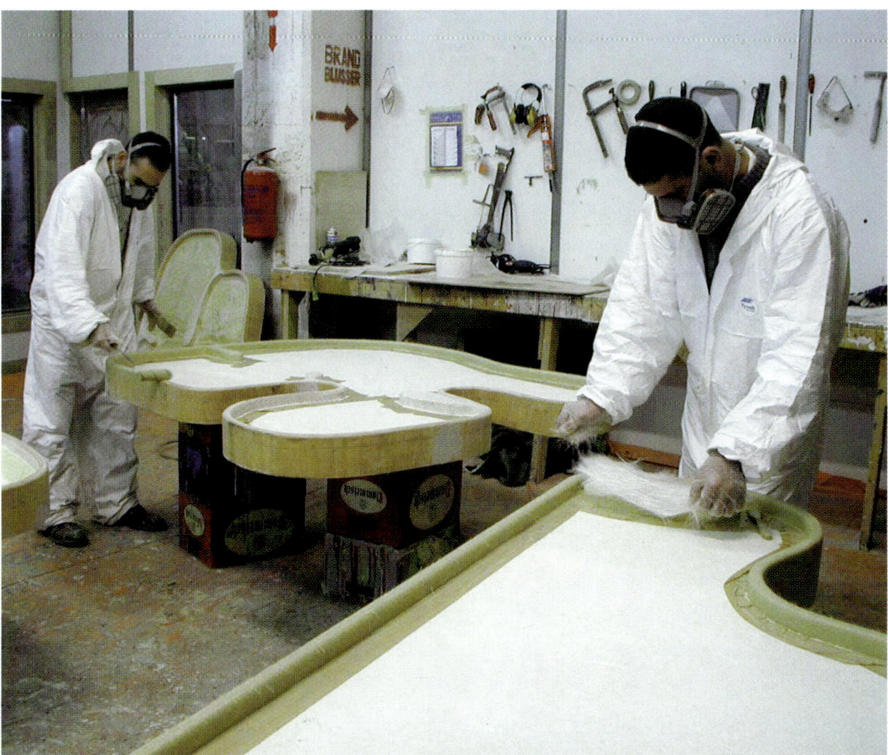

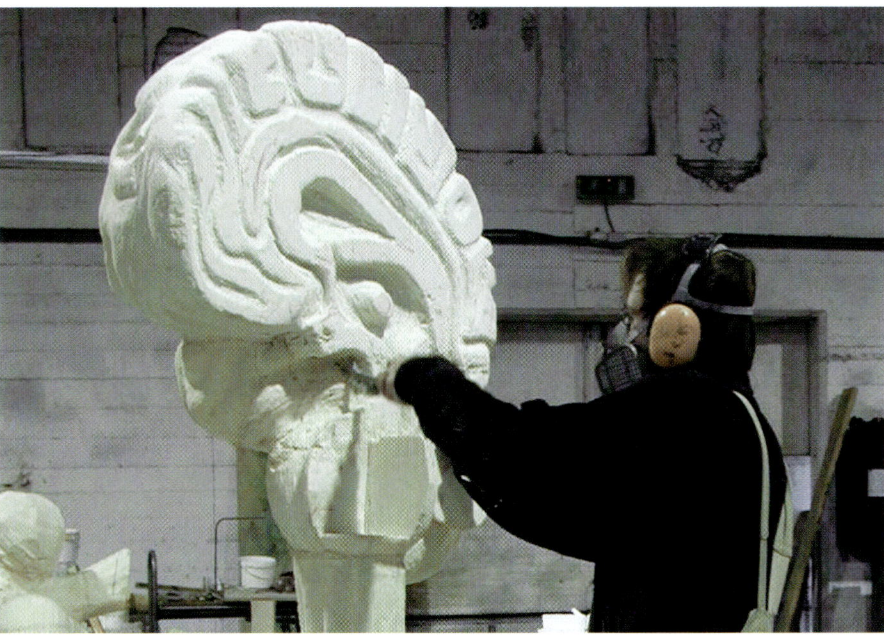

Sketches and studies for conducting the brain workshop in Atelier van Lieshout, Rotterdam

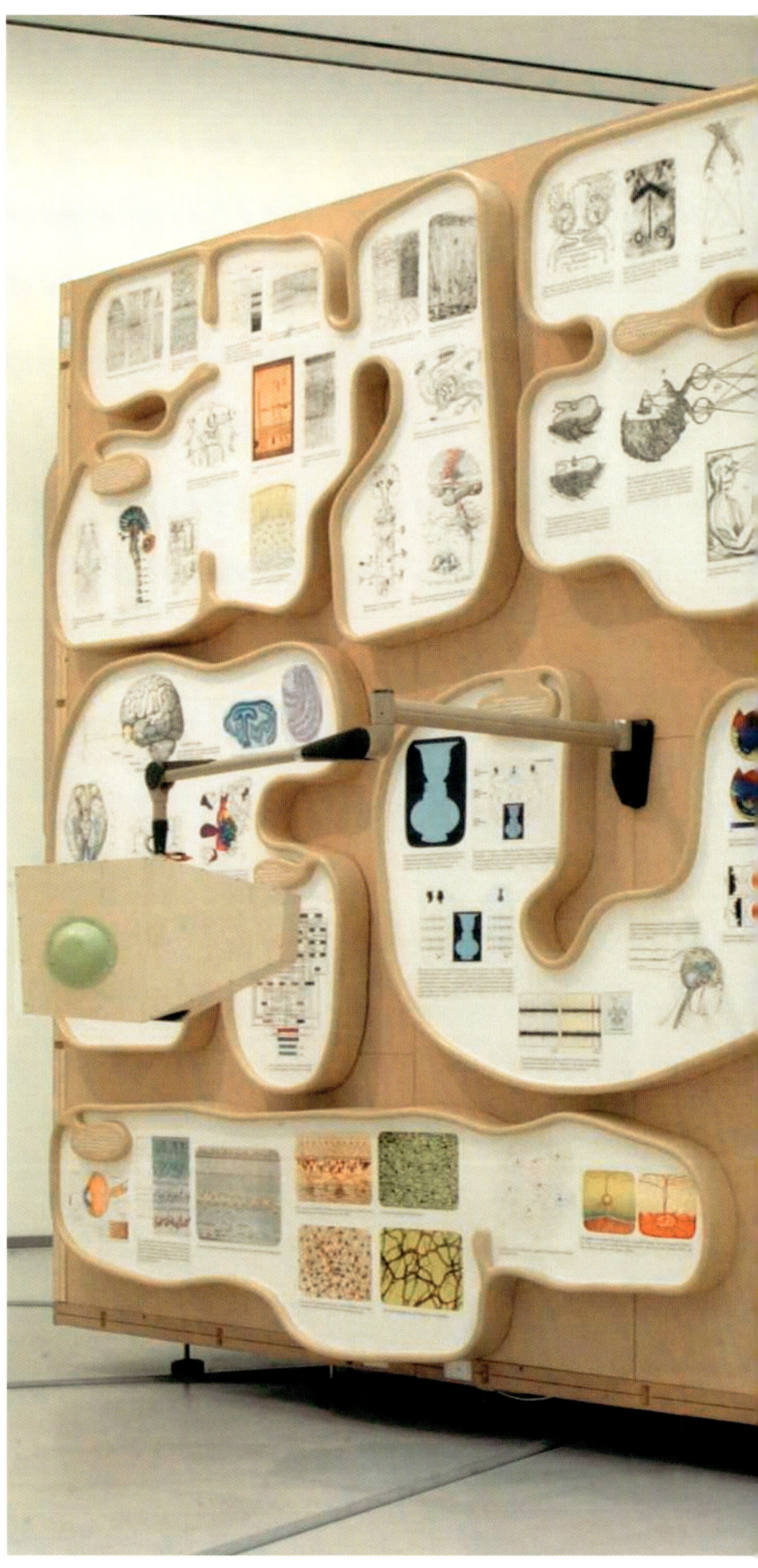

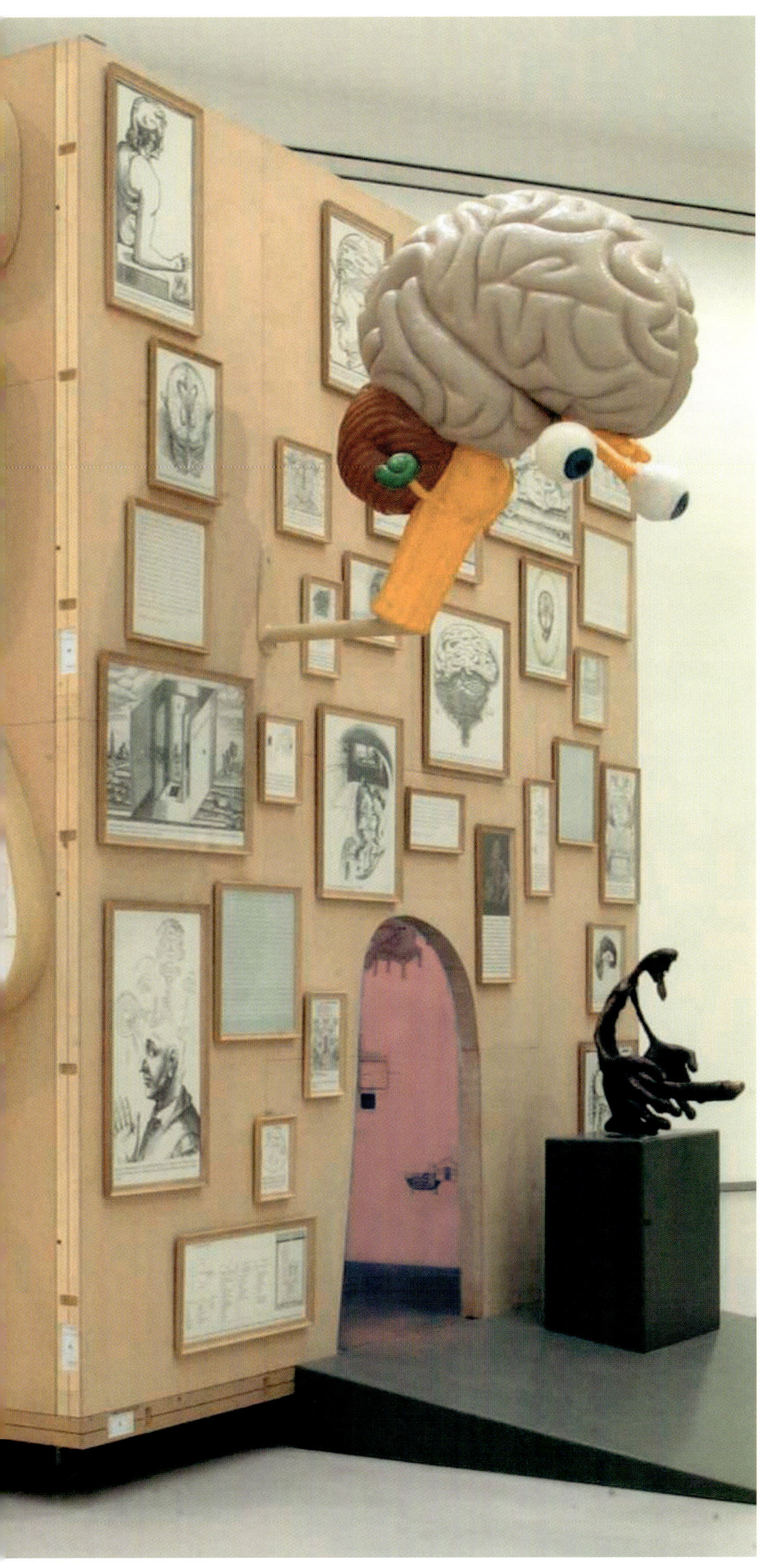

Atelier van Lieshout *Brain Pavilion*

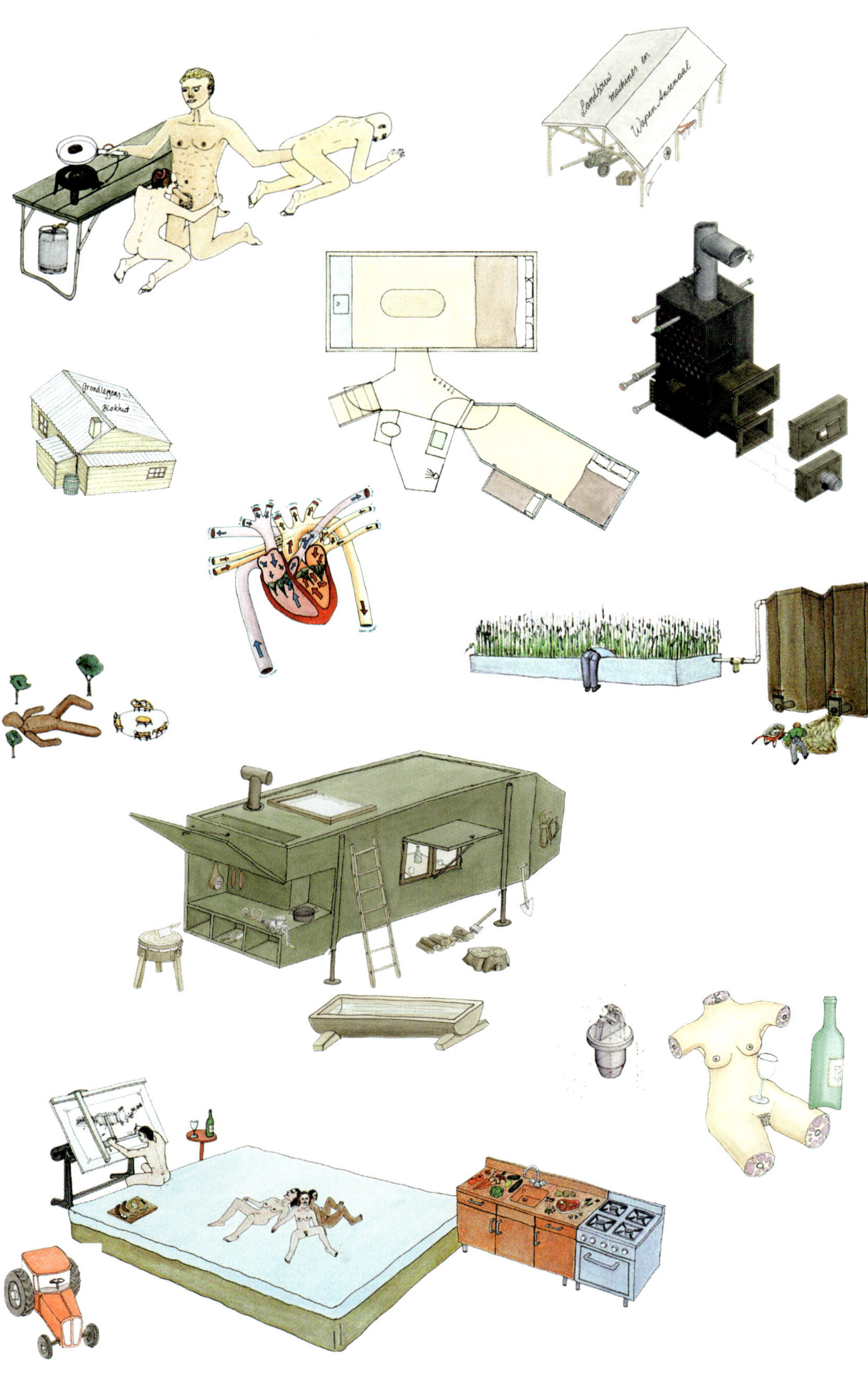
Landbouw machines en
Wonen-...
Grondlegers
Blokhut

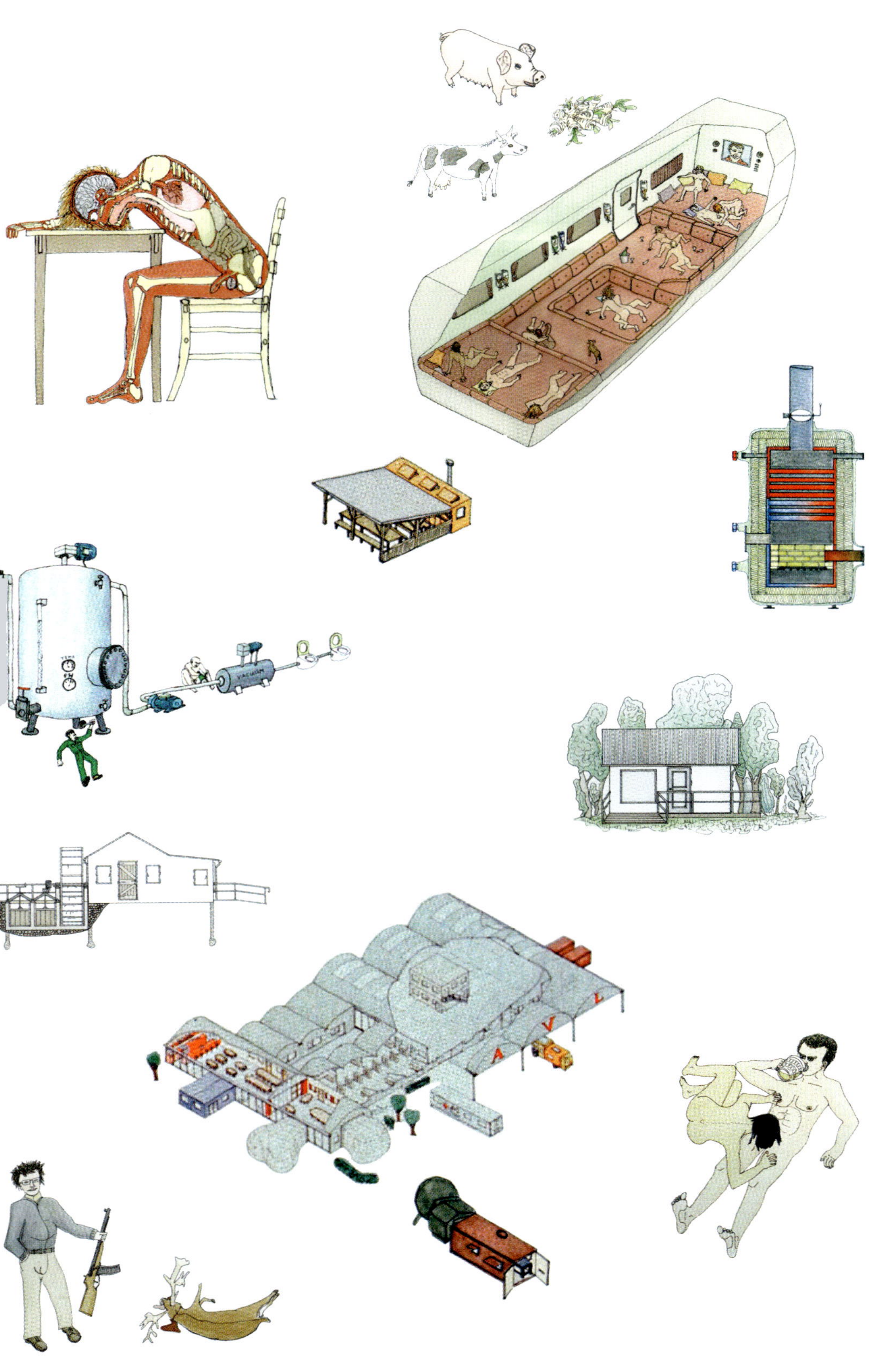

While the outer surface of the *Brain Pavilion* presents brain research from the third-person perspective, Joep van Lieshout unfolds his own subjective cosmos in the interior. The drawings include elements from the "free state" of AVL-Ville.

do I make a sculpture of it? And the other is the "soft" side of the brain, in other words, the question: Why are we the way we are? Why do I think as I do, why do I do something the way I do, and why do I say something in one way and not in another? The entire individual and personal component is the other aspect I am very interested in. In this project, that is the purpose of the interior of the pavilion, that is where we will portray, so to speak, my nature, my essence. For the brain from the outside, we have collaborated with scientists. I have also done some research myself and read many books; medical and popular-science books about the brain. And for the other side, for the interior of the pavilion, I am making drawings as an artist.

 How have you gone about designing the outer surface of your pavilion? Is it a matter of information design or is there a specific artistic statement you are making?

 No, initially it was not a matter of any specific artistic statement. Though actually one has first to define the exact meaning of the term artistic statement and the form in which it is presented. The form is primarily important to convey the scientific information. Indeed, this is the first objective of my interpretation. And I tried to design it as attractively as possible, in order to facilitate its reading as much as I could. By working with balloons and clusters which are connected to one another, we want, of course, to demonstrate that the information is also interconnected. I think it is important to be able to read the information in different layers, and I wanted to avoid a large, elaborate thread and the need for linear comprehension. One sees something and thinks: this is interesting, I'll read this, and oh, I'll read this too, and this as well, and this looks good, and this here also has an impact on me. I think it is very important that it is not a linear story, a linear narration, but instead allows one to absorb parts separately. We have tried to accomplish this with the design and the way the information is grouped. So perhaps a statement does enter into it after all, because the information is presented in an organic manner. Not hierarchically, but rather associatively and parallel – in other words, modelled somewhat on how the brain works. Indeed, that was how I wanted it.

 Is this a more intuitive procedure or the result of rational consideration of how the brain functions?

 In part it is intuitive, though in part it is also an entirely rational distribution of information. On the one hand, my sculptures are partially rational and scientific, and partially artistic and ironic. One is an anatomical model of the brain and correlates fairly precisely with reality. Another, for example, is the homunculus man, which is somewhat more pseudo-scientific. Although I have changed him; he now has, among other things, a very large cock – instead of the very small one he usually has in scientific drawings. So this is an ironic deviation, for in itself it is unclear whether it is meant seriously or not, and whether it is right or maybe not quite right. Room has been left here for uncertainty and irony. That is my job as an artist – without it art is not possible.

 As an artist, how do you feel about the confrontations you have had with scientists? What languages are used and how well does one understand one another?

 In this respect, we are similar enough, I think. Although science and art are very specialized today, so one can only understand a small part of science and even then, only if one is well-informed about it. It is exactly the same with art. It has a life of its own, and one has to be very familiar with it. Only people who are very specialized themselves are able to understand it. So that is why it is more difficult today to bring these spheres together – though perhaps attempts are not made often enough. For I do believe more possibilities exist. Artists and scientists are people who have learned to think in a particular way. The disadvantage is that they can only think in this one particular way. Perhaps by working together people can learn to think the way other people do and to make new discoveries as a result.

 What will take place inside the pavilion?
 A montage of existing works, of drawings, will be displayed, because these depict my soul, my mind. Certain drawings will be added, connecting it all together, and these will generate new pictures. All in all, it will look a bit like the Apocalypse or a painting by Hieronymus Bosch; information will be profuse. One will be able to read a lot into it.

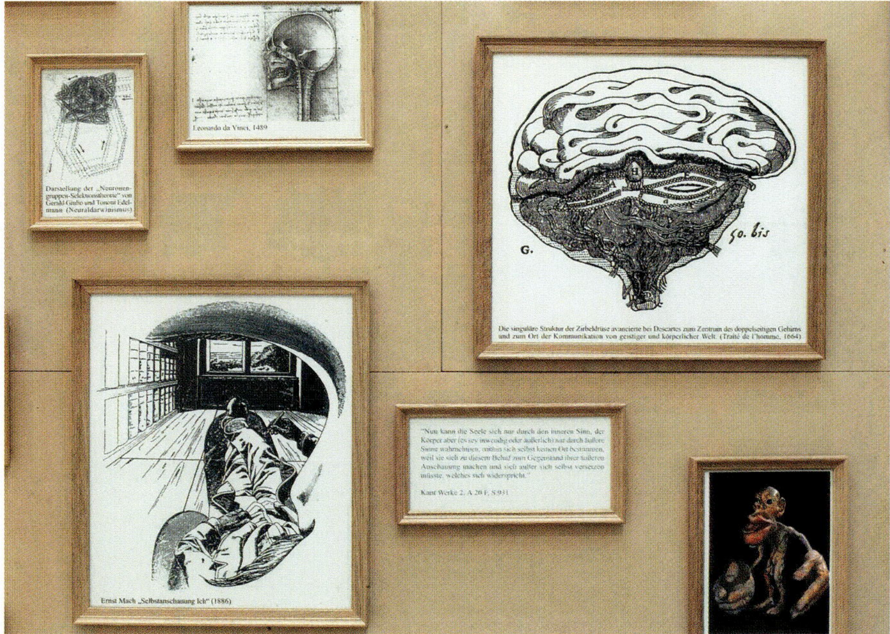

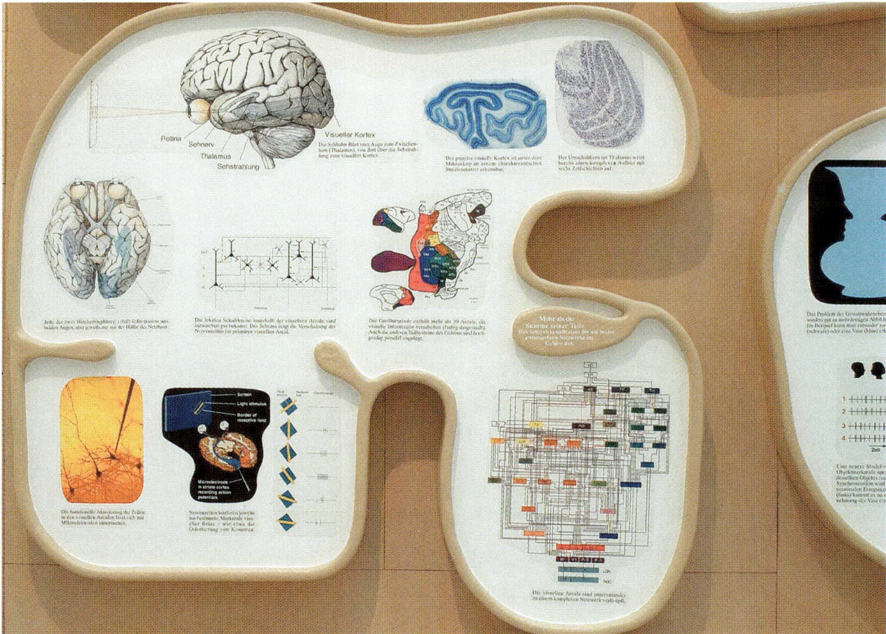

Scientific information is conveyed by means of cluster forms that bundle systematic and historical aspects of a topic. The pictures selected also underscore the meaning of scientific images and the processes resulting in them.

THOMAS SPRING: Your contribution "WildCards" is about designs and visions for the future of the knowledge society. You have invited ten artists and ten scientists to participate in this project. Their ideas are to be presented on oversized playing cards which visitors can pull out of a kind of depot. What relationship between artists and scientists did you take as your starting point?

CHRISTIANE DELLBRÜGGE: Artists and scientists are not equal players in their access to societal reality. Their working conditions differ fundamentally. Artists work on tasks they have set themselves and are not bound to an institute, a discipline or scientific truth. The downside of this independence is, however, that they have a smaller radius of activity. Artists move in a sphere whose rules they have not set; they use existing rules and try to change them by doing so. Science, on the other hand, determines what our future will be like and, as Meyer-Abich says, for this reason it is more political than what governments concern themselves with. Typical features of scientific work are teamwork, the application of specialized knowledge and equipment pools, the worldwide networking of know-how and the funds spent on research. Of course, in principle, the parameters are transferable and it would be an interesting experiment to swap the working conditions of these two spheres and see what came of it.

STEFAN IGLHAUT: There are different points of departure in a project where artists and scientists work parallel to one another and express themselves either parallel or in contrast to one another. How has this affected "WildCards", and what have you done with the two sides?

CHRISTIANE DELLBRÜGGE: We have placed subjective and radical positions next to one another. In doing so, we hope to open ourselves up to a fictional perspective. We are not interested in the foreseeable future that scientific and technical advances are taking us towards, but rather in hitherto inconceivable futures, ones which people catapult themselves into with an utopian leap.

RALF DE MOLL: For scientists, this means going beyond the boundaries of their disciplines or what is currently possible, and designing – instead of just analyzing or diagnosing. For artists, this means not just touching on sore points, but devising instructions, tools and models.

THOMAS SPRING: How did you go about looking for the scientists and the artists? What were your criteria? And what does one experience when addressing artists and scientists with such a project idea?

RALF DE MOLL: We started with artists whose works we already knew and whose methods we were familiar with. We had some premises related to content: for instance, we wanted Nana Petzet to participate, because she works on models for recycling and consumer resistance; Lucy Orta or Stephen Willats who explore tools for alternative behavior patterns; and Benjamin Foerster-Baldenius who deals with the re-appropriation of public space. From there we sought scientific positions with which we would be able to involve ourselves intellectually.

CHRISTIANE DELLBRÜGGE: Initially we wondered how we should talk to scientists and ask the right questions, and whether the right questions even existed. For a while we debated the possibility of falling back on philosophers, who work at the boundary between the virtual and the real anyway. But the longer we spend on the project, the greater is the response from committed scientists and the more "utopian windows" we see which scientists might open. We have discarded controversial topics that have been loaded with a kind of sex appeal by the media. For example, instead of inviting a genetic engineer to participate, we asked Hans Herren from ICIPE in Kenya. He is working on a shift in nature's balance, an ingenious re-arrangement of what exists so as to fight pests and pathogens. Or nutritionist Angelika Meier-Ploeger, who is investigating strategies for training consumption, and wants to alter consumers' behavior and agriculture by using aesthetic arguments.

STEFAN IGLHAUT: What role does the question of authorship play in this project? Will the artists and scientists be mentioned individually by name as authors under the umbrella of Dellbrügge & de Moll, or will the author be Dellbrügge & de Moll?

RALF DE MOLL: The 20 participants have authorship and with it they accept responsibility. Of course, the overall outcome will be a work by us, but that is another story. Birger Priddat, an economist and philosopher from Witten-Herdecke University, was the first scientist we visited, and he predicted the problems we would have with scientists. Aside from fearing they would ruin their chances for funding or would misdirect their energies, they also feared endangering their scientific authority by participating as authors in the "frivolous" context of an art exhibition.

THOMAS SPRING: What experience did you have with refusals and positive feedback? A scientific thesis which is presented in conjunction with art inevitably turns into something different from what it would be in a scientific or political context.

CHRISTIANE DELLBRÜGGE: There was one refusal by a renowned climatologist from Hamburg. We had asked him for a program, modelled on Julian Huxley's "If I were Dictator", a program to avert the climate catastrophe on a rational, scientific level, irrespective of diverse interest groups. In an earlier study, he had already developed political and economic concepts for a model. He believed such a program was technologically no problem at all and could be realized within the next five years without any financial losses. But he was not willing to pick up a pen and put his program to paper, and then figure as its author in the exhibition. He does not believe a scientist can be an advocate. He is a member of work groups with lobbyists from the fossil fuel industries, representatives of Greenpeace and politicians, and does not want to endanger his position. Don't you think he embodies the kind of scientist that Paul Feyerabend talked about, one for whom his career and the opinions of his colleagues are more important than his responsibility to society?

STEFAN IGLHAUT: So this climatologist had objections to your artistic concept, how are you going to deal with that? Perhaps cultures have become so removed from one another that concepts can in fact be ruined by publishing them in the wrong place. Has his reply had any repercussions on your concept and how you plan to proceed? Are you going to use a blank card to mark the site of incompatibility or simply seek other partners?

RALF DE MOLL: It is not a question of individual personalities, but of the problem itself. This discussion just increased our interest. We had to find someone whose thoughts were more radical and who was also willing to defend his position. At the Potsdam Institute for Climate Impact Research we found what we wanted. Ottmar Edenhofer and Herrmann Held are in the process of designing a "Marshall Plan" for the world. They assume we are not automatically heading toward a future, but can design the future. What kind of a future do we want and what means are required to attain it? These means do not have to come exclusively from the natural sciences and technology. The institute is working on a program in collaboration with scholars from the humanities, with economists, climatologists, etc., all of whom illuminate and tackle problems from different perspectives.

STEFAN IGLHAUT: How are the "WildCards" to be presented? Will the visitors be given an indication of what is art and what is science, of what are external contributions and what is by Dellbrügge & de Moll?

CHRISTIANE DELLBRÜGGE: The authors will be listed. And we will contextualize the contributions on subtext cards recognizable as such by their uniform design. Whether one is dealing with an artist or a scientist will be clear in some cases, in others it will not be. Some scientists are very visual and get straight to the point. Their inspiration for an idea

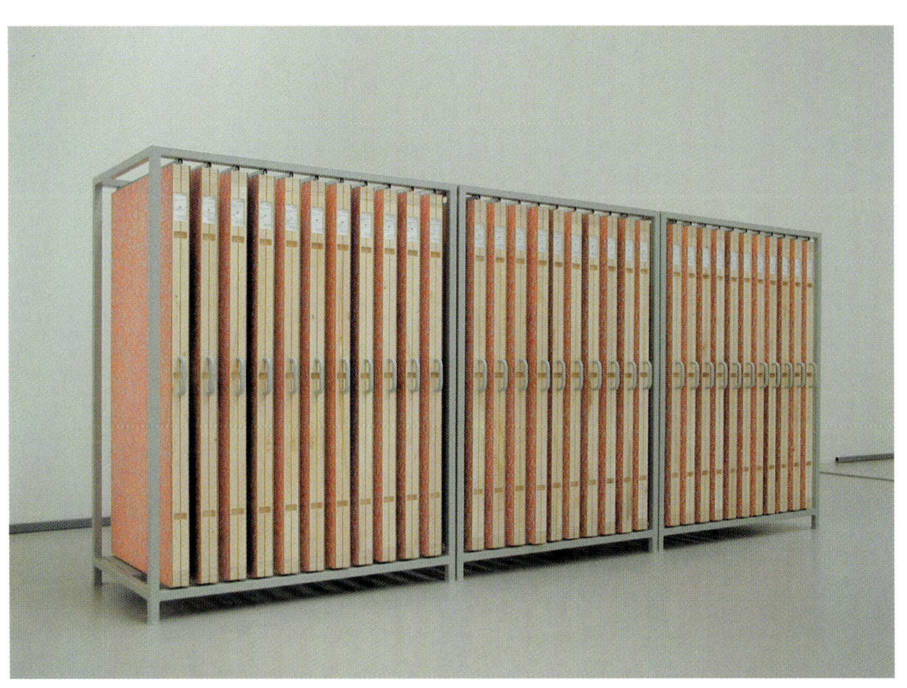

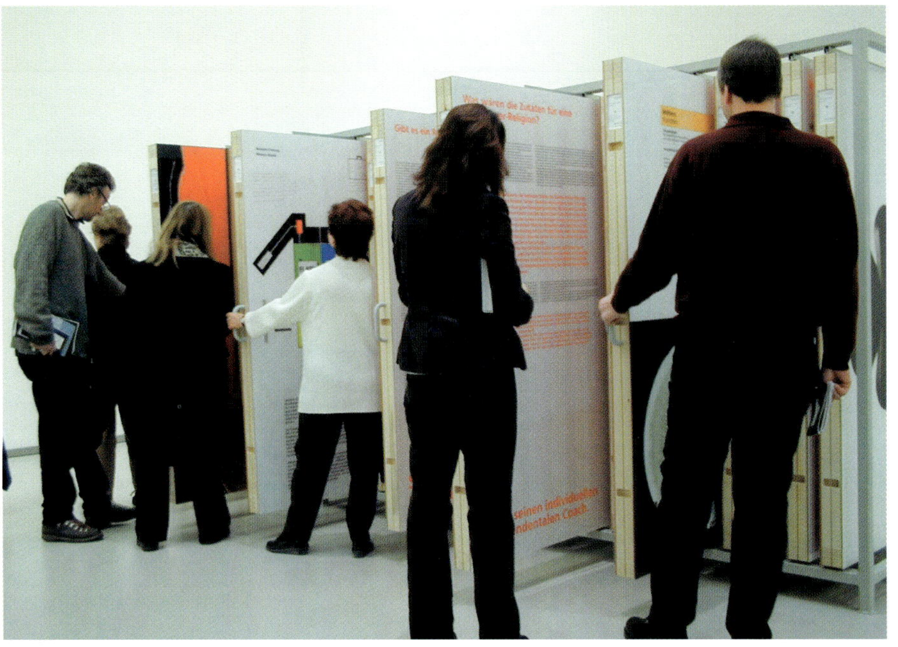

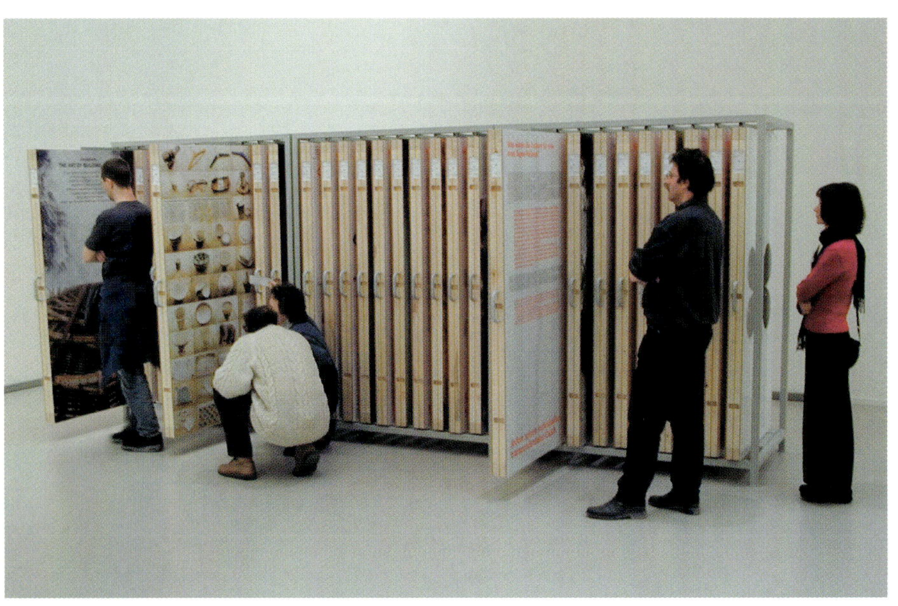

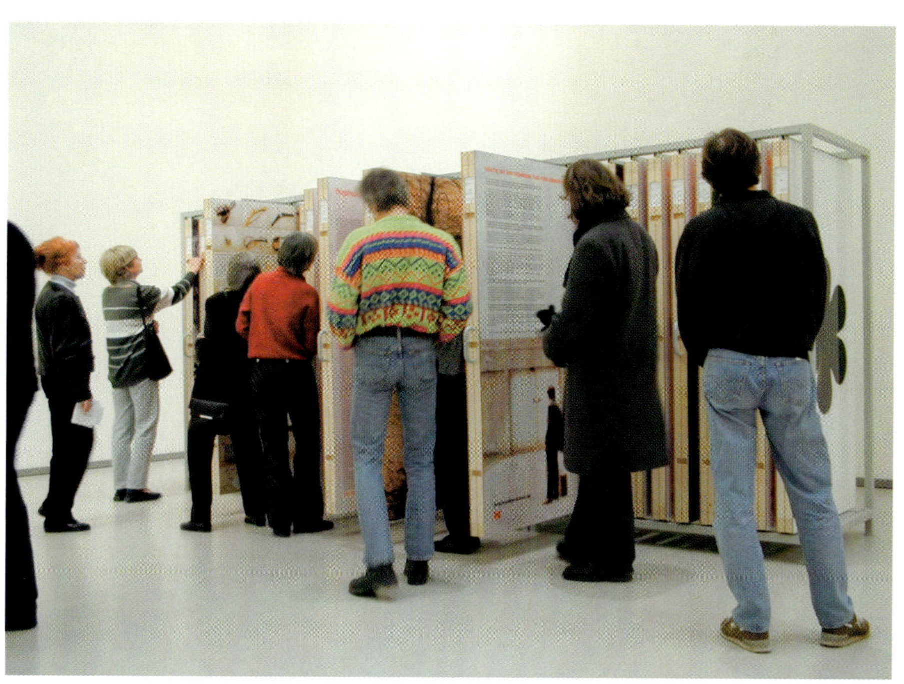

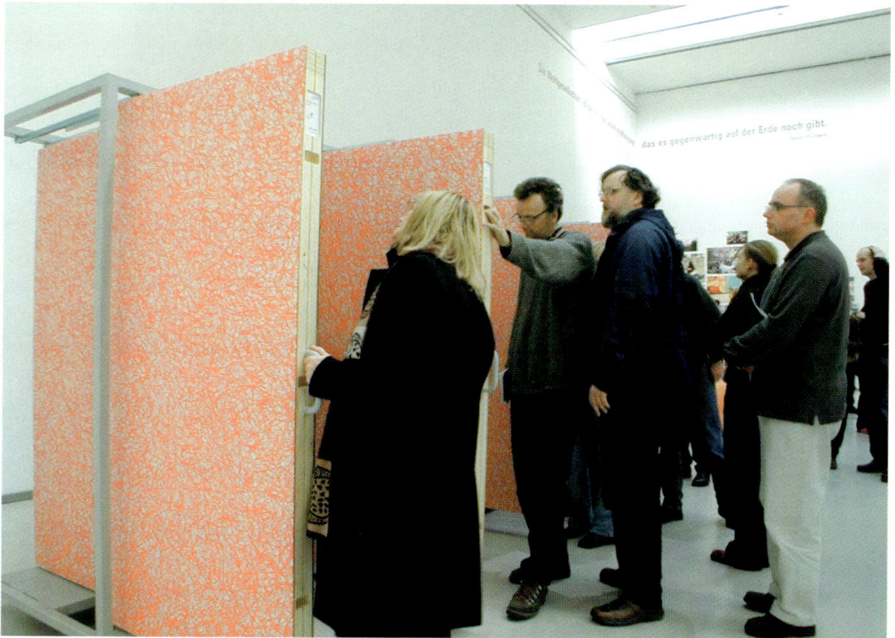

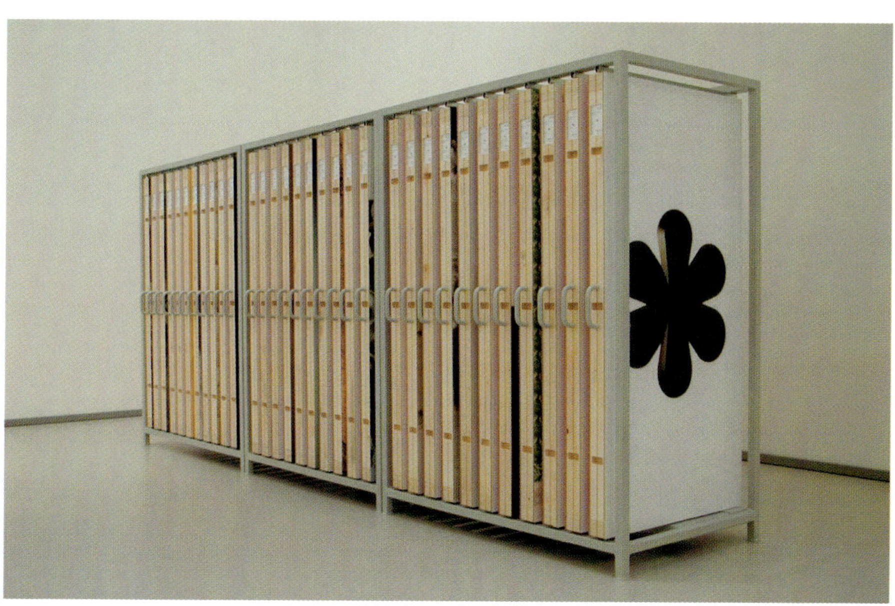

Dellbrügge & de Moll *WildCards*

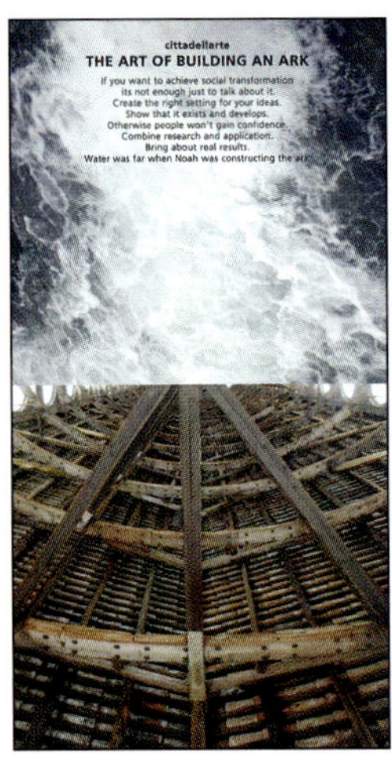

cittadellarte
THE ART OF BUILDING AN ARK
If you want to achieve social transformation
its not enough just to talk about it.
Create the right setting for your ideas.
Show that it exists and develops.
Otherwise people won't gain confidence.
Combine research and application.
Bring about real results.
Water was far when Noah was constructing the ark.

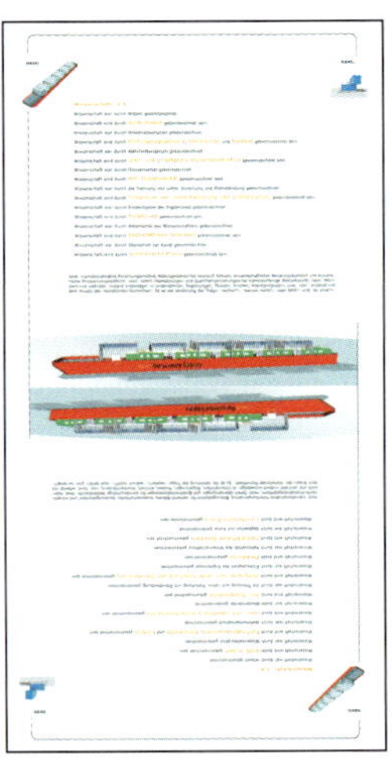

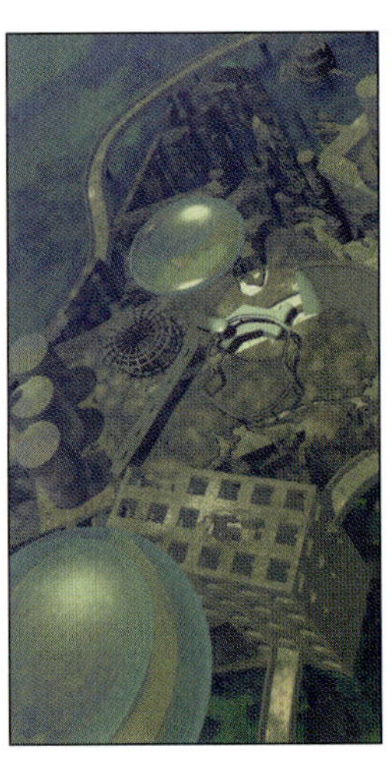

Kommst du mit in den Krieg?

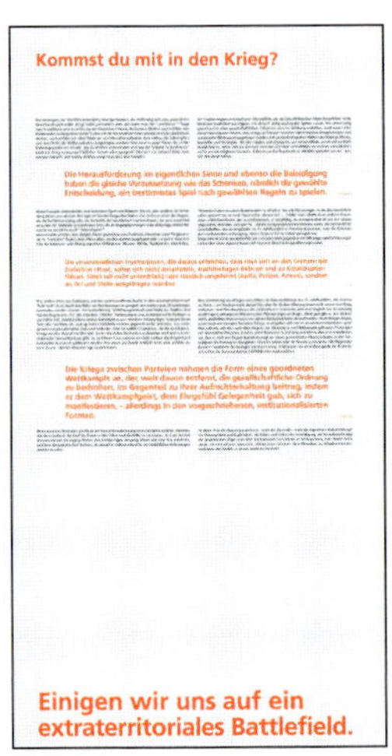

Einigen wir uns auf ein
extraterritoriales Battlefield.

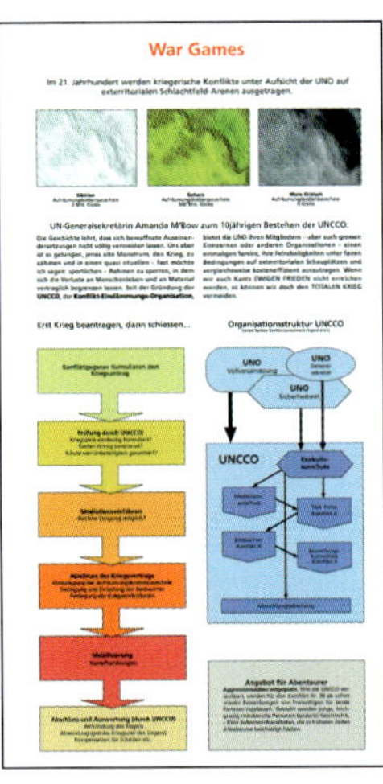

War Games

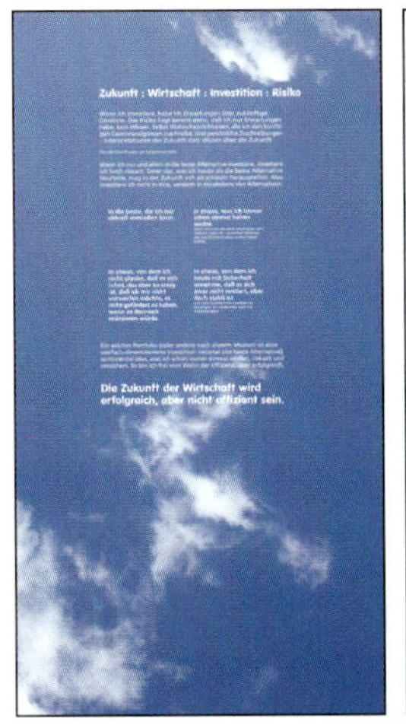

Zukunft : Wirtschaft : Investition : Risiko
Die Zukunft der Wirtschaft wird
erfolgreich, aber nicht effizient sein.

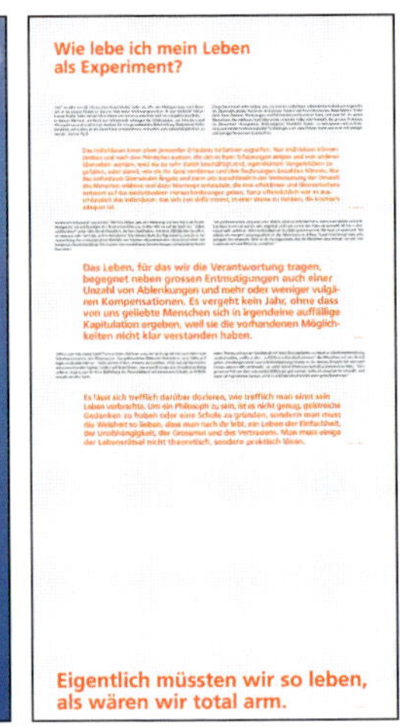

Wie lebe ich mein Leben
als Experiment?
Eigentlich müssten wir so leben,
als wären wir total arm.

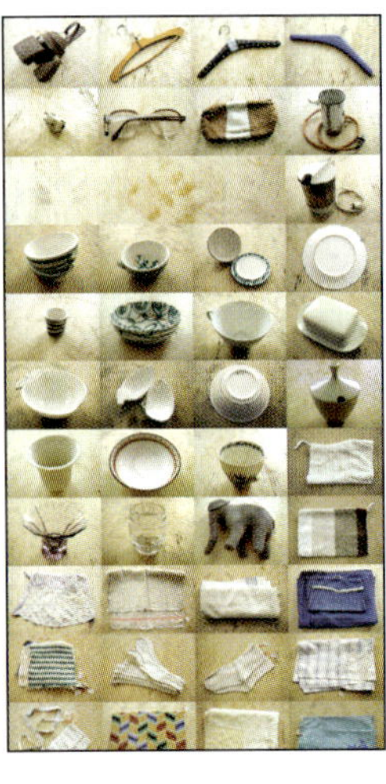

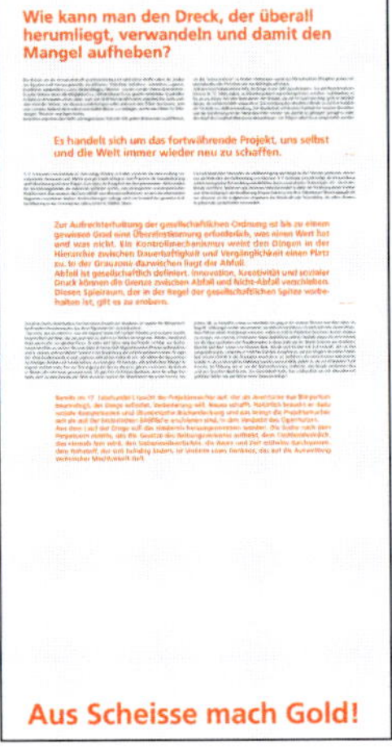

Wie kann man den Dreck, der überall
herumliegt, verwandeln und damit den
Mangel aufheben?
Aus Scheisse mach Gold!

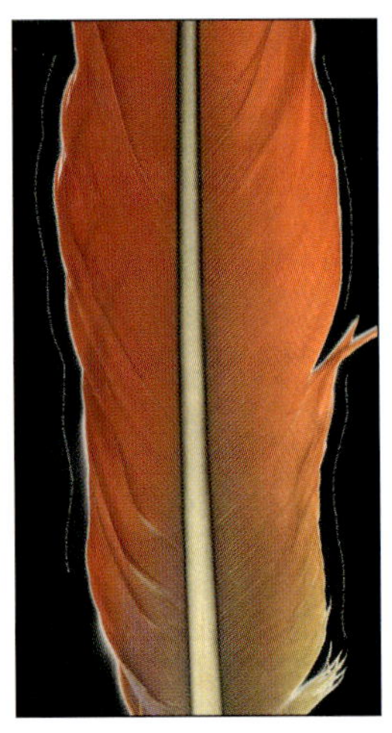

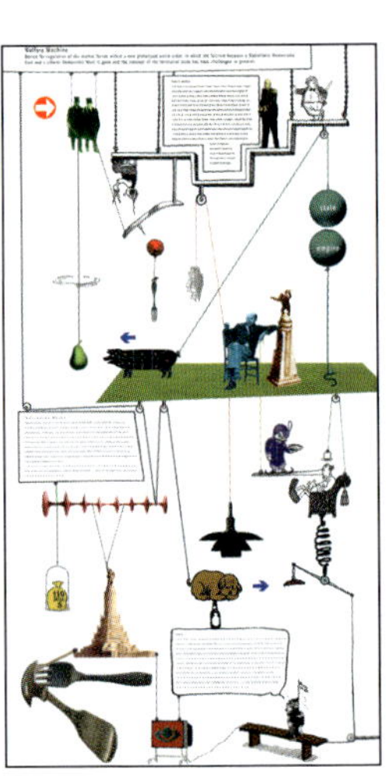

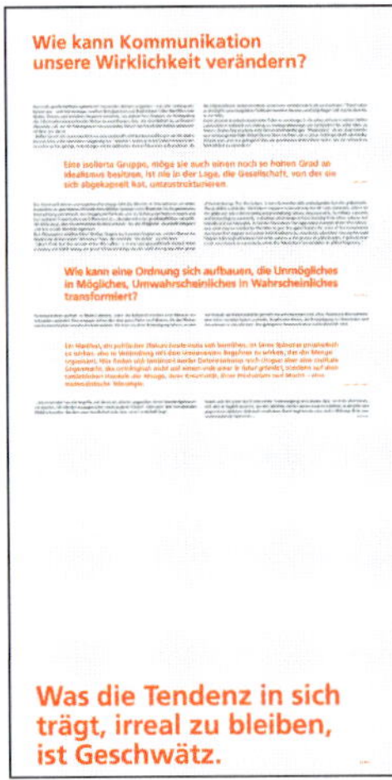

Wie kann Kommunikation
unsere Wirklichkeit verändern?
Was die Tendenz in sich
trägt, irreal zu bleiben,
ist Geschwätz.

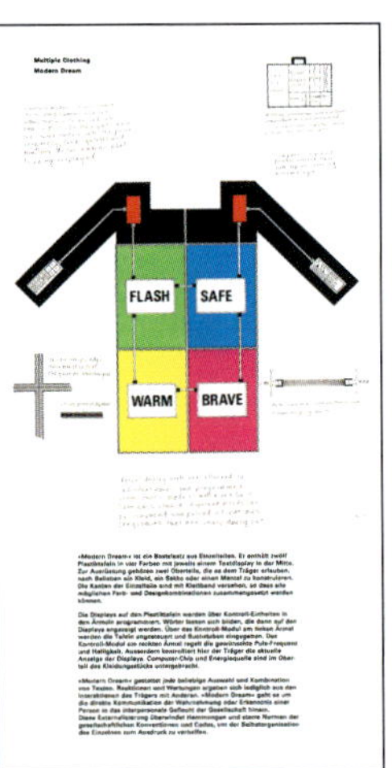

Multiple Clothing
Modern Dream
FLASH
SAFE
WARM
BRAVE

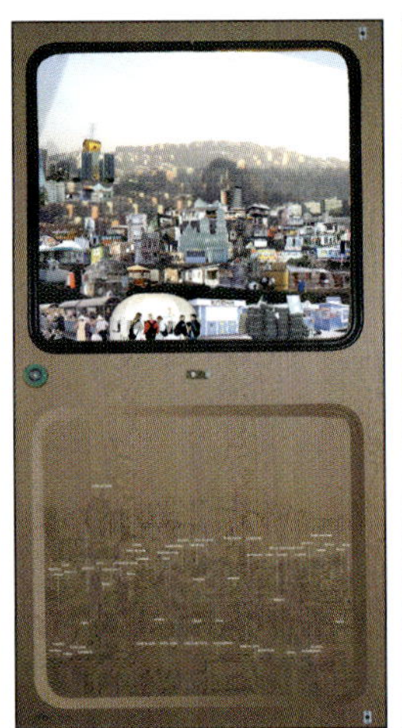

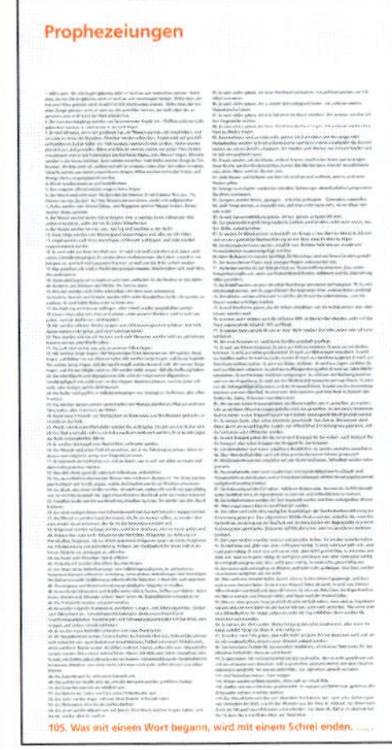

Prophezeiungen

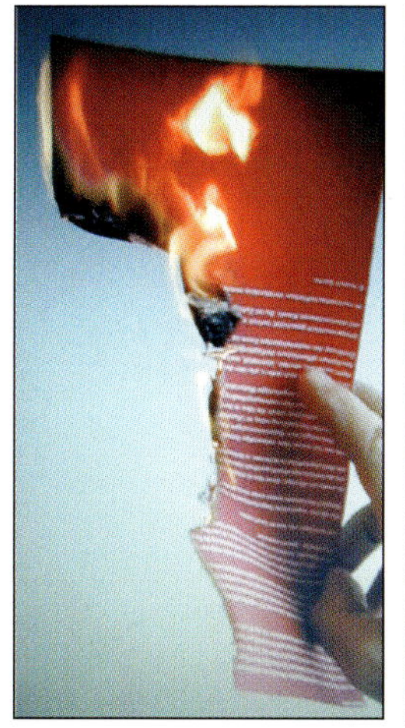

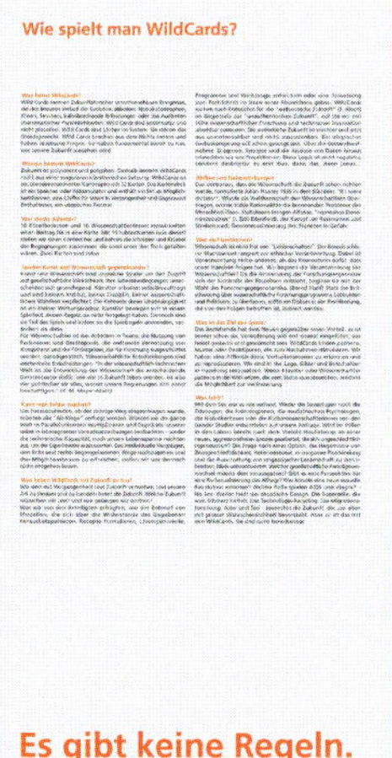

Wie spielt man WildCards?
Es gibt keine Regeln.

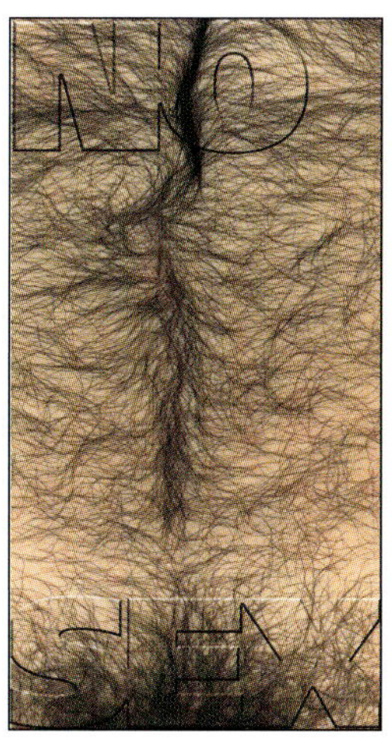

NO
SEX

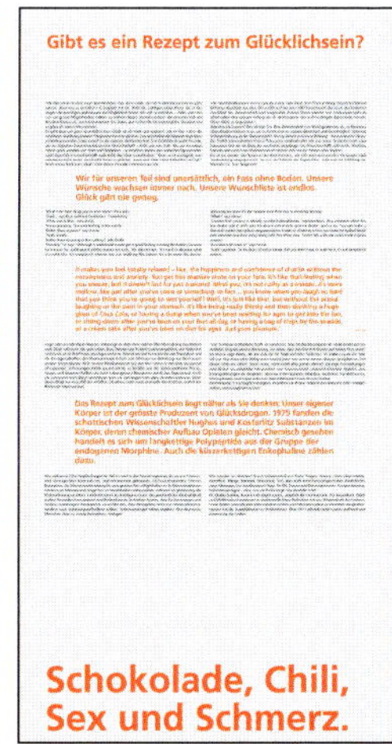

Gibt es ein Rezept zum Glücklichsein?
Schokolade, Chili,
Sex und Schmerz.

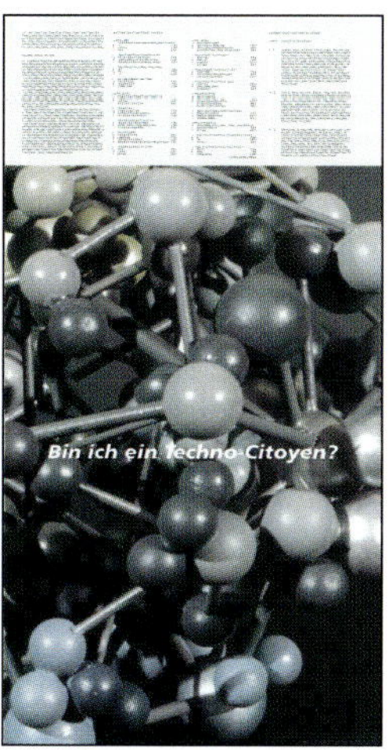

Bin ich ein Techno-Citoyen?

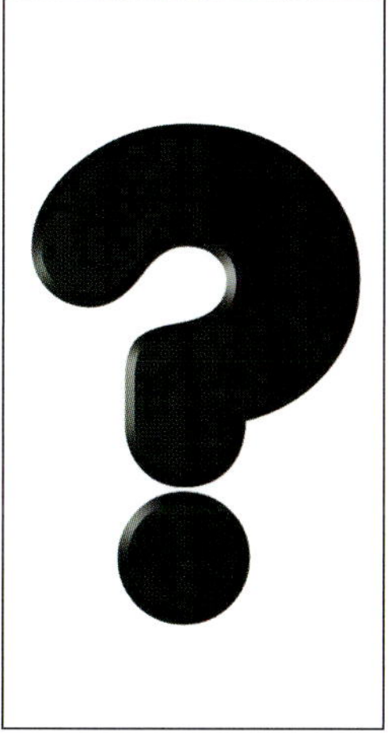

?

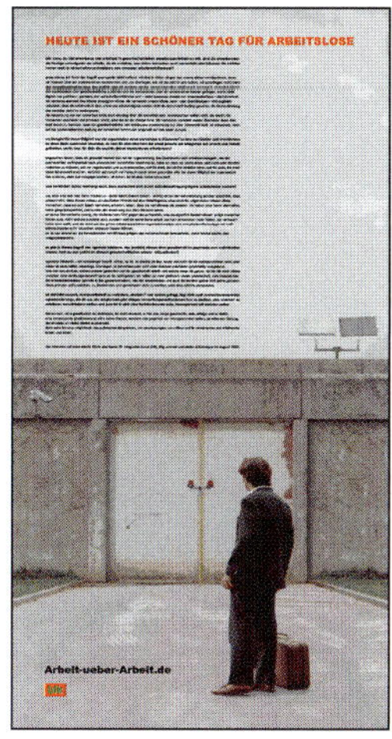

HEUTE IST EIN SCHÖNER TAG FÜR ARBEITSLOSE
Arbeit-ueber-Arbeit.de

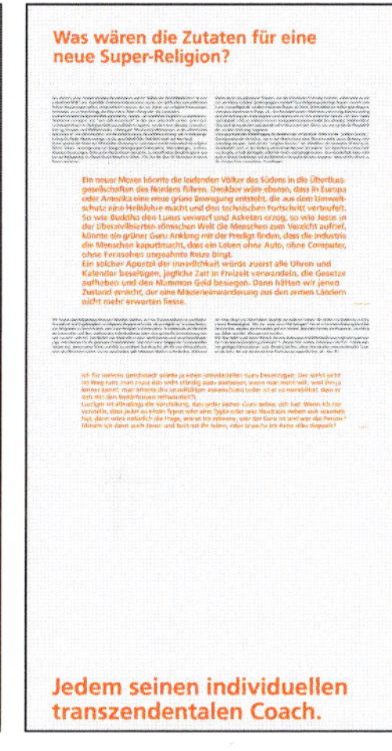

Was wären die Zutaten für eine
neue Super-Religion?
Jedem seinen individuellen
transzendentalen Coach.

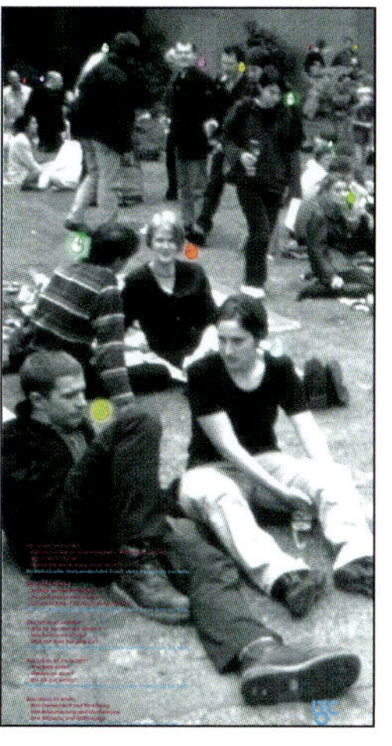

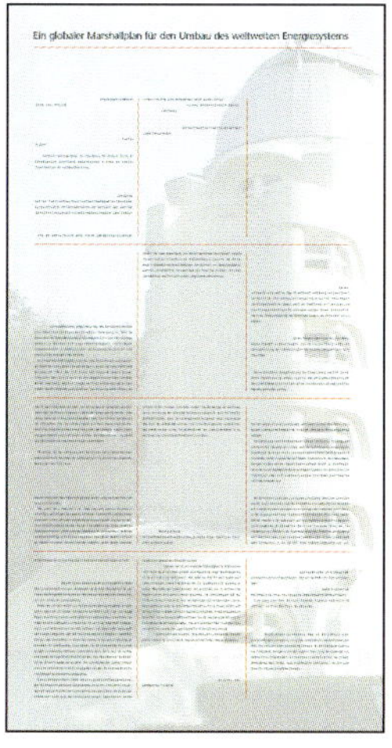

Ein globaler Marshallplan für den Umbau des weltweiten Energiesystems

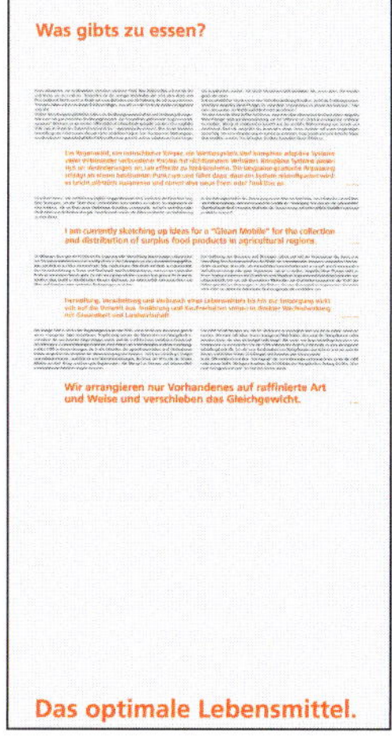

Was gibts zu essen?
Wir arrangieren nur Vorhandenes auf raffinierte Art
und Weise und verschieben das Gleichgewicht.
Das optimale Lebensmittel.

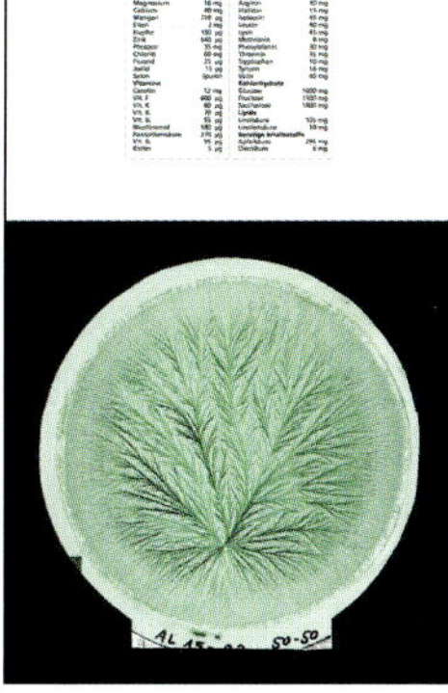

Möhren,
Karotten

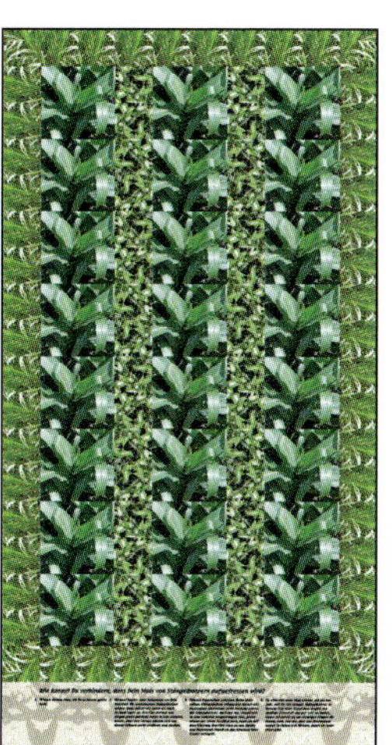

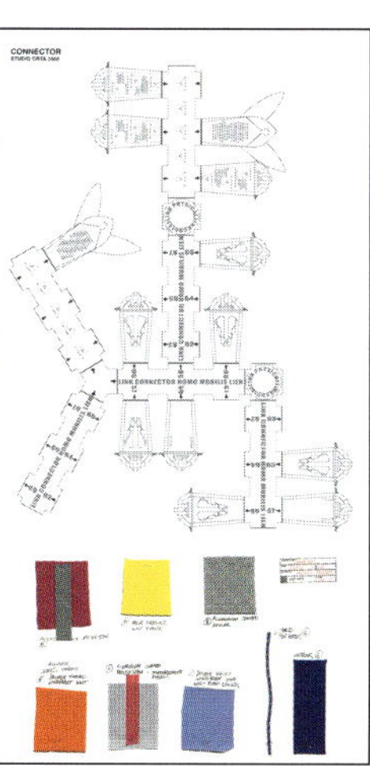

CONNECTOR

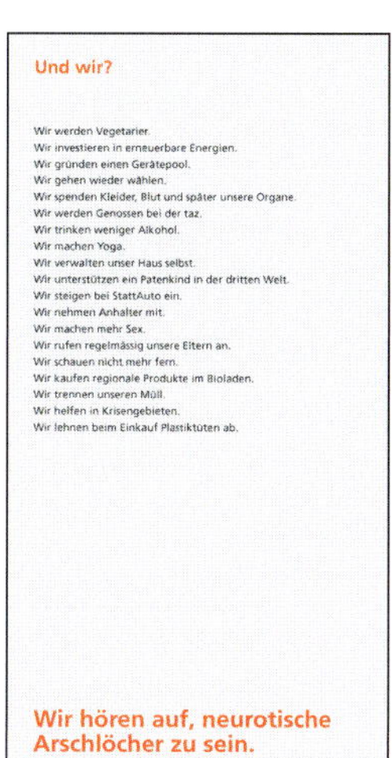

Und wir?
Wir werden Vegetarier.
Wir investieren in erneuerbare Energien.
Wir gründen einen Gerätepool.
Wir gehen wieder wählen.
Wir werden Kleider, Blut und später unsere Organe.
Wir werden Genossen bei der taz.
Wir trinken weniger Alkohol.
Wir machen Yoga.
Wir verwalten unser Haus selbst.
Wir unterstützen ein Patenkind in der dritten Welt.
Wir steigen bei StattAuto ein.
Wir nehmen Anhalter mit.
Wir machen mehr Sex.
Wir rufen regelmässig unsere Eltern an.
Wir schauen nicht mehr fern.
Wir kaufen regionale Produkte im Bioladen.
Wir trennen unseren Müll.
Wir helfen in Krisengebieten.
Wir lehnen beim Einkauf Plastiktüten ab.
Wir hören auf, neurotische
Arschlöcher zu sein.

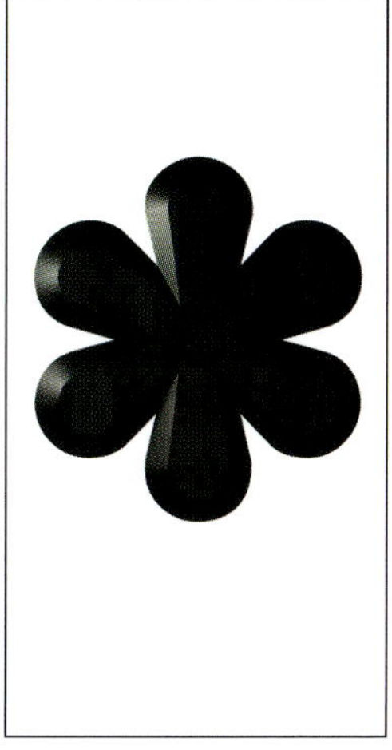

and its development partially resembles an artistic process, and is also marked by the moment when disjointed fragments suddenly converge to form a whole. And then one asks oneself how come one did not see this all along.

STEFAN IGLHAUT: How does this collaboration between you and the scientists actually work? Do briefings take place, and do the experts stick to them?

CHRISTIANE DELLBRÜGGE: After corresponding by e-mail, we visit our partners in person. Only by talking to them does it become clear whether we can actually work together. Usually we prepare a question as a guideline: we asked the psychologist of religion Sebastian Murken whether he could construct a "super religion" for us, one which distilled the best from different religious movements or conceived of the perfect charismatic leader. It took us a long time to find someone for the topic of war and conflict. So far no solutions have been found for the fact that we have not achieved a non-violent society. What models might we develop to deal with warlike aggression? Ultimately we found Angela and Karlheinz Steinmüller. She had been a mathematician and he was originally a physicist, they both became science-fiction writers in the GDR as well as futurologists at the Office for Future Studies. We confronted them with the question of whether or not it would be possible to design an exterritorial "battlefield" for the outsourcing of war.

RALF DE MOLL: We reversed the image of Utopia as an island isolated away from an evil world, making a good world possible. In this model, the weapons industry continues to rake in profits on the "battlefield"; young men who seek peak experiences and the proximity of death may prove their worth; conflicts in interest are fought out; poor and rich countries have equal chances to arm themselves – and all this without collateral damage. What must the rules be like, what weapons and what territory would be suited – Siberia, the Sahara or the moon? After initially exclaiming "What nonsense!", they said they were working at that very moment on a book about wild cards and that this, indeed, was a true wild card. Now they are designing a plan which will demonstrate how it might work.

THOMAS SPRING: Is this fiction science?

RALF DE MOLL: These are "patterns", models or thought configurations. In our culture we have an affinity for identifying and reproducing patterns of behavior. We are in the position to absorb images and translate them into action. That is our motivation in "WildCards".

The status quo constantly manifests itself in relatively redundant images. As an artist or a scientist, the moment I introduce "patterns" that do not correspond to the status quo, there is the possibility of something changing. One has to first conceive and formulate changes, before they can be transferred to behavior. How can "patterns" be developed that are so attractive that people reproduce them?

CHRISTIANE DELLBRÜGGE: Scientific decisions irreversibly change the conditions of our lives. Paul Feyerabend suggests that the funds for research projects should be distributed by the population that is forced to accept the consequences of scientific research. To find out if the right course has been taken, you would also have to take all courses that stray from it into consideration. If we were to multiply the entire world into parallel universes and observe duplicates of ourselves in experiments on a life-size scale, neither the capacity of computers nor our lifespans would suffice to analyze and evaluate the experiments. Nevertheless, we do not want to pass up the intellectual pleasure of pursuing courses which stray to the right and left, or of exploring the scope of possibilities.

STEFAN IGLHAUT: That sounds a lot like the transformation of society, which is an interesting field, too, of course. Do you ask about Utopias in "WildCards" and the kind of relationship artists and scientists have to them?

RALF DE MOLL: In 1998, when we worked on our Internet project "Hamburg Ersatz" (http://hamburg-ersatz.trmd.de), it was a question of utopian models, though of historical ones. At the time, the director of the Kunstverein in Hamburg, Stephan Schmidt-

Wulffen, commented: "Utopia – it's a term nobody dares to utter anymore." Utopian thought, however, has become prevalent again, even if people now prefer "vision" to "Utopia". The term also plays a role in science, because it has become necessary to dream up something in view of the climate catastrophe, the threat of war and politics' failure. When value systems collapse, people have to consider how they can develop alternatives. To do this one needs visionary thinking. We will use "WildCards" in the exhibition as a platform for the introduction of new ideas. We see ourselves as exemplary communicators and have abandoned the role of observers.

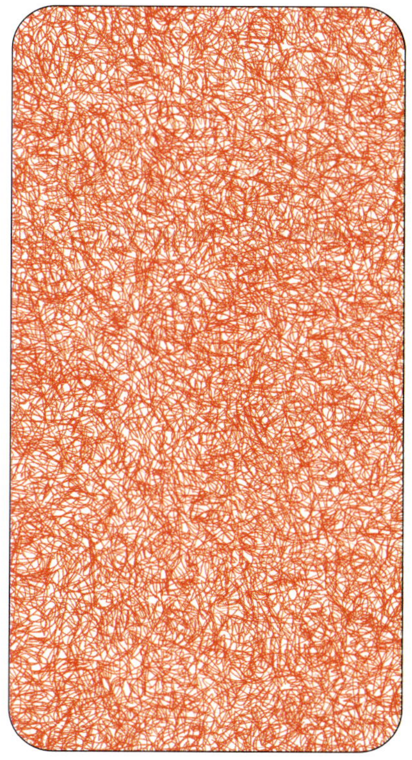

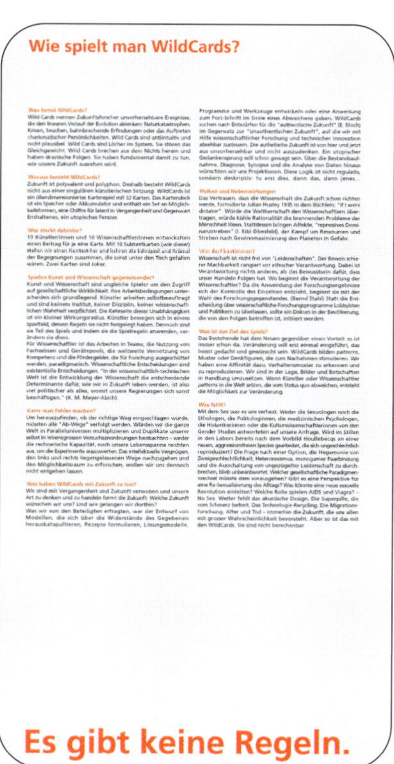

Wie spielt man WildCards?

Was heisst WildCards?

Wild Cards nennen Zukunftsforscher unvorhersehbare Ereignisse, die den linearen Verlauf der Evolution ablenken: Naturkatastrophen, Krisen, Seuchen, bahnbrechende Erfindungen oder das Auftreten charismatischer Persönlichkeiten. Wild Cards sind antiintuitiv und nicht plausibel. Wild Cards sind Löcher im System. Sie stören das Gleichgewicht. Wild Cards brechen aus dem Nichts herein und haben drastische Folgen. Sie haben fundamental damit zu tun, wie unsere Zukunft aussehen wird.

Woraus besteht WildCards?

Zukunft ist polyvalent und polyphon. Deshalb besteht WildCards nicht aus einer singulären künstlerischen Setzung. WildCards ist ein überdimensioniertes Kartenspiel mit 32 Karten. Das Kartendeck ist ein Speicher oder Akkumulator und enthält ein Set an Möglichkeitsformen, eine Chiffre für latent in Vergangenheit und Gegenwart Enthaltenes, ein utopisches Fenster.

Wer steckt dahinter?

10 Künstler/innen und 10 Wissenschaftler/innen entwickelten einen Beitrag für je eine Karte. Mit 10 Subtextkarten (wie dieser) stellen wir einen Kontext her und führen die Schnippel und Krümel der Begegnungen zusammen, die sonst unter den Tisch gefallen wären. Zwei Karten sind Joker.

Spielen Kunst und Wissenschaft gegeneinander?

Kunst und Wissenschaft sind ungleiche Spieler um den Zugriff auf gesellschaftliche Wirklichkeit. Ihre Arbeitsbedingungen unterscheiden sich grundlegend. Künstler arbeiten selbstbeauftragt und sind keinem Institut, keiner Disziplin, keiner wissenschaftlichen Wahrheit verpflichtet. Die Kehrseite dieser Unabhängigkeit ist ein kleiner Wirkungsradius. Künstler bewegen sich in einem Spielfeld, dessen Regeln sie nicht festgelegt haben. Dennoch sind sie Teil des Spiels und indem sie die Spielregeln anwenden, verändern sie diese.
Für Wissenschaftler ist das Arbeiten in Teams, die Nutzung von Fachwissen und Gerätepools, die weltweite Vernetzung von Kompetenz und die Fördergelder, die für Forschung ausgeschüttet werden, paradigmatisch. Wissenschaftliche Entscheidungen sind existentielle Entscheidungen. "In der wissenschaftlich-technischen Welt ist die Entwicklung der Wissenschaft die entscheidende Determinante dafür, wie wir in Zukunft leben werden, ist also viel politischer als alles, womit unsere Regierungen sich sonst beschäftigen." (K. M. Meyer-Abich).

Kann man Fehler machen?

Um herauszufinden, ob der richtige Weg eingeschlagen wurde, müssten alle "Ab-Wege" verfolgt werden. Würden wir die ganze Welt in Paralleluniversen multiplizieren und Duplikate unserer selbst in lebensgrossen Versuchsanordnungen beobachten – weder die rechnerische Kapazität, noch unsere Lebensspanne reichten aus, um die Experimente auszuwerten. Das intellektuelle Vergnügen, den links und rechts liegengelassenen Wege nachzugehen und den Möglichkeitsraum zu erforschen, wollen wir uns dennoch nicht entgehen lassen.

Was haben WildCards mit Zukunft zu tun?

Wir sind mit Vergangenheit und Zukunft verwoben und unsere Art zu denken und zu handeln formt die Zukunft. Welche Zukunft wünschen wir uns? Und wie gelangen wir dorthin?
Was wir von den Beteiligten erfragten, war der Entwurf von Modellen, die sich über die Widerstände des Gegebenen herauskatapultieren, Rezepte formulieren, Lösungsmodelle,

Programme und Werkzeuge entwickeln oder eine Anweisung zum Fort-Schritt im Sinne eines Abweichens geben. WildCards suchen nach Entwürfen für die "authentische Zukunft" (E. Bloch) im Gegensatz zur "unauthentischen Zukunft", auf die wir mit Hilfe wissenschaftlicher Forschung und technischer Innovation absehbar zusteuern. Die authetische Zukunft ist von hier und jetzt aus unvorhersehbar und nicht auszudenken. Ein utopischer Gedankensprung will schon gewagt sein. Über die Bestandsaufnahme, Diagnose, Synopse und die Analyse von Daten hinaus wünschten wir uns Projektionen. Diese Logik ist nicht regulativ, sondern deskriptiv: tu erst dies, dann das, dann jenes...

Risiken und Nebenwirkungen

Das Vertrauen, dass die Wissenschaft die Zukunft schon richten werde, formulierte Julian Huxley 1935 in dem Büchlein: "If I were dictator". Würde die Weltherrschaft den Wissenschaftlern übertragen, würde kühle Rationalität die brennenden Probleme der Menschheit lösen. Stattdessen bringen Affekte, "repressives Dominanzstreben" (I. Eibl-Eibesfeld), der Kampf um Ressourcen und Streben nach Gewinnmaximierung den Planeten in Gefahr.

Wie darf kontinuieren?

Wissenschaft ist nicht frei von "Leidenschaften". Der Beweis schierer Machbarkeit rangiert vor ethischer Verantwortung. Dabei ist Verantwortung nichts anderes, als das Bewusstsein dafür, dass unser Handeln Folgen hat. Wo beginnt die Verantwortung der Wissenschaftler? Da die Anwendung der Forschungsergebnisse sich der Kontrolle des Einzelnen entzieht, beginnt sie mit der Wahl des Forschungsgegenstandes. (Bernd Stahl) Statt die Entscheidung über wissenschaftliche Forschungsprogramme Lobbyisten und Politikern zu überlassen, sollte ein Diskurs in der Bevölkerung, die von den Folgen betroffen ist, initiiert werden.

Was ist das Ziel des Spiels?

Das Bestehende hat dem Neuen gegenüber einen Vorteil: es ist immer schon da. Veränderung will erst einmal eingeführt, das heisst gedacht und gewünscht sein. WildCards bilden patterns, Muster oder Denkfiguren, die zum Nachahmen stimulieren. Wir haben eine Affinität dazu, Verhaltensmuster zu erkennen und zu reproduzieren. Wir sind in der Lage, Bilder und Botschaften in Handlung umzusetzen. Wenn Künstler oder Wissenschaftler patterns in die Welt setzen, die vom Status quo abweichen, entsteht die Möglichkeit zur Veränderung.

Was fehlt?

Mit dem Sex war es wie verhext. Weder die Sexuologen noch die Ethologen, die Politologinnen, die medizinischen Psychologen, die Historikerinnen oder die Kulturwissenschaftlerinnen von den Gender Studies antworteten auf unsere Anfrage. Wird in Stillen in den Labors bereits nach dem Vorbild Houllebecqs an einer neuen, aggressionsfreien Spezies gearbeitet, die sich ungeschlechtlich reproduziert? Die Frage nach einer Option, die Hegemonie von Zweigeschlechtlichkeit, Heterosexismus, monogamer Paarbindung und die Ausschaltung von ungezügelter Leidenschaft zu durchbrechen, blieb unbeantwortet. Welcher gesellschaftliche Paradigmenwechsel müsste dem vorausgehen? Gibt es eine Perspektive für eine Re-Sexualisierung des Alltags? Was könnte eine neue sexuelle Revolution einleiten? Welche Rolle spielen AIDS und Viagra? – No Sex. Weiter fehlt das akustische Design, Die Superpille, die vom Schmerz befreit, Das Technologie-Recycling, Die Migrationsforschung, Alter und Tod – immerhin die Zukunft, die uns allen mit grosser Wahrscheinlichkeit bevorsteht. Aber so ist das mit den WildCards. Sie sind nicht berechenbar.

Es gibt keine Regeln.

The following artists and scientists have contributed to Dellbrügge & de Moll's "WildCards": Michelangelo Pistoletto with "cittadellarte"; Karen and Jörg van den Berg et al. and quartier vier with the project "next:the:science:faqtory", Universität Witten/Herdecke GmbH; Bittermann & Duka with "Eylandt"; Angela Steinmüller & Karlheinz Steinmüller with "War Games", Z_punkt GmbH Büro für Zukunftsgestaltung; Blank & Jeron with "o. T."; Birger P. Priddat with "economic's future", chair for economics and philosophy, Universität Witten/Herdecke; Nana Petzet with "Modell Tante Erika"; Godfrey B. Tangwa with "We-Culture", Université de Yaoundé, Cameroun; GLOBE, Cecilie Høgsbro Østergaard and Peter Holst Henckel with "Welfare-Machine"; Stephen Willats with "Modern Dream – Multiple Clothing"; Benjamin Foerster Baldenius with "Ausblick auf eine zweidimensionale Welt"; Hinrich Sachs with "Performance"; Harald Preissler, Joachim Reske with "Techno-Citoyen", Forschung Gesellschaft und Technik, DaimlerChrysler AG, Berlin / Palo Alto; buero für integrative kunst, Stefan Krüskemper, Jörg Amonat with "Arbeit über Arbeit"; Sebastian Murken with "Individueller Transzendentaler Coach ITC", study group for the psychology of religion, Forschungszentrum für Psychologie und Psychosomatik (FPP), Universität Trier; Ottmar Edenhofer with "Marshallplan", Potsdamer Institut für Klimafolgenforschung PIK, Institut globaler Wandel und soziale Systeme; Angelika Meier-Ploeger with "Zahl und Bild", FG Ökologische Lebensmittelqualität und Ernährungskultur, Universität Kassel; Hans Herren, Zeyaur Khan, Markus Knapp with "Push-Pull-Rezept", International Center of Insect Physiology and Ecology, ICEPE, Nairobi, Kenya; Lucy Orta with "Connector".

M+M

M+M stands for artistic collaboration between Marc Weis (born 1965) and Martin De Mattia (born 1963). M+M taught as guest lecturers at the Academy of Fine Arts in Munich during the winter semester 2000/2001, and they have been lecturers at the College of Design and Fine Art in Zurich since 2001.

PRIZES AND FELLOWSHIPS (SELECTION): 2002 USA-Fellowship from the state of Bavaria; 1998/99 fellowship for the Villa Massimo, Rome; 1997 Promotional Award from the state of Bavaria; 1994 working grant from the Kunstfonds e.V., Bonn; Botho-Graef-Art-Prize, Jena.

INDIVIDUAL AND GROUP EXHIBITIONS (SELECTION): 2002 Schauspiel, Frankfurt; "Stories", Haus der Kunst, Munich (catalog); "Kopfreisen", Kunstmuseum, Bern (catalog); "Das zweite Gesicht", Deutsches Museum, Munich (catalog); 2001 vpe-Projekt, Munich; "2115 km", Museum of Modern Art, Moscow (catalog); "Sala di consultazione", Institut Français, Florence; 2000 Marstall, Munich; "Vision-Ruhr", Zeche II, Dortmund; "Der körpererfüllte Raum fort und fort …", OK Centrum für Gegenwartskunst, Linz; "TALK-Show", Von der Heydt-Museum, Wuppertal and Haus der Kunst, Munich; "Serien und Konzepte", Museum Ludwig, Cologne; "Oreste", Italian Pavilion, Biennial, Venice; "Officina Europa" (European Factory), Bologna, Rimini a.o.; 1999 Galleria Neon, Bologna; 1998 Suermondt Ludwig Museum, Aachen; Galerija Skuc, Ljubljana; "Die Unruhe und die Zufriedenheit", Kunstverein, Karlsruhe; "Circuitos d'Agua", EXPO, Lisbon; "Transferit", open air project, Munich; 1997 "Video-Interieur", Kunstverein, Constance; "G-A-M-e", Galleria D'Arte Moderna, Bologna; 1996 Dany Keller Galerie, Munich; Galleria Neon, Bologna; Förderkoje, Art Cologne, Cologne; "Junge Kunst", Wilhelm-Hack-Museum, Ludwigshafen and Brandenburgische Kunstsammlungen, Cottbus.

CHRISTOPH KELLER

Christoph Keller was born in 1967 and grew up in Freiburg im Breisgau and in Canberra/Australia. From 1987–92 he studied mathematics, physics and hydrology in Freiburg, Berlin and Santiago de Chile. In addition, he produced texts and photographs for Die Zeit, Zitty, etc.. Subsequently he participated in an interdisciplinary art and video group Botschaft e.V. in Berlin. From 1996–99 Christoph Keller was a postgraduate at the College of Media in Cologne. Since 1999 he has lived and worked as an artist in Berlin.

PRIZES AND FELLOWSHIPS (SELECTION): 2002 PS1 Fellowship, New York; 2001 Kunstfonds Working Grant for Fine Art; 2000 Art Prize Ars-Viva from the Kulturkreis der deutschen Wirtschaft; 1999 Senate Fellowship for Fine Art, Berlin; 1995 Fellowship for Photography, Berlin.

INDIVIDUAL AND GROUP EXHIBITIONS (SELECTION): "LOOP", PS1, New York; "CAMP", Maebachi/Japan; "Encyclopaedia Cinematographica", Kunst-Werke, Berlin; "Alles auf Anfang", Hypo-Kunsthalle, Munich; "ars-viva: Kunst und Wissenschaft", ZKM, Karlsruhe; Ludwig Forum, Aachen; 2000 "ars-viva: Kunst und Wissenschaft", Moritzburg, Halle; "Berlin-Berlin", Nowosibirsk (photography in the round); "Encyclopaedia Cinematografica", Kunstbank, Berlin; "Produktivität und Existenz", Kunstamt Kreuzberg, Berlin; "dive-in", Luzerner Ausstellungsraum, Lucerne (photography in the round); 1999 "children of berlin", PS1, New York (photography in the round); "space", Schipper + Krome, Berlin (photography); "countdown", Berlin ("Continuous Present", computer-aided video installation); "Konstruktionszeichnungen", Kunst-Werke, Berlin; "retrograd – Filme der Charité Berlin 1900–1990", chronology of a history of medical film, Betacam SP, 32 min.; 1998 "tunnel & lightbox", Schipper + Krome, Berlin (inverse architecture); "Berlin-Biennale", Berlin (photography in the round); "medfilm – Ein Archiv der medizinischen Filme der Charité", "Nützliche Bilder", Oberhausen; 1997 "Was nun?", Schipper + Krome, Berlin (permanent installation "helioflex"); "Blue-Screen", Schipper + Krome, Berlin (photography in the round); 1996 "Tropic of Cancer", New York Art Gallery (Internet-travelogue-project) in collaboration with Felix S. Huber, Philip Pockock, Florian Wüst (www.icf.de/tcancer); "phototrop", Milchhof, Berlin (photography in the round on microfilm apparatus); 1995 "Patentamt-Panorama", WAPO-Projekt, Ars Electronica, Linz; "helioflex", dirty-windows-gallery, Berlin; "Kamtschatka", (video), S-VHS, 30 min., documentation of a geological expedition in Siberia; 1994 "Museum für Zukunft", contradictions between museum and futurology: collection of plans; models, scenarios, prognoses, visions. (www.icf.de/mfz); "Museum für Zukunft: Wir stellen um auf EDV", Media Biennial Leipzig, Galerie Schipper + Krome, Cologne; Künstlerhaus Bethanien, Berlin; "roto tv", (club videos 1994–89), presentations: Media Biennial, Leipzig, WMF-Club, Berlin, Friseur Berlin, Soundlab NY.; "Die dritte Generation", allgirls-gallery, Berlin.

ATELIER VAN LIESHOUT

Joep van Lieshout was born in Ravenstein in 1963 and studied at the Academy of Modern Art in Rotterdam from 1980 to 1985. Subsequently he worked for two years in the Studios '63 in Haarlem and spent a period of residence at Villa Arson in Nice during 1987. He founded the Atelier van Lieshout in 1995.

PRIZES AND FELLOWSHIPS (SELECTION): 2000 Wilhelminaring, Sculpture Award; 1998 Mart Stam 1998 Award; 1997 Anjerfonds – Chabot 1997 Award; 1996 87. Katalogförderpreis 1996, Alfried Krupp von Bohlen and Halbach Foundation; 1995 Bolidt Floor Concepts 1995, 1e prize; 1992 Prix de Rome Award; 1991 Charlotte Köhler Award.

INDIVIDUAL AND GROUP EXHIBITIONS (SELECTION): 2002 Camden Arts Centre, London; "Biennial of Sao Paulo", Sao Paulo; "Biennial of Sydney", Sydney; 2001 "Freistaat; AVL-Ville", Rotterdam; "PS1", New York; "La Biennale", Venice; "Sonsbeek 9", Arnhem; "Milano Europa 2000", PAC, Milan; "A-Portable. Women On Waves", Amsterdam (commission); "STAR-wagon", STAR Museum Veendam (commission); "Schwarzes und Graues Wasser", Bawag Foundation, Vienna; 2000 "Wonderland", St. Louis; "Over the Edges", SMAK, Gent; "Hangover 2000", performance and installation, EXPO, Hanover; "Visitor's Space Prison Hoogvliet", Rotterdam (commission); "Sound reflectors", Luxor theatre, Rotterdam (commission); "AVL-Men, public space", Knokke, Belgium (commission); 1999 Migros Museum für Gegenwartskunst, Zurich; "In the Midst of Things", Birmingham/Bourneville; "Arte all'Arte", San Gimignano; "USF", Contemporary Art Museum, Tampa/Florida; "Toilet-Units", Museum Boijmans Van Beuningen, Rotterdam (commission); 1998 "The Good, the Bad + the Ugly", Rabastens + Le Parvis / Tarbes and Walker Art Center, Minneapolis (commission); "Constructen ontwerpen voor stad en land", in collaboration with Birgitte Louise Hansen, De Paviljoens, Almere; "NL", Van Abbe Museum, Eindhoven; 1997 Museum Boijmans Van Beuningen, Rotterdam; "Sculpture Projects 97", Münster.

SOMMERER & MIGNONNEAU

Christa Sommerer was born in Ohlsdorf near Gmunden/Austria in 1964. She studied botany at the University of Vienna and art at the Vienna Academy of Fine Arts. Laurent Mignonneau was a student at the Academy of Art in Angoulême/France, where he was born in 1967. Both artists have worked as Artists in Residence within technological environments (1993 National Center for Supercomputing Applications, IL/USA and 1994 at the ICC-NTT Tokyo/Japan). They have been Invited Researcher and Artistic Director at the ATR Advanced Telecommunications Research Lab, Kyoto/Japan since 1995. In 2001 Sommer and Mignonneau spent a period working at the MIT (CAVS Center for Advanced Visual Studies, Cambridge, Boston/USA), before taking up their present positions as associate professors at the IAMAS Institute of Advanced Media Arts and Sciences, Gifu/Japan and as guest professors at the University of Kyoto. In 2001/2002 the artists were awarded doctorates for a thesis on Complex Systems, Artificial Life, Interface Design and Interactive Art. Contact: christa@iamas.ac.jp, http://www.mis.atr.co.jp/~christa

PRIZES AND FELLOWSHIPS (SELECTION): 2001 "World Technology Award for the Arts", London; 1999 "Honorary Award for Interactive Art and Netart", Prix Ars Electronica, Linz; 1995 "Inter Design Award", Japan Inter Design Forum, Tokyo; 1995 "Ovation Award", Interactive Media Festival, Los Angeles; 1994 "Golden Nica Award for Interactive Art", Prix Ars Electronica, Linz; 1993 "interActiva Award", Phillip Morris, Cologne; 1992/93 "Chicago Scholarship" Federal Ministry for Education and Art, Vienna; 1992/93 research grant, DAAD, Bonn.

INDIVIDUAL AND GROUP EXHIBITIONS (SELECTION): 2002 Maison Européenne de la Photographie, Paris; "Cibervision 02", Museo Conde Dugue, Madrid; "Navigate@art", Automobil Forum Unter den Linden, Berlin; "Situated Realities", Decker and Meyerhoff Galleries, Baltimore; "Art of Immersion", Animax Theater, Bonn; 2001 "L'homme transformé", Cité des Sciences et de l'Industrie, Paris; "Bo01 – City of Tomorrow", Malmö; "Microwave Media Art Festival", Hong Kong; "bits & pieces", Joseloff Gallery, Hartford; "Emerging Technologies", Siggraph02, Los Angeles; "Absolute Secret Sale: The Art of Secrecy", Espace Etude Tajan, Paris; 2000 "Living and Working in Vienna: 26 Positions of Contemporary Art", Vienna Art Gallery; "Alien Art", KIASMA Museum of Contemporary Art, Helsinki; "Media Art 2000 – Media City Seoul", Seoul Metropolitan Museum, Seoul; "Images and Signs of the 21st Century", Martin Gropius Bau, Berlin; "dot.jp", Museum of Modern Art, Home Page, New York; "Hard/Soft/Wet", Artspace Sydney: "Vision Ruhr Medienausstellung", Zollern Zeche, Dortmund; The Soros Center of Contemporary Art, Kiev; "Time Travel", Akademie der Künste, Berlin; "Play Zone", Millennium Dome, London; 1999 Cartier Foundation, Collection of Web-Art, Paris; "Biennal du Mercosul", Brazil; "Zeichenbau", Künstlerhaus Vienna; "Ars Electronica '99", OK Centrum für Gegenwartskunst, Linz; "The Millennium Motel", Siggraph '99, Los Angeles; "Cyber99", Centro Cultural Belem, Lisbon; 1998 Shiroishi Multimedia Art Center, Shiroishi Japan; "Videoformes", Clermont-Ferrand; 1997 ZKM, Collection of the Media Museum, Karlsruhe; "InterAct", Wilhelm Lehmbruck Museum, Duisburg, NTT-ICC InterCommunication Museum, Collection, Tokyo; "Arte Virtual – Realidad Plural", Museo de Monterrey, Mexico; "Center for the Arts", Yerba Buena Gardens, San Francisco; 1996 "Wunschmaschine Welterfindung", Vienna Art Gallery; "3D Vision", Tokyo Metropolitan Museum of Photography, Tokyo; "Biennale de Lyon", Museum of Contemporary Art, Lyon; 1995 "95 Kwangju Biennale", Kwangju, Korea; "Triennale di Milano", Palazzo dell'Arte, Mailand; "Revue Virtuelle", Centre Georges Pompidou, Paris; "Video Art", Museum of Contemporary Art, Warsaw; 1994 "ISEA 94", Museum of Modern Art, Helsinki; "Ars Electronica '94" – "Golden Nica Award", Linz; 1993 "InterActiva", Cologne; "Ars Electronica '93", Linz; "L'épreuve numérique", Palais de Tokyo, Paris; 1992 "Junge Szene", Vienna Secession.

DELLBRÜGGE & DE MOLL

Christiane Dellbrügge was born in Moline/USA in 1961, Ralf de Moll in Saarlouis during the same year. The two artists have worked together since 1984 and both studied at the State Academy of Fine Art in Karlsruhe.

PRIZES AND FELLOWSHIPS (SELECTION): 2002 Promotional Award for Fine Art, Art Prize of Berlin; 2002 EMARE, European Media Art Residency, Visual Research Centre, Dundee; 2000 International Media Art Prize ZKM/SWR, commendation; 1996 Art Prize Villa Romana, Florence; 1995 working grant from the Berlin Senate, grant for study abroad from the Berlin Senate, ICA Moscow; 1993–94 Artists in Residence, Kunst-Werke, Berlin; 1992 Fellowship from the Centre National des Arts Plastiques, Paris; 1991 Kunststiftung Baden-Württemberg; 1989 Kunstfonds Bonn; 1988–89 Artists in Residence, Künstlerhaus Bethanien, Berlin.

INDIVIDUAL AND GROUP EXHIBITIONS (SELECTION): 2002 "The gallery I'm dreaming of", Galerie Olaf Stüber, Berlin; "Kunstwerke '93", Sparwasser HQ, Berlin; "How do you feel", http://www.howdoyoufeel.de, Visual Research Centre, Dundee; 2001 "Plug-In", West-fälisches Landesmuseum, Münster; 2000 "Hamburg Ersatz Teile", Institut für moderne Kunst, Nürnberg; "Classical Chatroom Condition", log.in, Nürnberg "einräumen", Hamburger Kunsthalle cITy, ZKM Karlsruhe; "Models of Resistance", http://copenhagen-substitute.homepage.dk, Overgaden, Copenhagen; 1999 "Der Kunst im öffentlichen Raum gehört die Zukunft!", Galerie Sima, Nürnberg: "Pilot. The Audience from a Dis-tance", Museum van Bommel van Dam, Venlo; 1998 "Modell", Haus am Waldsee, Berlin; "Medialization", Edsvik kunst och kultur, Sollentuna, Sweden; 1997/99 "Ham-burg Ersatz", http://hamburg-ersatz.trmd.de, art in public spaces, Hamburg; 1996 "Substitut@ICA", Institute of Contemporary Art, Moscow "Ostseebiennale", Kunst-halle Rostock; "Are you talking to me?", Galerie Specta, Copenhagen; 1995 "T-Salon", Kunstraum Munich; "Der Diskurs findet hier statt", art in public spaces, Langenhagen; 1994 "Kunstkonsumentenprofile", Contemporary Art Center, Moscow; "Medien Bien-nale", Minima Media, Leipzig; 1993 "Parlare d'arte", AOCF 58, Rome; "Theorie wird Material", Media-MOO, MIT, Boston; 1992 "Génériques. Le visuel et l'écrit", Hôtel des Arts, Paris; 1991 "Ein Leben für die Kunst", Museum für Neue Kunst, Freiburg; 1989 "D&S Ausstellung", Kunstverein Hamburg.

GEWERK

The design office gewerk was founded in 1993; it has been run by partners Jens Imig, Birgit Schlegel and Stefan Rothert since 1995 and works in the areas of exhibition de-sign, graphic design and product development.

SELECTION OF PROJECTS: 2002 product development event fittings, interstuhl co., Tierin-gen; design of the exhibition "Offenes Geheimnis – Post- und Telefonkontrolle in der DDR", Museum für Kommunikation, Berlin/Hamburg/Frankfurt; 2001 design of the ex-hibition "Blaues Gold", Gasometer Oberhausen; design of the exhibition "Wunderbare Werbewelten – Marken, Macher, Mechanismen", Museum für Kommunikation, Berlin/Frankfurt/Hamburg/Nürnberg; since 2000 "Hörstelle Berlin – Radiogeschichte vor Ort", our own city environment project in collaboration with the Deutsches Tech-nikmuseum Berlin; design of the memorial at Münchner Platz, Dresden, and the memo-rial Pirna-Sonnenstein, Pirna; design of the bodywork and development of various mod-els for the Velotaxi GmbH (cycle rickshaws); Corporate Design for the bcc (Berliner Con-gress Center), Berlin; 2000 interior design, Tivola Verlag GmbH, Berlin; since 1999 de-sign of the Berlin Wall Documentation Center, Berlin; 1999 design of the exhibition "Sport im Rampenlicht – 100 Jahre Werder Bremen", Focke Museum / Landesmuseum Bremen; company presentation for Lufthansa Consulting, Cologne; 1998 design of the exhibitions "Automatenwelten", Museum für Kunst und Gewerbe, Hamburg; "Wil-helm Wagenfeld – Wegbereiter der Moderne", Wilhelm-Wagenfeld-Haus Bremen and Design Zentrum Bremen; 1997 own exhibition project "Fühlbox Fühlbar", Ham-burg/Berlin/Maastricht; design of the exhibition "automobilemoden", Focke Museum / Landesmuseum Bremen; since 1996 design of the Bautzen Memorial.

AUTHORS

PROF. DR. ANDREAS K. ENGEL Since 2002, full professor of physiology and director of the Institute of Neurophysiology and Pathophysiology at Hamburg University. 1987–2000, postdoctoral fellow and head of the junior research group at the Max-Planck-Institute for Brain Research in Frankfurt. From 2000–2002, head of research group "Cellular Neurobiology" at the Research Centre Jülich. Fellow at the Institute for Advanced Study Berlin during the academic year 1997–1998.

STEFAN IGLHAUT Exhibition curator of science + fiction. From 1990 to 1996, project director for the new media / media art of the Siemens Kulturprogramm, Munich. 1991, cofounder of Medienlabor München e.V., and member of the board until 1996. 1994–1997, curator of the "Mediensalon" at the Bavarian State Theater / Marstall. 1996–2000, exhibition director in the Theme Park of the World Exhibition EXPO 2000. He has run his own exhibition office Iglhaut + Partner Berlin since 2001.

PROF. DR. EVA KIMMINICH Academic in the fields of cultural science and Romance languages, academic assistant for various interdisciplinary research projects and advisor to the German Society for Semiotics on matters concerning youth culture. Since April 2002, she has been responsible for the research project "Hass und Hoffnung. Medienkultur-wissenschaftliche, semiotische und kultur-anthropologische Aspekte der französischen und frankophonen Vorstadtkultur" sponsored by the VolkswagenStiftung at the France-Center in Freiburg.

PROF. DR. JÖRG P. KOTTHAUS came to the Ludwig-Maximilians-University Munich via the University of California and the University of Hamburg, and has been a professor of experimental physics in Munich since 1989. He is spokesman and founding member of the Center for NanoScience (CeNS), an interdisciplinary association of physicists, chemists and molecular biologists.

PROF. DR. ULRICH KREMPEL After his doctorate in the arts and lecturing posts in Duisburg, Essen, Osnabrück and Kassel, Ulrich Krempel transferred the Kunsthalle Düsseldorf. 1986, exhibition director of the Museum Folkwang Essen and of the Art Collections of North-Rhine Westfalia in Düsseldorf in 1988. He has been the director of the Sprengel Museum Hanover since 1993. In 1996 he also became an honorary professor at the College of Fine Arts in Braunschweig.

DR. WILHELM KRULL After working as a DAAD lector at the University of Oxford and in leading positions at the Science Council and the Max-Planck-Gesellschaft, he has been General Secretary of the VolkswagenStiftung since 1996. He is also a member of the Education Council and of the Scientific Commission in Lower Saxony as well as being on the university boards of Constance and Marburg.

DR. MARTIN ROTH A cultural scientist who studied in Tübingen and Berlin, he was director of the German Hygiene Museum in Dresden from 1991–2000 and director of the EXPO 2000 Theme Park from 1996–2000. In 1995 he was elected president of the German Museums Federation and president of the Cultural Foundation of Saxony. Since October 2001, Dr. Martin Roth has been the general director of the State Art Collections in Dresden. In 2001/2002 he was a guest professor in the Faculty of Architecture at the University of Karlsruhe.

THOMAS SPRING Exhibition curator of science + fiction. He studied fine art and philosophy. From 1986 to 1994, he was editor at the Berlin publisher Argon, from 1996 to 1998 managing director of the Kulturwerk GmbH for the promotion of art. From 1999 onwards, direction of the project "Future of Work" in the Theme Park of EXPO 2000. Since 2001, he has been running the agency scheinprojekt – culture, concept, management.

EXHIBITION ORGANIZATION AND ACKNOWLEDGEMENTS

Exhibitions are always the work of many, and that is particularly true of the project science+fiction, since an integral part of its program was collaboration between artists and scientists. This exhibition would not have been possible without the often quite selfless commitment and concern for the success of the experiment demonstrated by the participating scientists, artists, and colleagues from museums. Particular acknowledgement should be directed towards the colleagues of the VolkswagenStiftung here. We would like to express our warmest personal gratitude to all those involved in the realisation of the exhibition.

VOLKSWAGENSTIFTUNG General Secretary Dr. Wilhelm Krull

EXHIBITION COMMITTEE Prof. Dr. Christina von Braun, Humboldt-University Berlin; Prof. Dr. Horst Bredekamp, Humboldt-University Berlin; Prof. Dr. Andreas Engel, University of Hamburg; Prof. Dr. Jörg Kotthaus, Center for Nano Science, University of Munich; Prof. Dr. Ulrich Krempel, Sprengel Museum Hanover; Dr. Wilhelm Krull, VolkswagenStiftung; Dr. Martin Roth, State Art Collections Dresden; Prof. Dr. Wolf Singer, Max-Planck-Institute for Brain Research, Frankfurt am Main; Prof. Dr. Peter Weingart, Institute for Research in Science and Technology, Bielefeld

CONCEPT AND DIRECTION OF THE EXHIBITION Stefan Iglhaut und Thomas Spring

EXHIBITION LOCATIONS SPRENGEL MUSEUM HANOVER; CENTER OF ART AND MEDIA TECHNOLOGY KARLSRUHE; CAESAR, CENTER FOR ADVANCED EUROPEAN STUDIES AND RESEARCH, BONN; GERMAN HYGIENE MUSEUM DRESDEN; THE NOBEL MUSEUM, STOCKHOLM; THE DEUTSCHES MUSEUM, MUNICH

ACADEMIC ASSISTANCE AND PROJECT COORDINATION Anna Echterhölter

PICTURE EDITING FOR THE WALL INSTALLATION SKETCHES SCIENCE / ART Anja Casser

PICTURE EDITING FOR THE WALL INSTALLATION GLOBAL IMAGES Karen Fromm

PICTURE RESEARCH Felix Hoffmann; Hanna Rose Shell

PRESS AND PUBLICITY WORK VOLKSWAGENSTIFTUNG Dr. Christian Jung, Julia Förster

PROJECT SUPERVISION VOLKSWAGENSTIFTUNG Katja Ebeling

TRANSLATIONS Nina Alpers; Nikolaus Schneider; Elvira Willems

SCIENTIFIC GUIDANCE AND COOPERATION BRAIN RESEARCH Prof. Dr. Tobias Bonhoeffer, director and scientist at the Max-Planck-Institute for Neurobiology, Martinsried; Prof. Dr. Dr. Olaf Breidbach, Institute of the History of Medicine, Natural Sciences and Technology at the Friedrich-Schiller-University Jena; Dr. Jens Eilers; Max-Planck-Institute for Brain Research, Frankfurt/M.; Dr. Dr. Martin Linden, Max-Planck-Institute for Brain Research, Frankfurt/M.; Dr. Lars Muckli, Max-Planck-Institute for Brain Research, Frankfurt/M.; Dipl. Psych. Marcus J. Naumer, Max-Planck-Institute for Brain Research, Frankfurt/M.; Prof. Dr. Wolfgang Schlote, Edinger Institute for Neurology at the Johann Wolfgang Goethe University Frankfurt/M. GLOBALIZATION Prof. Dr. Rainer Alsheimer, University of Bremen; Prof. Dr. Klaus Dicke, Friedrich-Schiller-University Jena; Prof. Dr. Christian Floto, IWF Wissen und Medien, Göttingen; Prof. Dr. Wolfgang Frindte, Friedrich-Schiller-University Jena; Prof. Dr. Lydia Haustein, Göttingen; Prof. Dr. Wilhelm Heitmeyer, University of Bielefeld; Prof. Dr. Eva Kimminich, University of Freiburg; Dr. Sybilla Nikolow, University of Bielefeld; Dr. Hartmut Rudolph, IWF Wissen und Medien, Göttingen; Dipl-Ing. Peter Wittenburg, Max-Planck-Institute for Psycholinguistics, Nijmegen. NANOSCIENCES CeNS, Center for Nanoscience, Munich; Dr. Martin Benoit, Center for Nanoscience, Munich; Prof. Dr. Thomas Beth, University of Karlsruhe; Dr. Monika Kaempfe, Center for Nanoscience, Munich; Prof. Dr. Dietmar Manstein, University of Heidelberg; Prof. Dr. Christoph Meinel, University of Regensburg

SCIENTIFIC FILMS ON THE TOPIC OF BRAIN RESEARCH THE FUNCTIONAL IMPORTANCE OF SYNCHRONIZATION PROCESSES IN THE BRAIN Text and Concept: Andreas Engel. ANIMATION DENDRITIC SPINE Concept: Tobias Bonhoeffer, Florian Engert, Max Planck-Institute for Neurobiology, Martinsried. Text: Andreas Engel. ANIMATION GROWTH CONES Concept: E. Birgbauer, University of California, San Francisco and the Company of Biologists Ltd. Text: Andreas Engel. BRAIN VOYAGER Text and Concept: Rainer Goebel, Max-Planck-Institute for Brain Research, Frankfurt/M. RECOGNIZING OBJECTS Text and Concept: Lars Muckli and Marcus J. Naumer, Max-Planck-Institute for Brain Research, Frankfurt/M. VOICES BECOME VISIBLE Text and Concept: Vincent van de Ven, David E.J. Linden, Rainer Goebel, Clinic for Psychiatry and Psychotherapy I, Johann Wolfgang Goethe University and Max-Planck-Institute for Brain Research, Frankfurt/M.

PROJECT ON RAP-CULTURE Concept: Prof. Dr. Eva Kimminich; Graffiti: kobo + stek, Agentur graco

DESIGN AND SCENOGRAPHY OF THE EXHIBITION gewerk, Berlin: Jens Imig, Stefan Rothert, Birgit Schlegel. TEAM Tanja Büsching, Petra Funk, Christine Neumeister, Christine Bentele, Inga Finke, Katja Kirchhoff, Markus Rüegger, Susanne Schmidt

PRODUCTION gewerk für Produktion: DIRECTION OF PRODUCTION / PROJECT COORDINATION Barbara Höffer. PRODUCTION ASSISTANT Hendrik Unger. PLANNING OF CONSTRUCTION AND REALISATION Tobias Solcher. TECHNICAL PLANNING Jörgen Pisarz, Event Engineering, Berlin. MEDIA / DATA FORMATS Manfred Schmitt, ubik media, Berlin

AUDIO-STATIONS Martin Kamratowski

MODEL CONSTRUCTION Ernst Dullemond, Martin Kamratowski

OBJECT SET-UP Claudia Rannow

EXHIBITION CONSTRUCTION Ausstellungsmanufaktur Hertzer GmbH, Berlin

LENDERS FRAMEWORK CeNS, Munich; Cochlear GmbH, Hanover; Deutsche Kinemathek – Film Museum Berlin; Deutsches Museum Munich; Dommuseum Salzburg, Austria; Germanisches Nationalmuseum Nürnberg; Greenpeace Deutschland, Hamburg; Heinrich Heine University Düsseldorf; Herzog August Bibliothek, Wolfenbüttel; State Museum Hessen Darmstadt; Humboldt-University, Berlin, University Library, Berlin; Institute for Anatomy, Medical Faculty of the Humboldt-University, Berlin; Museum of Art History, Vienna, Austria; Chair of Systematic and Topographic-Clinical Anatomy; Martin Luther University Halle, Mathematical Collection; Max, Binia und Jakob Bill-Stiftung, Adligenswil, Switzerland; Neurological Institute of the Johann Wolfgang Goethe-University, Frankfurt/M.; Silvia und Ralf Mörtel, Taunusstein; Veterinary Faculty, Munich; Ulmer Museum

WALL INSTALLATION SKETCHES SCIENCE/ART Archives of the Berlin-Brandenburgische Akademie der Wissenschaften; Buckminster Fuller Institute, Sebastopol (USA); Deutsches Museum Munich, Archives; Frau Folkens, Robert Koch-Institute Berlin; Frau Kraus, Österreichische Friedrich und Lillian Kiesler-Privatstiftung; Galerie Klosterfelde, Berlin; Herr Rohrwild, Hermann-Oberth-Raumfahrt-Museum; Konrad Fischer Galerie, Düsseldorf; State Library of Lower Saxony, Hanover; Reiner Matysik; Sabine Groß; Sigmar Polke or Galerie Erhard Klein; Steven Pippin; Foundation Archives of the Akademie der Künste, Berlin, Art Collection; Stiftung Weimarer Klassik State Library of Bavaria Munich; Tate Gallery London; Warburg Institute Archive, London; Françoise Xenakis, Paris

WE WOULD ALSO LIKE TO THANK THE FOLLOWING FOR THEIR SUPPORT AND COOPERATION Lars Bauernschmitt, Visum Foto GmbH; Bernd Beier, Media Technology at the TU Berlin; Dr. Martin Boss, Institute for Classical Archaeology, Erlangen; Dr. Reinhard Breuer, Alice Krüßmann, Spektrum der Wissenschaft; Jolanda Canoica, Pro Litteris, Zurich; Prof. Dr. Clausen, Rosemarie Clausen, Estate; Deniz Erol and Sven Graf, Cutter; Dell Magazines: A Division of Crosstown Publications for permission to print the title page of Astounding Science Fiction (1941), Street and Smith Publications, Inc.; John Ferry, The Estate of R. Buckminster Fuller, Santa Barbara; Frau Frey, special plaster models Laja Canaria, Taunusstein; Markus Frehrking, Galerie Frehrking Wiesehöfer; Dr. Rolf Giesen, Frau Ohlrogge and Herrn Siefert, Deutsche Kinemathek, Film Museum, Berlin; Dr. Glüber, State Museum of Hessen Darmstadt; Dr. Sabine Haag, Museum of Art History, Vienna; Frau W. Hauser, Deutsches Museum, Munich; Paul Holtkamp, Warburg; Cornelia Horsch, Berlin; Christian Jerger, Berlin; Ulrike Joas, Berlin; Dr. Peter Keller and Dr. Reinhard Gratz, Cathedral Museum, Salzburg; Leonore Leonardy, schauspielfrankfurt; Gisela Lerch, Berlin; Isabelle Leuchenet, Photo Library Altidude, Paris; Dr. Klaus Maurice, Traunstein; Museum in Progress, Vienna; Fritz Nepputh, Historisches Schreibmaschinenmuseum, Einbeck; Herrn Panse, Factory 7 Picture Archives, Stuttgart; Gary Pressel, AdTech, Houston; Harald Richter, Institute for Microelectronics, Stuttgart; Dr. Karin Richter, Martin Luther University, Halle; Sentilo Rieber, AVZ of the University Library Freiburg; Dr. Stefan Roller, Ulmer Museum; Jody Russell, NASA Johnson Space Center, Houston; Prof. Dr. Meinhard Schilling, TU-Braunschweig; Prof. Dr. Schnalke, Museum of Medical History, Berlin; Herrn Schulz, Cochlear GmbH, Hanover; Jochen Schumm, Dieter Kaufmann, Herrn Loebe, Frau Luebke and all the participating colleagues from Volkswagen Nutzfahrzeuge, Hanover; Markus Sommer, Somso Modelle, Coburg; Herrn Stühmeier, Heinz Nixdorf Museumsforum, Paderborn; Herrn Talib, Mevlana Mosque, Berlin; Frau Tillessen, Picture Press, Hamburg; Patrick Weisser, Med-El Deutschland GmbH, Berlin; Dr. Johannes Willers and Wiebke Glöckner, Germanisches Nationalmuseum, Nürnberg; Dr. Wittenberg, Staatsbibliothek zu Berlin – Stiftung Preußischer Kulturbesitz; Gabriele Yonan, Berlin; Delius Ziannis, Kinowelt, Munich; Fotografia dei Musei Civici di Palazzo Farnese (Museo Archeologico); Proprietà del Comune di Piacenza